PF
1404
.D36
1988

# Dialogue Journals: Writing as Conversation

by
Kathy Everts Danielson

CONCORDIA COLLEGE LIBRARY
BRONXVILLE, N. Y. 10708

59955

Library of Congress Catalog Card Number 88-60076
ISBN 0-87367-266-6
Copyright © 1988 by the Phi Delta Kappa Educational Foundation
Bloomington, Indiana

This fastback is sponsored by the Decatur Illinois Chapter of Phi Delta Kappa, which made a generous contribution toward publication costs.

The chapter sponsors this fastback to recognize the good teaching and dedicated service provided by educators everywhere.

# Table of Contents

| | |
|---|---:|
| Introduction | 7 |
| Dialogue Journals in the Elementary Classroom | 9 |
| Dialogue Journals in the Content Areas | 12 |
| Dialogue Journals and the Reading Curriculum | 17 |
| Dialogue Journals at Hone | 21 |
| Developing Fluency in Writing Through Dialogue Journals | 24 |
| Practical Considerations in Using Dialogue Journals | 26 |
| Conclusion | 29 |
| Bibliography | 30 |

# CONTENTS

PREFACE TO THE SECOND EDITION — vii
PREFACE TO THE FIRST EDITION — ix

## PART I. THE MEDICAL INTERVIEW

1. THE PHYSICIAN-PATIENT RELATIONSHIP — 3
2. PROCEDURES AND PROCESSES OF MEDICAL INTERVIEWING — 22

## PART II. WHAT TO LEARN IN HISTORY-TAKING

3. THE HISTORY OF THE PRESENT ILLNESS — 41
4. THE FAMILY HISTORY — 75
5. THE PERSONAL HISTORY — 88
6. TOPICS FOR FULLER DISCUSSION — 116

## PART III. THE TECHNIQUE OF HISTORY-TAKING

7. HOW TO TAKE THE HISTORY — 137
8. HOW TO HELP PATIENTS TALK FREELY — 172
9. HOW TO GUIDE THE INTERVIEWS — 189
10. VARIATIONS IN INTERVIEWS — 215
11. DIFFICULTIES AND FAILURES IN INTERVIEWING — 248
12. INTERVIEWING MEMBERS OF THE PATIENT'S FAMILY — 264

INDEX — 275

# PREFACE TO THE SECOND EDITION

The continued demand for this book has provided the impetus to revise some of the chapters in line with recent advances in our knowledge of interviewing and has resulted in a Second Edition.

Although we have known for centuries that different physicians obtained different histories from the same patient, the discrepancies were usually attributed to capriciousness—or even wickedness—on the part of the patient. The patient, it was sometimes thought, enjoyed showing up the lowly student or intern by giving a different history to the resident or professor. We know now that the matter is not that simple. Some discrepancies in the histories given by the same patient on different occasions are due to simple lapses of memory, while others derive from differing experiences on the part of the interviewers in knowing what to ask. Probably many more, however, stem from the patient's differing responses to the different interviewers as persons. And still more discrepancies arise from the different ways in which the interviewers unconsciously, but differently, guide the patient to reveal or suppress relevant information. We have known that physicians as interviewers can influence patients to emphasize different aspects of their complaints and histories; but we have learned only recently how powerful and also how subtle and completely unconscious (for both patient and physician) such influence may be.

A former generation also thought that the patient's knowledge of his own history was stable within himself, even if he revealed different amounts and aspects of it on different occasions. But this, too, has proved to be an oversimplification. Some memories of past events are fixed and do not change. It has been shown, however, that some memories change in important ways and extents. A person's current situation strongly influences the way he regards and remembers the earlier events of his life, or even those experienced not so long ago. Accordingly, a patient in the middle of some serious illness or other important life stress may give one account of particular events when he is ill and a quite different one just a few weeks later when he feels better. Furthermore, both these accounts may differ from what the patient had said about the same events some years or even a few months earlier.

Interviewing and pathology, including psychopathology, must be learned concomitantly. Mere skill in interrogation is of little value in medicine until the student knows the meaning of different symptoms so that he can pose relevant questions. A trained lawyer knows how to question witnesses, but he does not know how to talk with sick people any more than the average physician knows how to examine a witness in court. At the same time, a knowledge of pathology alone is nowadays quite insufficient equipment for guiding patients to yield the maximal information for their own benefit. The student must practice and learn interviewing as a separate medical discipline. And there are many aspects to be mastered.

The beginner must learn early to be aware of how his conduct in the interview can influence what the patient tells him. He also should learn how much the patient's past experiences with other persons may influence his reaction to the interviewer apart from anything the interviewer may do or say. Thus I urge that this book be read both before and after the reading of books on pathology (including psychopathology), just as the latter should be read before and after this one. In this way, by combining his reading with practical experience in interviewing and examining patients, the student can best integrate his knowledge of interviewing with other medical disciplines.

Since this book covers a wider range of interviewing than history-taking, it has seemed appropriate to change the title of the Second Edition in order better to express its aims and contents.

I extend cordial thanks to the Medical Department of Harper and Row, Inc., for the care taken in the production of this edition.

I. S.

*Charlottesville, Virginia*

# PREFACE TO THE FIRST EDITION

In the autumn of 1958, the Association of American Medical Colleges held its first Institute on Clinical Teaching for the discussion among medical teachers of the goals and methods of their teaching. The participants in this Institute came from every medical school of the United States and Canada and showed a remarkable diversity of skills and backgrounds as well as of aims in medical teaching. Although they did not agree on many things, these teachers did almost unanimously agree on one matter, namely, that medical graduates must know how to gather information from patients. The young physician can add other skills to this one as he continues his training and experience after graduation, but if he has not acquired comfort and dexterity in history-taking and interviewing by the time he graduates from medical school, he will practice medicine with incomplete data for which no other skill can compensate him or his patients.

Progress in psychological medicine with the increasing recognition of important psychological factors in a large number of illnesses (sometimes estimated as high as 75 per cent of all illnesses) has restored history-taking to the significance it had in the scheme of medical examination before the development of modern laboratory investigation. For history-taking and interviewing are the physician's chief tools for the psychological evaluation of his patients. Moreover, the past twenty years have brought considerable improvement in our techniques of interviewing; a student or physician should no longer depend upon slight adaptations of his social conversations, but should master definite principles and techniques.

Considering the agreement on this subject among the participants in the Institute and the increasing improvement in techniques of interviewing, it is surprising that our literature contains so little to instruct the student in history-taking and interviewing. Physical diagnosis, which also must be learned largely by imitation and practice, is the subject of several excellent textbooks. Yet these deal only briefly with history-taking and

## PREFACE TO THE FIRST EDITION

interviewing. And even textbooks of psychiatry, which offer outlines for psychiatric examinations, usually give little guidance in these subjects.

For these reasons I think that this book may prove useful to medical students and to practitioners for whom a textbook can enhance the value of personal instruction and practice. I will welcome comments from teachers and other readers of this book who can suggest ways in which I may improve it further to suit the needs of medical students and practitioners.

I have consulted and used many books and articles on the subject of interviewing; the references adequately document them, but I wish to emphasize my indebtedness here also.

A number of colleagues have given valuable suggestions or have read and helpfully criticized portions of the manuscript. For this help I wish to thank Dr. Robert A. Matthews, Jefferson Medical College; Dr. Charles Watkins and Dr. Frederick H. Davis, Louisiana State University School of Medicine; Dr. Andrew Kerr, Jr., New York State University College of Medicine at Syracuse; Dr. William Locke, Tulane University School of Medicine; and Dr. William Parson, University of Virginia School of Medicine.

I am grateful to the editor and publishers of *GP,* the journal of the American Academy of General Practice, for permission to use again some material of mine previously published in that journal. I wish to thank the editor of *Psychosomatic Medicine* for permission to republish some figures first published in that journal.

To my wife I am indebted for helpful suggestions and valuable encouragement. Mr. Louis E. Lascola, Department of Medical Illustration, Louisiana State University School of Medicine, and Mrs. Douglas Candland, Department of Medical Illustration, University of Virginia School of Medicine, have drawn the illustrations, and I am grateful to them for this helpful contribution. Mrs. Eunice Stevens and Miss Susan Downing of Paul B. Hoeber, Inc. gave me valuable suggestions about the organization of some of the material in the book and about improvements in its presentation. And finally, special thanks go to Mrs. Roger H. Fellom, my former secretary, and Mrs. Joseph Bodine, my research assistant, for their careful work during many revisions and the preparation of the final manuscript.

I. S.

*Charlottesville, Virginia*

# THE DIAGNOSTIC INTERVIEW

# 1

# THE PHYSICIAN-PATIENT RELATIONSHIP

Medical interviews have two main purposes: to find out what is wrong with the patient and to alleviate or cure the illness. The physician must know something about the illness before he can intervene successfully. This knowledge he gains through listening to the patient and examining him. The relationship between the physician and patient importantly influences the communications between them and the examinations conducted. It is the medium, so to speak, in which interviews and examinations occur. A constructive physician-patient relationship cannot substitute for technical skill in history-taking and interviewing. It is, however, a requirement of the best interviews; and an understanding of the principal variations in relationships between physicians and patients forms an essential component of technical skill.

The physician-patient relationship is actually a shifting complex of behavior exhibited by a physician and his patient when they are together, and often also when they are apart. The relationship between a physician and any one of his patients will vary widely from time to time; even wider variations occur in his relationships with different patients. And each patient varies in his relationships with different physicians.

The physician-patient relationship influences the interviews and examinations in several ways. First, the relationship affects what the patient will tell the physician. When two people talk together what they say depends not only on what they wish to talk about, but also on the thoughts they have about each other. We confide in our friends, not in our hostile critics. This principle applies with more than usual strength to medical interviewing because the subjects of discussion include matters both intimate and important. Our society does not endorse the public discussion of many of these subjects and they often become on this account alone charged with a great deal of emotion when we finally bring them forth to utterance. It might be supposed that patients would want to tell the physician everything that could possibly influence their health. Many do want to do so and succeed. But others do not want to, or want to talk freely but cannot. Patients can conceal facts of extreme importance to health and even life because they fear what the physician may say or find during his examinations. Yet despite these obstacles outside and within themselves, most patients do have a capacity for confiding in physicians. To foster this confidence the physician needs to know what patients think of him and what he can do to modify those thoughts which get in the way of their talking freely.

Secondly, the physician's knowledge of the relationship between himself and the patient guides him in what he can say to the patient or ask him to do while preserving the patient's cooperation. The physician can say some things to the patient at the end of an interview that he could not say in its first five minutes. He can say some things to the patient after ten or twenty interviews that he cannot say in the first interview. The difference lies in the different degrees of attachment of physician and patient to each other. For example, when a strong relationship ties the physician and patient, the physician can be bolder and more incisive without disturbing the patient. He can even make clumsy mistakes and the patient will forgive him for what would, in the earlier phases of their acquaintance, have been major crimes. To give another example, an older physician can more readily adopt a "fatherly" attitude towards a young patient than can a younger one. In this way he can, if the need arises, be authoritative more easily than can a younger physician.

Thirdly, the patient's behavior with the physician provides an important paradigm of his behavior with other people. The degree to which the patient's behavior with the physician typifies his behavior with other persons varies greatly. In many instances this behavior is rather accurately representative; in many other instances much less so. As the initial strangeness between physician and patient passes away and they become less guarded, more typical behavior comes forward. Even then, however, the patient's behavior towards the physician will differ somewhat or perhaps greatly from his behavior with other people. This slight disadvantage does not outweigh one unusual feature of the patient's behavior with the physician, namely, that the physician can observe it directly. He does not have to hear about it second hand from the patient or his family. Consequently, the data are less distorted and more useful.

Fourthly, an understanding of the relation of the physician and patient contributes indispensably to psychotherapy, but a further discussion of this lies outside the scope of this book.

## FACTORS INFLUENCING THE RELATIONSHIP BETWEEN PHYSICIAN AND PATIENT

A number of different factors influence the behavior of the patient and physician with each other. These include the patient's past relations with other people; the needs of the patient; the physician's personal characteristics and behavior; the amount of time which physician and patient spend together and the experiences they share. The following sections will discuss each of these in turn.

### *The Patient's Previous Relations with Other Persons*

What the patient has learned in previous relations with other people always influences his present relationships. His relationships with his parents have particular importance because they occur earliest in his experience. The patient may develop a relationship with the physician which resembles the pattern of his relationship with his parents. A constructive, friendly relationship between the patient and his father facilitates the development of a friendly relationship between the patient and the physician. On the other hand, if the patient's father was harsh and punitive towards the patient as a child, the patient may expect the physician to be critical of him. Particularly important in this connection is the past experience of the patient in confiding his thoughts and feelings in other people. If in the past, his confidences have met with anger, derision, or other unpleasant responses on the part of his confidants, the patient will probably have become cautious when talking to other people. This makes him guarded in what he tells the physician.

Although every patient's past experiences shape his relationship to the physician, patients vary widely in the extent to which earlier experiences influence them. Some patients approach the physician as if he were a duplicate of their mothers or fathers. Other patients can discriminate much more clearly and perceive the physician as he is. Still other patients, probably the majority, perceive the physician rationally in some or most respects, but in other respects they confuse the physician with a parent.

The physician should notice attitudes on the part of the patient which, being unprovoked by the physician's behavior, probably arise from the patient's past experiences. Irrational attitudes towards the physician suggest that the patient confuses the physician with someone in his past experience. When psychotic patients misidentify the physician in this way, their confusion may include every aspect of the physician; the patient may literally visualize (i.e., hallucinate) the physician as the patient's mother, father, or whoever may be the original person with whom the physician is confused.

With nonpsychotic patients, misperceptions are usually much less inclusive and much less obvious. They rarely go so far as a false visualization of the physician, although patients may falsely perceive individual items of the physician's appearance, such as erroneously giving him or taking away a moustache. Most such misperceptions by nonpsychotic persons consist in assigning to the physician attitudes and capacities which he does not have. Thus, he may have attributed to him a maternal solicitude for his patients which he does not have and cannot realistically be expected to have. Such a misperception may be expressed, for example, in the patient's making inordinate requests of the physician for signs of approval and affection. Because such misperceptions are isolated and patchy rather than inclusive, they may escape notice. But their detection is no less important on that account.

Conditioning experiences giving rise to inappropriate responses to other people, including physicians, do not occur only in early childhood. Later experiences may equally well promote erroneous generalized responses. Some persons can readily see the individual differences between different persons who superficially resemble each other. Other persons make frequent and serious generalizations about other persons or groups of persons on the basis of limited or even individual experiences. Thus after an unpleasant experience with a physician some patients continue with the same physician; others change to another physician, while still other patients respond with generalized distrust of all physicians and have nothing more to do with them.

The physician can make such faulty generalizations as readily as his patients. For example, a physician may first perceive the aforementioned patient as a sick person requiring the physician's professional skill. However, as the patient's demands for special attentions continue, the physician may come to perceive the patient as if he were an important figure of the physician's early life. The demanding patient may remind him unconsciously of the demands for affection made by his own mother when he was young. The physician may have reacted toward these demands with resentment and may react similarly towards his demanding patient. The physician needs to become aware of his own patterns of behavior in order to avoid exhibiting inappropriate responses himself.

## The Needs of the Patient

In any illness for which the patient seeks medical aid, he needs the physician. But the patient may have special requirements which make the physician more necessary than usual to him, and these will strengthen his attachment to the physician. For example, in severe physical illnesses, especially those which threaten life, the physician becomes much more important to the patient than in the treatment of minor illnesses. Similarly, when the patient has been much deprived of affection or attention, his hunger for these may seek satisfaction from the physician. Anxiety nearly always increases the attachment of the patient to the physician.

## The Characteristics and Behavior of the Physician

Two physicians who show apparently identical attitudes and behavior towards the patient (insofar as this is possible), may still elicit quite different responses from him. These differences arise from subtle but important differences in the physicians themselves, and in the roles to which the patient assigns them. Among the factors of importance in this connection three deserve mention.

### The Physician's Position as an Expert and as One Having Authority over the Patient

As mentioned above, the patient needs the physician, and the physician's expertness in medicine supplies the rational aspect of the relationship. However, less rational aspects of the patient's perception of the physician as an expert may influence his behavior towards the physician. For example, the patient may confide in a specialist various items he has withheld from a family physician or another specialist on the mistaken grounds that the other physician would not understand, or "would not want to listen to all that." Thus, if the patient wishes to discuss physical symptoms, but believes the physician he addresses (for example, a psychiatrist) has no interest in physical symptoms, that physician may hear nothing about physical symptoms unless he inquires specifically about them. The patient may, however, talk freely of personal matters to this physician. When the same patient sees an internist, he may speak quite freely about his physical symptoms, but omit mention of his anxieties. Thus he may avoid talking to either physician of matters which he has arbitrarily decided lie outside each physician's interest and skill. In this way the patient may interfere, unconsciously perhaps, with the attainment of a comprehensive view of his illness.[11] Physicians need to remember that patients communicate different needs and show different behavior to different people. The difficulties created by this tendency to adjust words to the listener can be reduced if the physician remains alert to it. And, he does not need to follow the patient's expectation of him. Patients can be guided by psychiatrists to talk of physical symptoms. Similarly, internists and general practitioners can help patients to talk freely about psychological symptoms and difficulties. They do this because, when they have a genuine interest in all aspects of their patients, they communicate this breadth of interest to the patients.

The authority of the physician and his power to influence the patient's life also shape the patient's attitude towards him. Here again rational and irrational may blend. The physician certainly does have some real authority, e.g., the power of commitment to a mental hospital, and his recommendations for treatment, although they can be refused, actually carry an enormous weight. To this the imagination of the patient frequently adds authority which the physician does not have or does not intend to use. For example, an anxious patient with a psychological disorder may perceive a psychiatrist only as someone who can send him to a mental hospital. This perception may interfere seriously with the patient's ability to talk to a psychiatrist. It frequently happens that medical students elicit from patients information which the more experienced professors never hear from the patients directly. A probable factor in this is that the patients see the students as "beginners" or "underdogs," and certainly as powerless to affect them. The professors, on the other hand, are seen as the powerful makers of potentially harmful decisions. Other factors no doubt enter into these relationships, such as the fact that the students spend much more time with the patients than the teachers.

### Personal Characteristics of the Physician

The personal characteristics of physicians lend themselves in various ways to the misperceptions mentioned above. For example, when the physician himself is an elderly man, the patient can more readily relate to him as he did towards his own father. If the patient is older than the physician, he may adopt a parental attitude towards the physician, behaving towards him as he does towards his son. As much as any such factor, the sex of the physician influences the responses of the patient towards him. Patients of either sex may be inhibited from discussing certain topics with a physician of the opposite sex or may exhibit other patterned responses towards a physician of the opposite sex. Other aspects of the physician's personal appearance may also influence the patient's behavior towards the physician. If a medical student appears on the wards without a tie or dressed appropriately for the beach, the patient may be pardoned if he confuses the student with his young son and responds accordingly.

### The Physician's Behavior toward the Patient

What the physician does influences the patient as much as what he is. The necessary professional behavior of the physican may elicit certain previously patterned responses on the part of the patient. For example, the physician's way of asking questions may quite unintentionally resemble closely the sweet, but all too often firm, insistence of the patient's mother as she questioned her little boy when he came home from school. In addition, unprofessional or neurotic behavior on the part of the physician can weaken the patient's confidence in him.

The patient's observation of the physician's competence strengthens his attachment to the physician. Physicians need to remember that a display of competence must usually precede a firm attachment of the patient to the physician. Inexperienced physicians sometimes misunderstand the connection between the patient's ability to talk and his relationship with the physician. They often believe that first they must establish and consolidate an ineffable "relationship" with the patient, after which the patient will talk freely. But this is to put first things second, at least partially. The relationship of the patient and the physician is created from the fantasies of the patient and from the constructive working together of the patient and the physician. The patient's fantasies, important as they are, provide the least substantial foundation for the relationship; fantasies alone can never sustain a constructive relationship for long. In order to promote an effective relationship with the patient, the physician must therefore be about his business of helping the patient. Initially this consists in listening to the patient and helping him talk. Certainly the patient becomes able to talk more freely after he has become attached to the physician. But this attachment depends upon the physician's ability to help the patient talk freely in the first place. Nothing helps the patient talk so much as his actually talking.

We can summarize the influence of the physician's personal characteristics on the patient by saying that he (the physician) acts as a complex conditional stimulus (or group of stimuli) for the patient. The more closely he resembles in his appearance and behavior the significant persons of the patient's past life, the more he will evoke the responses they evoked. Some of the physician's resemblances to these people derive from what he is and what he must do to carry out his work. These aspects of himself he cannot alter to suit the patient, but must remain aware of their possible effect. Other resemblances of the physician to the significant persons of the patient's past life may lie in what we may call the physician's nonmedical behavior. The inappropriate and irrational ingredients of the physician's professional behavior may resemble similar behavior in the patient's parents, for example, and may stimulate habitual responses to them.

The physician needs to remember that the patient responds to him both for what he does and for what he is. If he forgets this last kind of response he may think the patient's irrational responses related to something he has done and forget that they may occur simply because the physician reminds the patient (usually unconsciously) of important persons in his past life.

### Duration of the Relationship

As already mentioned, the contacts of the physician and patient over one or many interviews gradually strengthen the relationship between them as the patient increasingly experiences the physician's interest and acceptance. The longer the patient experiences such interest and acceptance, the stronger becomes his attachment to the physician, and the more readily he can confide and talk about formerly disturbing topics.

These conclusions are founded upon observations of the physiological components of anxiety which accompany the discussion of particular topics with the same and different physicians. For example, when a patient first talks about a disturbing subject with a physician, he often shows marked signs of anxiety, such as tachycardia and tachypnea. Further discussions of the same topic with the same physician bring a gradual decline in anxiety. Eventually the patient can become quite comfortable in talking about this topic with this physician. If, however, a new physician brings up the same topic with the patient, the signs of anxiety may return, although usually not to the same degree as upon the occasion of the first discussion with the first physician.

The physician should remember that if he sees the patient every day for an hour the patient may have become strongly attached to him at the end of a week. If he sees the patient only for a few minutes once a week it may take years for the development of an equal attachment. Medical students and psychiatrists usually develop strong relationships with patients. Several factors enter into this, including the fact that they spend more time with their patients than do most other groups of physicians.

As the attachment of patient and physician increases, less rational behavior, previously inhibited, can also come forward. Usually the full unfoldment of such irrational attitudes does not occur until a degree of intimacy or intensity in the relationship has occurred. In earlier phases of the relationship, the participants are more likely to cast themselves in the roles which they think the social occasion demands. These require the best behavior of which the patient is capable and he usually shows it. The largest strawberries are always found at the top of the basket. In later acquaintance, both physician and patient may reveal aspects of themselves which they initially hide from each other.

For example, if a patient has been indulged excessively by his parents, he may come to expect such indulgence from others. In his initial contacts with the physician he may act towards the physician with seemingly realistic appraisal of the physician's professional role, his skills and his limitations. Later, however, the patient may shed these attitudes and reveal his underlying expectation that the physician will treat him with indulgence as did his parents. He may express this attitude by taking up the physician's time unnecessarily, making frequent telephone calls at night, consulting the physician for all kinds of advice unconnected with the physician's chief area of expertness, and in many other ways. When the physician does not respond in the manner of the patient's parents, strong emotional reactions may be evoked in the patient. He may become anxious, angry, depressed, or show other emotional responses similar to those shown in his childhood in similar situations with his parents.

## Shared Experiences

Frequently the patient lives through important experiences with the assistance of the physician. Of such a nature are operations, pregnancies and deliveries, serious illnesses (both physical and mental), deaths, or some acute domestic crisis. And to this list must be added confession and acceptance, by no means the least important of shared experiences. The sharing of such experiences nearly always strengthens the attachment of the patient to the physician.

An important aspect of the above factors is that they are all in play at the same time. This may seem to make the subject of the relation between physician and patient intolerably complex, but a recognition of all the factors will in the end lead to less complexity than attempts at oversimplification. It is unhelpful to think that the physician represents to the patient nothing but his father. It is equally unhelpful to forget that the patient's previous experiences have influenced his attitude towards the physician. The present is never only a repetition of the past, nor is it altogether new. Similarly, the physician must remember that the patient responds to the physician both according to the stereotype (often fantastic) he has formed of physicians and also as an individual person. He responds to what the physician actually does and also to what he thinks the physician ought to do. In short, the patient's behavior with the physician mixes the past and the present, the rational and the irrational; the physician must study all these components.

## THE PATIENT'S ATTITUDE TOWARD THE PHYSICIAN

The signs of a strong attachment of the patient to the physician differ in no way from the signs of attachment in other relationships. The patient shows pleasure in seeing the physician and in talking to him. He readily listens to the physician's suggestions and cooperates in other treatments. Such attitudes on the part of the patient greatly facilitate the physician's work. Unfortunately these attitudes alternate with others or are entirely replaced by them. The physician must observe the occurrence of attitudes in the patient towards him which may interfere with treatment. Among such harmful attitudes are both excessive attachment and insufficient attachment to the physician.

### *Excessive Attachment of the Patient to the Physician*

An excessive attachment on the part of the patient for the physician means an unreasonable expectation of what the physician can do. The patient clings to the physician because he believes the physician can do everything for him; accordingly, he himself does less. The physician can hardly avoid disappointing the patient's fantasies with resultant anger and discouragement on the part of the patient. He is then further behind than he might have been because he has done so little for himself while expecting the physician to do so much more than the physician could.

To avoid such difficulties, the physician must detect the signs of excessive attachment as soon as possible. Among useful clues, the physician may notice excessive eagerness on the part of the patient to talk to him and him only, with perhaps a stubborn reluctance to cooperate with anyone else such as other physicians or nurses. The patient may also ask for much advice, especially on matters outside the physician's province, or about which the patient should be able to make up his own mind. Unrealistic fantasies about what the physician can accomplish may be suggested by failure of the patient to do as much for himself as he can, although other motives can account for this also.

### *Insufficient Attachment of the Patient to the Physician*

Sometimes the patient fails to become attached to the physician in the usual way. Usually in such cases the patient has a deep mistrust of other people which he has learned during previous experiences with other people, not necessarily but sometimes with other physicians. The signs of such mistrust include the failure of the patient to talk freely to the physician, or to cooperate adequately in the treatments which the physician recommends. The patient may display overt irritation, sullenness or anger towards the physician.

As indicated above, lack of cooperation in treatment arises from different motives and other factors. Excessive dependency and distrust of the physician frequently interfere, and the physician should think of them early. The patient may despair about his condition, and so believe treatment futile. Because the patient thinks the physician can do nothing, he may not become attached to the physician since he does not associate the physician with the hope of any relief. This process occurs often in patients with severe depressions and other psychoses, and in many other patients to whom ignorance and panic bring despair about their diseases.

Suggestions for managing insufficient attachment of the patient to the physician have been deferred to the discussion in Chapter 11 of the approach to the involuntary patient.

## THE PHYSICIAN'S ATTITUDE

The physician's attitude, even more than his behavior, has an important influence on his relationship with his patient; it is responsible for success or failure in his part of the interview, that of encouraging the patient's spontaneous flow of talk, removing the obstacles in his way, and directing him towards significant topics.

### Self-Study

The great importance of the physician's attitude for the success of interviewing (and all the practice of medicine) requires the physician to learn all he can about himself. He should try to become as much aware as possible of the thoughts and feelings that arise in him when he is with, or thinking about, the patient. Such self-study has several values.

By becoming more aware of his reactions to the patient, the physician can much more effectively control unsuitable responses on his part. For example, if he becomes aware that the patient has induced some anxiety in him, he may manage to control the expression of such anxiety and thus avoid further increasing the patient's fears. Similarly, the awareness of irritation, anger, or discouragement in himself may help him to check displays of these to the patient.

The physician's own thoughts and feelings provide useful clues to the patient's psychological state. The patient may induce important emotions in the physician in two ways. First, he may influence the physician through emotional resonance. Everyone tends to affect the people around him and induce in them the moods and emotions which he has. So if the physician finds himself feeling anxious or depressed, he may use this as a hint of the presence of the same condition in the patient.

Secondly, the patient's behavior towards the physician may induce reactions in the physician. A patient may appear to answer inquiries cooperatively, but his manner may communicate irritability and anger towards the physician. The latter may find himself becoming increasingly tense as the interview continues. If the physician studies his own feelings in the presence of the patient he may obtain important clues to the patient's motivations and adaptations. To give further examples, if the physician finds himself made anxious by the patient, he should consider the possibility that the patient is, perhaps unconsciously, trying to frighten him. Or if the physician finds himself strongly moved to offer a great deal of reassurance and sympathy to the patient, he should consider whether the patient is not unusually eager for such reassurance and sympathy.

Thirdly, the physician will find that his observations of the effect of the patient on him are extremely valuable as an index of the effect the patient has on other people. If he annoys the physician or extracts much sympathy from him, he is probably affecting other people in the same way. Such observations may provide clues to important aspects of the patient's psychological functioning. The physician cannot assume that the patient's behavior towards him exactly duplicates his behavior with other people; everyone behaves somewhat differently with each other person. Nevertheless, behavior tends to form patterns, so that much of what the patient shows the physician pertains to his behavior with other persons.

The physician should also study his thoughts and emotions with different patients for what they tell him about himself. When he makes inferences about the patient's psychological state from observations of his own, he should always consider to what extent factors in his own personality or current stresses in his life may have induced the feelings he observes in himself. He should not mistake tension arising from other preoccupations with that induced by the patient's anxiety or other behavior.

Also, the physician should become as much aware as he can of the complex motivations (never single) which enter into his relations with different patients and colleagues. He should conduct a continuing research into his own attitudes, seeking to reinforce helpful ones and expunge harmful ones.

*Desirable Characteristics of the Physician*

The appropriate attitude for promoting interviews includes several desirable ingredients. We take for granted that the physician brings to each interview dignity, graciousness, and good manners. But in addition, skilful interviewing requires also that the physician have and show interest, acceptance, warmth, and flexibility.

The attitude of the physician is never conveyed in a direct verbal statement. It does not help for the physician to say something like: "You can trust me. I am interested in you and am for you." Many patients have come to distrust words as expressions of attitudes. They judge the physician by his behavior so he might as well spare himself the awkward silence which might greet any such remarks as those of the above example. What he cannot say in words he must show instead in his actions.

**Interest**

The interest of the physician in the patient encourages the patient to talk. It tells him he is talking to someone who wants to help. And interest in the patient can be feigned only with difficulty and risk. Patients can usually distinguish a physician who is genuinely interested in them from one who appears interested because he wishes to give that impression. Fortunately, few physicians need to simulate, because most are genuinely interested in their patients. The interest springs from a wish to ease suffering and from curiosity about disease. Some physicians restrain the expression of an interest in their patients as persons, believing this to be an unprofessional intrusion into the affairs of the patient. On the contrary, if the physician expresses his interest in a professional manner, he has few greater assets for helping his patients.

The physician's interest in the patient tells the patient that the physician is trying to understand him. That the physician tries to understand sometimes means more to the patient than whether he succeeds. For all good physicians know, and most patients sense, that medical understanding of human ills remains quite imperfect. The patient knows that the physician will help him with what understanding he does have, and part of the patient's response to the physician's interest derives from the hope of relief brought by expert knowledge and skills. But the patient knows little or nothing of pathology or the science of medicine, and he can only respond in a general and expectant way to the kind of understanding based on expert knowledge and training.

Yet the patient responds also to the physician's interest as an expression of a different kind of understanding, that of any human being who shows kind interest in the suffering of another and tries to care for him. Even the simplest and perhaps stumbling efforts of the physician to enter the patient's world and come to know something of what he experiences kindle the patient's affection. No one can ever actually share the experiences of another person; but the effort to do so always brings one person closer to another. The ability to make this effort can itself become a kind of expertness because it draws the patient closer to the physician and so enables him to talk more freely and cooperate more fully in the treatment. This ability has little connection with the other kind of understanding which comes with expert knowledge. Anyone who watches the success of inexpert, unsophisticated medical students in gaining the friendship and trust of their patients can have no doubt about this. Knowledge can lead to healing; kindness is healing itself.

### Complete Acceptance of the Patient

The patient will reveal his inner feelings only to someone who, he feels, accepts him unconditionally. The patient's suffering drives him to seek help by talking about his symptoms and difficulties to the physician. With respect to physical symptoms, the patient can usually talk freely. But often he will wish to conceal his psychological symptoms because these usually include feelings, attitudes, and activities of which he is ashamed. Previous experiences have too often taught him that confidences can be turned against him. Consequently, the patient's wish to confide often conflicts with his fear that to do so may bring pain. He wonders if the physician will treat him the way other persons have done. From this arises the need for the physician to have and show complete acceptance of the patient whatever he may say.

The physician naturally reacts emotionally to many things the patient says. Some of the patient's statements may arouse in him feelings of disgust, anxiety, embarrassment, sorrow, or other emotional states. It would be asking the impossible, and also the undesirable, to expect the physician never to show such feelings. But he should strive to become aware of his reactions to what the patient says. Then he should gradually try to bring under control those emotions which can interfere with the patient's ability to talk. He should not, for example, allow what the patient says to evoke expressions of anger, surprise, or disgust as these will surely deter the patient from further confidences. He may laugh with the patient, but never at him. Nor should he permit, if he can help it, the expression of negative emotions with which the patient may have temporarily infected him. Thus, if the patient's anxiety or depression make the physician anxious or depressed, the physician should try to avoid communicating this to the patient. Some patients may become alarmed by the knowledge that their emotions have affected the physician. They think that this proves they are "bad" or destructive.

The physician must learn to conceal any moral judgments he may have about the attitudes or behavior of the patient. He will be most successful in this if he looks upon all behavior as having a meaning and serving a purpose for the patient. He will be unsuccessful if he considers only its effect on those around the patient or on society. Such an approach does not necessarily imply approval of all the patient's attitudes and behavior, but rather a complete acceptance of the patient notwithstanding them. Without this prevailing tolerance, sooner or later suggestions of moral judgment will infiltrate the manner and remarks of the physician. The physician's judgmental thoughts will be conveyed in subtle ways to the patient and will deter the patient from further revelations of his feelings. The physician should be moral, but not a moralist.

Many patients fear that another person may not accept them because of their hostile thoughts and attitudes about persons toward whom they have been expected to have only loving thoughts and attitudes. The acceptance of the patient, communicated by the physician's manner and remarks, can aid in drawing out the expression of his emotions. If the physician asks with a smile: "Did that make you mad?" the patient will usually admit being angry if he was. But if, as the physician asks this same question, his face appears forbidding or critical, the patient may say: "No, that didn't make me mad. That didn't bother me at all. I never gave it another thought."

The physician should show his acceptance of the patient by phrasing his questions tactfully at all times. Similarly he must, at least initially, accept the patient's own evaluation of his experiences. If the patient says people are reading his mind, the physician may wish to say: "Are you sure they are reading your mind?" or "Why do you say a thing like that?" More tactful questions would be: "Why should they read your mind?" and "Who are they?"

The physician should always convey to the patient an assumption that the patient is trying to be objective. He knows that the patient will rarely succeed in this. "The nearest we can come to being impartial," said G. K. Chesterton, "is to admit that we are partial." But few persons can do this. Nearly everyone prefers to insist that he is unbiased. The physician should not challenge this assumption in the patient, at least initially. He should remember that people tend to develop the qualities which others attribute to them. So the assumption by the physician of the patient's objectivity tends to make the patient strive to be more objective.

THE VALUE OF THE PATIENT'S EXPERIENCES FOR HIM. Acceptance of the patient means also the attempt to understand the value for the patient of all the experiences he has had or wants to have. A narrow range in the experience of the physician may constrict his sympathies for experiences important to other people. Some physicians can compensate for their own limited range of experiences by recognizing the value to others of those experiences they have missed themselves. Other physicians seem unable to do this and thus deprive some of their patients of the opportunities for talking which they need. For example, a physician who has had no religious experiences himself may become bored when the patient tries to discuss his religious conflicts, or may devalue the patient's religious experiences, or seek to "explain" them. Such an attitude removes his usefulness to the patient for discussing this topic. The desired attitude has nothing to do with whether the physician is himself outwardly religious. The atheist may better understand the meaning of a religious experience to the patient than a firm believer. What counts is the ability to appreciate the meaning of the patient's experiences for him.

### Warmth and Empathy

From the recommendation of complete acceptance of the patient it should not be thought that the ideal attitude is one of judicial aloofness. The physician should have and show empathy, which is the ability to feel what another person is feeling. The patient should be helped to feel that his reactions are natural under the circumstances, even if they have not been entirely satisfactory for himself or others.

One can hardly exaggerate the importance for a successful interview of the physician's communication of friendly feelings for the patient. No one can say that a particular form of interviewing surpasses others. A kindly, warmhearted physician can use an apparently crude question and answer method while developing an extremely strong and therapeutic relationship with his patient. Conversely, an insensitive, aloof physician may use a more "modern" nondirective, nonquestioning technique of interviewing and annoy the patient beyond endurance. Interviewing, although this should hardly need stating, cannot be learned from a book, but only from personal experience. A book can say what should be done; unfortunately, it can tell little about how or when to do it. Personal experience does teach this and teaches also that the method of interviewing can vary widely without impairing the results;

but the attitude of the physician towards the patient cannot. Nothing can substitute for a friendly attitude towards the patient.

The physician may, however, vary the amount of warmth he shows according to the circumstances. Some patients need more encouragement than others. Yet the physician need never sympathize sentimentally with the patient in his misfortune. Wise patients will prize understanding more highly than sympathy; and sympathy will only corrupt the foolish ones. Nor should the physician identify himself completely with the patient so that he comes to believe and say to himself: "Anyone would have become sick if he had gone through what you did." If the physician begins to lose his objectivity, he may also lose his ability to help the patient. His task is to understand the patient's reactions without necessarily believing that they are the only possible reactions to the situation the patient is in. The patient must have a physician who believes he (the patient) did the best he could at the time; he also needs a physician who is aware of alternative, and possibly better, methods of handling problems.

When the physician tries to communicate greater friendliness and warmth to the patient, he should remember possible misunderstandings of his gestures by the patient. Thus he may think it helpful and it sometimes is, to touch a patient or use the patient's given name. But some patients may interpret the physician's physical contact as a sexual advance; others may construe his use of their given names as belittling them or treating them like children who are called by their first names. A knowledge of different cultures and a tactful sense of the immediate situation will assist the physician to do what is helpful more than technical rules.

### Flexibility

THE SELECTION OF TOPICS. This book will emphasize many times the need for flexibility. Efforts to compress the interview into a rigid pattern inevitably lessen the patient's freedom to talk. In fact, the physician can sometimes obtain good results if he follows no outline whatever and merely keeps in mind the general goal of knowing as much as he can about the patient's illness and about the patient as a person. Usually, however, the physician will follow some outline in its broad headings. Certain basic facts of the present illness he must obtain. These usually the patient gives to him agreeably as he asks for them. But beyond such basic facts lie many other matters which the patient needs to talk about and the physician needs to listen to. Here the physician should let the patient run much more freely. If he does this and offers gentle guidance only, he will eventually learn everything he needs to know. On the other hand, if he forces the patient to talk in a certain order or way, he may hear only conventional and unrevealing fragments. He may get pieces of paper torn from a book instead of a whole volume.

If, during any interview, the patient becomes extremely anxious or confused, the physician may often give him time to relax by inquiring in more detail than usual about neutral matters. Thus even more than the necessary amount of time can be spent in the description of the patient's physical symptoms or the exact nature of his work. If the conversation happens to light upon a topic about which the patient talks with more ease, such as a hobby, the physician may linger with it until the patient relaxes further. Then he may again approach other more difficult subjects.

THE PHYSICIAN'S RESPONSES. The flexibility of the physician has natural limits. He need not assume roles or feelings other than those which come naturally. However, he may, within the limits of his own mood, vary his emotional responses to the patient according to the patient's condition. To an anxious patient, the physician should offer firm reassurance. To a depressed patient, the physician should show quiet optimism, but not exuberant cheerfulness. If the patient is angry or suspicious, the physician should be friendly, but not ingratiating or defensive.

One can be rather sure that a jocular mood is always out of place in a professional consultation. A sense of humor can relieve some of the anxieties of the practice of medicine. But its inappropriate exhibition to the patient can prove harmful. For example, if things afterwards turn out badly, the patient may understandably reproach the physician with taking grave matters too lightly.

THE USE OF LANGUAGE. The physician must show flexibility by suiting his language to the patient's comprehension. He should prefer simple everyday words like "mad," "angry," and "help" to technical terms such as "hostile," "dependency," and "security." The use of strange technical words may startle the patient out of his flow and start him ruminating about what the physician means by such words. The physician should note the patient's expressions for common emotions, physical organs, symptoms, and illnesses. Then, when he understands the sense in which the patient uses these terms, he should employ them himself in his remarks to the patient. If he does not use terms which have the same meaning for him and the patient, confusion may result.

The choice of language should be governed by the goal of achieving maximal communication with the patient. This requires that the language in which the two communicate be as natural as possible for both participants, not just for one of them. There should be no need to translate "four-letter words" into polite English if the patient uses such words first. On the other hand, the physician should not necessarily use such words if the patient does not. The physician should not adopt the accent or language of a slang or dialect in order to promote rapport by a show of fellowship. The patient will often detect such artificial maneuvers and may resent them as patronizing to him.

## References and Suggestions for Further Reading

1. ALEXANDER, M., and FRENCH, T. M.: *Psychoanalytic Therapy*. Chapter 5, The Transference Phenomenon. New York, The Ronald Press Co., 1946.
2. BAKER, A. A., and Thorpe, J. G.: Placebo responses. *A.M.A. Arch. Neurol. & Psychiat.* 78:57, 1957.
3. BARTEMEIER, L.: The attitude of the physician. *J.A.M.A.* 145:1122, 1951.
4. BREUER, J., and FREUD, S.: *Studies in Hysteria*. Trans. by A. A. Brill. New York. Nervous and Mental Disease Monographs, 1950 (originally published 1895).
5. DOLLARD, J., and MILLER, N. E.: *Personality and Psychotherapy*. Chapter 17, Transference: Generalized Responses in the Therapeutic Situation. New York, McGraw-Hill, Inc., 1950.
6. FREUD, S.: The dynamics of the transference. *Collected Papers*, Vol. 2, Chapter 28. Trans. by Joan Riviere. London, The Hogarth Press, 1935.
7. FREUD, S.: Further recommendations in the techniques of psychoanalysis: Observations on transference love. *Collected Papers*, Vol. 2, Chapter 33. Trans. by Joan Riviere. London, The Hogarth Press, 1924.
8. FROMM-REICHMANN, F.: *Principles of Intensive Psychotherapy*. Chapter V, The Initial Interview. Chicago, University of Chicago Press, 1950.
9. GLIEDMAN, L. H., GANTT, W. H., and TEITELBAUM, H. A.: Some implications of conditional reflex studies for placebo research. *Am. J. Psychiat.* 113:1103, 1957.
10. IMBODEN, J. B.: Brunswik's theory of perception. A note on its applicability to normal and neurotic personality functioning. *A.M.A. Arch. Neurol. & Psychiat.* 77:187, 1957.
11. KASPER, A. M.: The psyche doctor, the soma doctor, and the psychosomatic patient. *Bull. Menninger Clin.* 16:77, 1952.
12. MEARES, A.: *The Medical Interview*. Springfield, Ill., Charles C Thomas, 1958.
13. STEVENSON, I., and MATTHEWS, R. A.: The art of interviewing. *GP* 2:59, 1950.
14. STEVENSON, I.: *The American Handbook of Psychiatry* (edited by S. Arieti). Chapter 9, The Psychiatric Interview. New York, Basic Books, Inc., 1959.
15. SULLIVAN, H. S.: *The Psychiatric Interview*. New York, W. W. Norton Co., Inc., 1954.
16. WITTKOWER, E. D., and WHITE, K. L.: Bedside manners. *Brit. Med. J.* i:1432, 1954.

# 2

## PROCEDURES AND PROCESSES OF MEDICAL INTERVIEWING

The physician can influence his relationship with his patients by attention to certain practical aspects of the interviews and to certain processes common to all or most medical interviews. The importance of these procedures and processes merits their discussion here before the following chapters describe details of the data to be collected and the techniques for collecting them.

### ARRANGING THE INTERVIEW

In planning and conducting interviews, the physician should always consider the convenience and comfort of the patient. Even before they meet, physician and patient may have talked on the telephone. The physician then can demonstrate his interest in the patient by the attention he gives to the patient's preliminary statement of his symptoms and by arranging for a full interview. These arrangements should include a time convenient for the patient and explicit directions to the patient for reaching the clinic or office of the physician.

The physician should arrange for privacy during the interview, and keep the period as free as possible from interruptions or other distractions. Privacy in the conduct of an interview on a ward may require special efforts. Nevertheless, some degree of privacy can usually be arranged. Many patients on wards are well enough to be taken to a small side room. Others can be surrounded by screens which provide some break against the escape of sound. Sometimes the general hubbub of the ward provides a noise which masks the sounds of the interview. Patients often think that other patients have more interest in their personal affairs than they do, and we should respect their uneasiness on this matter. A patient may find talking to the physician difficult enough; he may find talking in a room full of other strange and possibly curious persons quite impossible. The clinic and office meet requirements of privacy more readily. Here the physician should concern himself more with the prevention of interruptions and with allowing himself adequate time for the needs of the interview.

It may be helpful for the physician to arrange the seating in the room so that the patient and he can easily see each other's faces, but do not have to do so. Many shy patients talk much more readily when not being stared at. The patient should not have to look into the bright light of a window or lamps.

One of the principal advantages of the physician in the eyes of his patient is that he is more detached from the patient's illness than members of the patient's family. So the patient often feels a freedom in talking whch is unusual and welcome to him. If then the physician invites or permits a member of the family to be present during the interview, the situation ceases to be unique. The interview can become too readily a repetition of familiar exchanges which the patient has already had with the relative in question. Relatives will often crowd themselves into the physician's office under one or another pretext, most often that the patient lacks their own superior clarity of expression in explaining his difficulties. The physician must usually resist such intrusions gently, but if need be, also firmly. And this applies even when the interview seems likely to be confined to the patient's physical symptoms. The physician cannot predict what reticence the patient may have about physical symptoms, or when he may be ready to make one of those useful digressions into his personal life which the physician should always seek to encourage.

Some exceptions to the above rule occur. Sometimes small children become restless away from a parent. However, parents should not be permitted to intrude simply because the patient is a child. Also with some elderly patients, some psychotic patients, or patients speaking a foreign language only, the physician may need a relative to help him communicate with the patient.

When a physician excludes a patient's relative from an interview, he should tell the relative that he will perhaps see him later. Assuming the patient agrees to this during the interview, the physician can then talk with the relative after he has talked to the patient. Further remarks on talking with relatives have been made in Chapter 12.

The physician should always note the circumstances of the patient's arrival at the office. These often provide important clues to significant attitudes on the part of the patient towards his illness and towards members of the family. Thus the physician should note whether the patient telephones or writes himself to make his appointment or whether someone else does this for him. Similarly one should note whether the patient comes alone or with a relative. Excessive dependency may often be first and best demonstrated by the manner of the patient's coming for medical examinations and treatment.

## STARTING THE INTERVIEW

At the beginning of any interview, the initiative lies with the physician. He should introduce himself and then, if the interview takes place in an office, he should lead the patient to the office and indicate a comfortable chair for the patient. If the interview takes place in a hospital, after the introduction the physician should arrange himself and the patient so that both can talk comfortably without straining to see or hear each other.

If the patient has been referred by a colleague, a few sentences will serve to inform the patient that the physician is already acquainted with his case but wishes to hear more. The physician may say, for example: "I'm Dr. Smith. Dr. Jones has told me a little of your symptoms and asked me to see you, but I'd like to hear about them from you directly."

If the patient has referred himself, the physician may simply say: "Tell me about your illness (problem)." "Why have you come to see me?" "Why did Dr. Jones send you to me?" "What brought you to the hospital?" or "Tell me what brings you here." Often such remarks will start the patient talking. Sometimes he may appear puzzled and need more direction. The physician could then say: "You must have been feeling bad or you would not have come to see me, so tell me about your symptoms and also about yourself." The last phrase indicates to the patient whose complaints are physical that the physician is interested in the person who has these complaints. Thus a remark of this sort early in the interview helps to prepare the patient for a comprehensive study. Moreover, it encourages the patient to talk spontaneously about everything which comes to his mind without fear of boring or irritating the physician.

Certain opening moves by the physician should be avoided. For example, the physician should not open the conversation with: "What's wrong with you?" or with "What is the matter with you?" The information he seeks with such questions is certainly important, but the timing and the phrasing are incorrect. At the beginning of an interview, the patient is far from ready to say what he thinks is wrong with himself. He wants to tell about his symptoms and start the treatment. He has come to the physician to find out what is wrong. Apart from this the reference to "something wrong" carries connotations of inadequacy and even moral defect. The patient may think he is being judged and condemned for being ill. Furthermore, the examples above may promote in the mind of the patient the notion that there is some one thing wrong, the correction of which will bring health. Patients commonly entertain such ideas of a single cause. The physician often works hard to get them to think of multiple causes and processes rather than single causes and anatomical defects. Nothing is gained by using language which encourages the patient's original line of thought.

## Putting the Patient at Ease

The patient's predicament at the beginning of the interview must be kept in mind. He is ill and usually does not know in what way or how seriously. Ignorance augments his fears, and fears further disturb his mental and physical functioning. In this state he is obliged to meet another person, more often than not for the first time, and provide that other person not only with a coherent account of his own symptoms, but with a great many other details, many of them highly intimate, of his past and present life. To make matters worse, the patient often cannot see the relevance of most of this detail to his current suffering. The physician himself often does not know which details will eventually become relevant and which will have to be discarded.

If the interview takes place in a hospital, the patient's anxiety and confusion may already have been compounded by his contacts with a large number of entirely strange people who pass busily back and forth across his view, and who seemingly never stop unless to ask him a question or give him an instruction.

In the absence of any physical emergency, the physician should attend first to the emergency of the patient's initial anxiety brought about by the circumstances described above. This anxiety is most readily reduced by the simple presence of the physician who, by his interest in the patient, offers the prospect of relief. The patient's anxiety usually soon recedes as he becomes absorbed in telling his story.

Sometimes the physician's presence and interest in hearing the history is not enough by itself. Then the physician may need to make other moves to reduce the patient's anxiety before the interview can proceed satisfactorily. If the patient shows marked anxiety, the physician should sometimes ask the patient about this directly. He can say, for example,

"You seem very upset about something. Can you tell me what it is?" More often the patient shows a lesser degree of anxiety which interferes with the interview, without blocking it entirely. The physician should always give the patient plenty of time to get used to talking to him before he pushes the interview into personal matters. The patient can often be put at ease by prolonging the introductory amenities, perhaps with a conversation about mutual acquaintances. The physician should help the patient to relax by sustaining the conversation himself and asking questions about the symptoms and the patient's current life. A markedly anxious patient should not be expected to talk fluently or to bear responsibility for filling silences in the conversation. The physician should keep the initiative and fill the silences with his questions. The patient then does not feel pressed to speak because the physician is already speaking. So extensive questioning, which might later be avoided as interfering with the patient's spontaneity, may in this situation carry the patient along until he can regain his composure and freedom to speak easily. Questioning designed to relieve anxiety should be directed away from the sources of the anxiety into some neutral area such as, for example, the details of the patient's job.

## PHASES OF HISTORY-TAKING

An interview or series of interviews forming part of an examination ordinarily shows several phases somewhat divided from each other by a difference in topics discussed, by different willingness on the part of the patient to talk, and hence also by different needs for activity by the physician.

At the beginning of the first interview, both physician and patient wish to discuss the chief complaints and the details of the present illness. The patient may have some anxiety about these subjects, but nevertheless wishes to talk of them. With little activity from the physician, the patient will usually give an account of his current symptoms or troubles as he sees them. In this phase of the interview, the physician should listen with as few interruptions as possible. For the most part he should restrain curiosity about details in favor of preserving the patient's spontaneity. He cannot expect to understand everything, but can make mental or written notes of questions to which he may return later.

In the next phase of the interview, the physician wishes to learn more details of the present illness, in order to obtain a clearer understanding of the main symptoms and any associated disturbances. He also wishes to understand the environment in which they have occurred. During this phase the physician may also find it convenient to review the patient's past health, including a survey of the health and functioning of his different physical organs. So at this point the physician necessarily questions the patient more fully. The patient often does not understand the reasons for this questioning, but he usually follows the physician's leads. The topics discussed are relatively free of anxiety for him.

In the next phase, the physician may ask the patient to tell him something of his family background. The physician may need to ask questions in this area also, in order to give the patient leads about the specific information he wants. The patient can usually talk most easily about the physical health of the members of his family. After this, he may be led to talk about the personalities of these people. Finally, through transitions, he may be encouraged to talk about his experiences and relationships with them. This forms part of the personal history and the topic may provide a good channel into it.

In the final phase, the physician wishes to explore the personal history and the specific psychological problems of the patient which may contribute to the total disability. Then he should try to stop questioning and again draw out the patient's spontaneous remarks. Often he can do this easily, for many people like to tell the story of their lives to someone who is interested. Nearly always, however, the story eventually reaches people and events which are still associated with painful feelings and then the patient may become less eager and often positively reluctant to talk about these subjects. So here he will again need the active help of the physician. Frequently the physician must explain to the patient the reasons for talking about these painful subjects.

These common phases of interviews have not been mentioned with the intention of insisting that every interview will or must follow the same pattern. Here, as always, the principle of flexibility should supersede any formal outline of procedure. Many times the physician will find opportunities to pass from the present illness directly into a discussion of the personal history. The family history may then come later and the details of the patient's current life situation conclude the survey. The physician should expect variations in the patient's ease of talking and his own activity should show responsive variations. Some patients, for example, will talk easily about themselves and with difficulty about their families. Other patients will be quite garrulous about their families and reticent about their own feelings.

The various topics of the history may be discussed in one interview, or only completed after many interviews. It is unusual to complete a history and evaluation of a disorder in one interview, although the attempt must sometimes be made. Usually several and perhaps up to six or ten interviews will be required. But the actual time spent is not so important as the skills used and the results obtained. Here also, the different abilities of patients to reveal themselves influence results as much as the aptitude and the experience of the physician. But he needs these qualities in making smooth and unnoticed the transition from one topic to another, so that, for example, the patient will start talking about his personal life instead of his symptoms without being aware of the change of subject.

The physician needs skill for every aspect of history-taking and interviewing, but more for some than others. Because the patient wishes to talk about his major symptoms and has little or no anxiety in doing so, he willingly shares the task of making this part of the history-taking successful. In contrast, the sensitivities and easily aroused anxieties of the patient when he is led to discuss his psychological difficulties or personal life pose special problems for the physician. The physician has to uncover and bring into the open essential data without increasing the patient's discomfort excessively and certainly without threatening the patient's attachment to him.

## DURATION, NUMBER, AND FREQUENCY OF INTERVIEWS

Several factors limit the duration of interviews. The time which the physician has available naturally influences the duration. So does the willingness of the patient to talk. If a patient shows signs of being restless or dissatisfied with the course of an interview, it may be wiser to break it off and resume another day when he may be more approachable. It often happens that a patient who is initially reluctant to talk about himself (other than his symptoms), becomes much less so after an interval, even before the physician sees him again. So when the physician approaches the patient a second time, he may be surprised to find the patient much more eager to talk than he was at first.

The physician must always remember that talking about personal problems evokes the emotions which were originally associated with the people and events discussed. Strong emotional states are always more tiring than weaker ones. The associated muscle tension of strong emotions can cause considerable fatigue. An hour of history-taking about a physical illness may be less fatiguing than ten minutes spent in re-living some traumatic event of the past. For this reason, few interviews should last longer than an hour, or an hour and a half. If more time than this is needed, the patient and physician should usually arrange to meet again. Occasionally, when the patient has a strong wish to talk, a longer interview of two or more hours may be helpful; but such lengthy interviews are not usually needed for the initial examination of a patient.

As the physician should avoid interviews which are too lengthy, so he should not cut them too short. As mentioned later in Chapter 8 in connection with encouraging the patient to express his emotions, the patient always needs some time in which to relax so he can talk freely. Usually, he talks much more freely in the last fifteen minutes of an interview than in the first fifteen minutes. In a truncated interview lasting only ten or fifteen minutes, he may never reach the point of talking as freely as he should. Nevertheless, brief interviews may be helpful sometimes and they should not be discarded simply because longer ones are infeasible.

For all the abovementioned reasons, therefore, it generally happens that effective interviews last sometime between half an hour and an hour.

The physician should give whatever time a thorough history requires. But he is not required to give all this time in the initial interview. This is rarely possible. All the relevant historical data can rarely emerge in the hour or so likely to be allotted to a preliminary examination. The physician should therefore do what he can in the first interview and continue the work in succeeding ones. It is often possible to form a preliminary opinion of the patient's disorder at the first interview. Upon the basis of this, some tests or some preliminary treatments may be proposed. When the patient returns for the tests or treatments, the physician can interview him each time, and each time can somewhat extend his acquaintance with the patient and understanding of him.

Or the physician at the initial interview may propose further interviews to the patient. He may say to the patient: "There seems to be a lot more to go into which we cannot do today. Suppose we arrange another time (or several more times) when we can talk about these things further."

For history-taking interviews when there is no urgency, there are some advantages to meeting at about weekly intervals. The lapse of a week nearly always brings something new for the patient to talk about, and from talking about the seemingly small events of the week, the patient often learns to connect symptoms and life situations. When the physician talks with the patient more often, less has happened between visits, and so the interviews may lack material from the patient's current life. Such material is particularly valuable for exposing fluctuations in symptoms and their relationships to stresses.

Moreover, frequent interviews tend to make the patient more dependent upon the physician. Like everyone, patients generally have expectations of another person in accordance with the amount of time they spend with that person. The more time they spend with the physician, the more they think he is interested in them, and the more they tend to expect him to do for them.

At times, however, more frequent interviews are desirable. When the patient has a great deal of material from his past or present life which presses for expression, the physician may see him every day for a few days. Then, when the pressure diminishes, the interviews can be spaced further apart. Also, if the patient seems markedly anxious and in need of much support, daily interviews may be needed. But this would be a requirement of psychotherapy, not of history-taking.

### ENDING THE INTERVIEW

Interviews should not end abruptly. The patient's need to express himself fully should be respected. He should not be cut off bluntly in the middle of some important recital. In the first place, this is plainly rude, and indicates lack of interest on the part of the physician. Secondly, the patient may leave the office in an emotionally disturbed state. If the patient has been much agitated or angry about what he was saying, the disturbance may distract him sufficiently to make it dangerous for him to drive a car or walk in traffic. Therefore, no patient should be allowed to leave an office in a markedly disturbed condition. There are two alternative courses for preventing this. If the physician has time, he can allow the patient to talk himself out until the patient has relaxed again, and then he can terminate the interview. But a busy physician has other demands on his time, and cannot always hear the patient through a long account. Therefore he should warn the patient about five minutes before he must close the interview. He can say something like: "I can see this subject is extremely important to you, and think we are going to have to go into it a lot more. Unfortunately, I only have about five minutes more which I can spend with you today, so we may have to leave some of it." With such comments, the patient nearly always begins to move away from the distressing subject so that by the time the five minutes are up, he is once more composed and ready to leave the office.

Even when the patient is not especially disturbed by the interview, he should be given a chance to say anything which may be important to him before the interview closes. The physician can say, for example: "We're going to have to stop there, I'm afraid, unless there is something else you particularly wanted to mention before we stop." Upon this the patient may talk a little further, although usually taking the physician's hint that the interview is to end.

At the end of an interview a patient may wish to express some anxiety-laden thought which he had previously inhibited. It is as if a balance between inhibition and expression is finally broken as the patient sees the end of the interview approaching and decides he will risk the dangers of revealing his anxiety. At this point, however, he may still hesitate while looking towards the exit. Because such reserved items are specially charged with anxiety, the physician should help the patient to verbalize them. Useful remarks to encourage this are: "Is there anything else you would like to tell me?" and "Is there anything else I should know about you?" Sometimes the physician can helpfully say: "You look as if you had something else on your mind. Let's take a few minutes to hear about that." Then the patient will nearly always tell this special fear and the interview can end.

The physician can usually distinguish these special fears reserved for the end of the interview from the holding maneuvers of loquacious patients who will not let the physician go. The inhibited fears usually require the physicians' active encouragement before they are expressed; the merely garrulous patient often requires rather firm discouragement before the interview can end.

The physician should usually give the patient a chance to ask any questions he may have. For example, he can say: "I know I've asked you a lot of questions. Perhaps you have some you'd like to ask me." To this the patient may reply with some questions which also tell the physician more about the patient. The patient's questions reveal areas of confusion, conflict, or anxiety for him. The physician should not, however, use the patient's questions only for his own information. He should answer the questions considerately and with all possible accuracy, although there may be some he cannot answer.

Many patients hesitate to open themselves freely to physicians in a first interview. They need time to evaluate the physician's trustworthiness and also often to consider the relevance of the many personal matters he may inquire about. For such patients the following technique often proves useful. At the initial interview the physician carries the patient into the territory of his emotions and life situation as far as the patient can comfortably go. If appropriate, the physician can throw out for the patient's consideration some suggested correlations (based on inferences from the data) between the patient's symptoms, emotions, and life situation. These suggestions the patient frequently rejects as quite irrelevant, and reverts to such explanations as "overwork," "the menopause," "low blood pressure," or whatever comforting diagnosis he or she has assigned to the symptoms. At this point the physician can say: "Well, I think the things we've been talking about (here naming the life stresses or emotions) are important in your illness and may be the main source of your symptoms. Let's leave it there today, but I would like you to think over all the things we've talked about between now and the next time I see you. I think you'll find you have a lot of other thoughts about it all and these will help us work it out better." The interview can then end with the physician and patient arranging to meet again in a few days or a week. The patient will nearly always think much in the interval about the subjects discussed. Often he may eagerly request another interview before the scheduled one. And when he and the physician do meet he may pour out much more information, often confirmatory of the physician's preliminary opinion. Apparently in the first interview the patient's initial anxiety, augmented perhaps by the first confrontation with correlations between symptoms and emotions, interferes with the patient's ability to think clearly and also evokes a defensive rejection of such correlations. After the interview the patient relaxes somewhat and has time to reflect on its contents and to bring into his awareness a great many associated ideas which had previously been excluded by his acute anxiety. At the next interview he can usually think and talk more freely because he is usually more relaxed.

The patient sometimes wishes to know his diagnosis or his prognosis or the proposed treatment early in the study and even after only a history-taking interview. The physician can tell the patient something of whatever he knows at the time. If he knows too little to form a definite opinion of the case, he should say so frankly without offering false reassurances designed to cover the delay. The patient is much more likely to resent evasion or unwarranted reassurances than a frank statement that a definite opinion cannot yet be offered. Most patients would prefer to forego unfounded reassurance and wait longer for reassurance soundly based on a complete study. However, even when the physician cannot furnish the patient with a complete formulation of the problem, he can usually provide some reassurance which may reduce the patient's concern considerably. Such reassurance should certainly not be withheld from the patient. The physician can usually offer some such remark as: "Nothing you have told me has given me any cause to worry about the outcome," "You haven't told me anything yet to make me think you have a serious illness," "If you had a really serious illness, you would have different symptoms from those you have, but let's do some more examinations to make sure," or "What we have found out so far about your symptoms still seems to show you much more healthy than ill." Statements of this kind, provided they fit the facts, can help the patient without committing the physician to a position which may later become untenable.

It is particularly harmful to tell a patient who has consulted the physician because he is having symptoms: "There is nothing the matter with you." Obviously the patient would not have come if there was nothing the matter with him. It may well be the case that the patient has no major physical disease and that his physical symptoms are largely or entirely manifestations or accompaniments of emotions such as anxiety or depression. If the patient has mistakenly thought he had a severe physical illness, he will have to be educated to a different opinion. But this should usually be done gradually. If he is emotionally disturbed, is dimly aware of this possibility but frightened of it, and has accepted his physical symptoms as acceptable alternatives, to deprive him suddenly of this explanation for his illness may be quite frightening. I know of two depressed patients who have committed suicide after being told, following physical examinations, that there was "nothing the matter."

Finally, the ending of each interview should include some plan for continuing. It way be that some treatment can be proposed; or it may be that further interviews are needed. In any case the patient should be told what to expect next as explicitly as possible. If treatments are proposed, they should be accompanied by explanations of the illness and specific recommendations. If further interviews are proposed, the exact time and place of the next one should be settled with the patient before the interview ends. Under no circumstances should the physician walk away from a patient's bed, or let the patient walk away from his office, without the patient clearly understanding the next step in the examination or treatment.

## BEGINNING LATER INTERVIEWS

In later interviews, the physician should greet the patient and then let him talk first. Or the physician should ask the patient some open question which permits him to talk about whatever is uppermost in his mind. Useful questions of this kind are: "How are things?" "What's been happening since I saw you last?" or "How have you been?" In responding to questions of this kind, the patient will feel free to talk about some current difficulty which is on his mind or which has arisen since the previous interview. It may be that something important has happened to him and he may want to talk first of this. A breezy greeting by the physician may jar a patient whose father has died the week before. Also, if the physician opens the interview with a focusing question, the patient may feel obliged to conform to the physician's selection and may never return to whatever lies at the top of his mind at the time. If, however, the patient has no current matter to talk about, the physician can then ask a more directive question.

Sometimes it is helpful to bring the patient back to the end of the last interview and say: "Last time we had to stop before you had time to say everything that was on your mind. Perhaps we can go on where we left off." Or the physician may say: "After you left here, you probably thought of a lot of things you did not have a chance to say. Let's go into those now." If to such inquiries the patient responds unproductively, the physician can then direct the patient towards whatever specific topics of the history or the patient's current life need further elucidation.

## MAKING NOTES

The preference of the physician and sometimes the attitude of the patient should decide whether notes are taken during an interview or examination. The great advantage of a verbatim, or almost verbatim, account of the patient's remarks is not to be abandoned lightly. The principal reason for sacrificing this advantage, however, is its interference with the free flow of the patient's remarks and with the ability of the physician to attend to the emotional coloring of these remarks. Few physicians can take detailed notes without diminishing their participation in the interview or their observations of the patient. Some patients approve the physician's taking notes as a sign of his special interest in their cases. Other patients, not exclusively paranoid ones, are concerned about who has access to the physician's notes. If they see detailed notes being written down, they cease to talk freely until reassured that the notes are confidential and not accessible to anyone else. Still other patients associate the taking of notes with filling out a questionnaire which means to them being treated in a routine way, or as a number rather than as a person.

The physician may, if he wishes, start all interviews with some notes. The patient's name and some of the basic identifying data are going to be written down anyway at the first interview. The physician may then continue to take some notes as the interview progresses. He will soon learn whether this distracts or disturbs the patient, or whether he himself cannot listen adequately if he takes detailed notes. In either of these cases he can then abandon note-taking altogether or confine himself to notes of headings only. If a patient objects to the taking of notes, the purpose of the notes may be briefly explained to him with reassurances of their inaccessibility to anyone but the physician. If the patient then still objects, the note-taking should be abandoned altogether.

The excellent reasons for not always making notes in the patient's presence do not preclude the making of adequate records after the patient leaves the office. The physician should then, or as soon as possible, make a full and systematic written record of his interview and examination of the patient.

If the physician makes notes immediately after the interview, he can often capture many of the exact words and phrases of the patient. Direct quotations of the patient's remarks increase the value of the records.

The physician should remember that society has conferred upon him the privilege of learning about the intimate affairs of his patients. But this privilege does not extend to the large number of other persons who may work with the physician, come in contact with the patient, or have some interest in him. The physician is responsible for seeing that material which the patient has confided in him does not reach unauthorized persons.

## RECOGNIZING THE LIMITATIONS OF INTERVIEWS

Even skillful interviewers frequently fail to elicit important information from patients. The missing information is not necessarily only in the area of personal relationships, feelings, and thoughts. Different interviewers have been found to elicit quite different histories of such symptoms as cough, sputum, pain, and dyspnea from patients who could be expected to have the same incidences of such symptoms.[3] Errors are, however, probably greater in eliciting the histories of personal relationships and emotional functioning. Investigations have shown that different psychiatrists may have markedly different effects on patients, even when they are ostensibly using a uniform approach.[4,7] This being so, patients as they give their histories are much influenced as to the types and amounts of information they give.

The frequent gaps in initial histories naturally suggest the value of going over the history more than once with the patient. However, there are hazards here also. First, the second history given by the patient may not be more accurate than the first one if the two differ. Secondly, questions tend to introduce errors that are not found in a freely given narrative.[8,11] This results from the common reluctance to admit ignorance. Under questioning the patient (just as witnesses in court) tends to fill in the gaps of memory with statements which may be quite false, but which at least temporarily satisfy the patient's and the physician's longing for a complete picture. This process of filling in the gaps of memory is usually quite unconscious on the part of the patient, but the physician needs to be aware of its possible occurrence during reviews of the history, especially with questioning of the patient by him. Children and uneducated adults when questioned are particularly likely to fill in gaps of memory with invented answers. Therefore, in considering a review of the history the physician needs to weigh the benefits from the new information likely to emerge against the disadvantage resulting from the possible introduction of new errors and distortions.

## THE USE OF QUESTIONNAIRES IN HISTORY-TAKING

Several questionnaires have been devised to cover systematically the topics of the medical history. The patient can fill them out before he first meets the physician either at home or in the waiting room.

The Cornell Medical Index (CMI) was the first successful questionnaire of this type.[1, 2] In comparison with history-taking interviews the CMI performs well. Patients' answers to this questionnaire permitted physicians to identify 94 per cent of the diagnostic areas or systems in which diseases were later found after further history-taking and examinations of the responding patients. Furthermore, the physicians studying the answers to the questionnaire were able to indicate correctly the actual disease found in 87 per cent of those cases in which the area of disease was lo cated through use of the questionnaire.[2] Kanner, has developed a somewhat more extensive questionnaire the answers to which can be rapidly printed out by a secretary or by a programmed typewriter.[9]

Such questionnaires have two important advantages which will almost certainly make them used more widely in the future. They save time for the physician, thereby increasing his usefulness to the public and sometimes reducing the cost of his services to the individual patient. And they cover every organ and every important symptom systematically thus avoiding the errors that can occur from failure of systematic coverage in history-taking during an interview. With certain patients they have the additional advantage of obtaining information about emotionally charged topics which the patient would not reveal if he were talking face-to-face with the physician, even though he knows the physician will read his answers to the questionnaire.

Medical-history questionnaires also have important limitations. They are not infallible and skillful history-taking by the physician may bring out points omitted in answering a questionnaire. Also by noting the emotional accompaniments of the patient's answers to questions the physician gains valuable information about the patient that he cannot obtain from reading the patient's answers to the questionnaire. And finally, the questionnaire cannot facilitate the development of a strong doctor-patient relationship which is the essential core of all treatment. Indeed, occasionally the questionnaire may be seen by the patient as an impersonal device on the part of the physician, although most patients seem to respect the thoroughness which its use implies.

### References and Suggestions for Further Reading

1. BRODMAN, K., ERDMANN, A. J., LORGE, I., and WOLFF, H. G.: The Cornell Medical Index: An adjunct to medical interview. *J.A.M.A. 140*:530, 1949.
2. BRODMAN, K., ERDMANN, A. J., LORGE, I., and WOLFF, H. G.: The Cornell Medical Index-Health Questionnaire. II. As a diagnostic instrument. *J.A.M.A. 145*:152, 1951.
3. COCHRANE, A. L., CHAPMAN, P. J., and OLDHAM, P. D.: Observers' errors in taking medical histories. *Lancet 260 (vol.1)*:1007, 1951.
4. DIMASCIO, A., BOYD, R. W., GREENBLATT, M., and SOLOMON, H. C.: The psychiatric interview: A sociophysiologic study. *Dis. Nerv. Syst. 16:*4, 1955.
5. FROMM-REICHMANN, F.: *Principles of Intensive Psychotherapy*. Chapter V, The Initial Interview. Chicago, University of Chicago Press, 1950.
6. GARRETT, A.: *Interviewing: Its Principles and Methods*. New York, Family Service Association of America, 1951.
7. GOLDMAN-EISLER, F.: Individual differences between interviewers and their effect on interviewees' conversational behavior. *J. Ment. Sci. 98*:660, 1952.
8. HUNTER, I.M.L.: *Memory: Facts and Fallacies*. Harmondsworth, England, Penguin Books, Ltd., 1957.
9. KANNER, I. F.: Programmed medical history-taking with or without computer. *J.A.M.A. 207*:317, 1969.
10. MEARES, A.: *The Medical Interview*. Springfield, Ill., Charles C Thomas, 1958.
11. STERN, W.: *General Psychology from the Personalistic Standpoint*. Trans. H. D. Spoerl. New York, The Macmillan Company, 1938.
12. STEVENSON, I.: *American Handbook of Psychiatry* (edited by S. Arieti). Chapter 9, The Psychiatric Interview. New York, Basic Books, Inc., 1959.
13. STEVENSON, I.: *The Psychiatric Examination*. Boston, Little, Brown and Company, 1969.
14. SULLIVAN, H. S.: *The Psychiatric Interview*. New York, W. W. Norton Co., Inc., 1954.
15. WHITEHORN, J. C.: Guide to interviewing and clinical presonality study. *A.M.A. Arch. Neurol. & Psychiat. 52*:197, 1944.
16. WITTKOWER, E. D., and WHITE, K. L.: Bedside manners. *Brit. Med. J. i*:1432, 1954.

# PART II

# WHAT TO LEARN IN HISTORY-TAKING

# 3

# THE HISTORY OF THE PRESENT ILLNESS

The physician in approaching his patient should have some specific ideas about the information he wishes to elicit from his interviews and examinations. He will not often obtain his history cast in the form which it will finally take when he records it. But this makes all the more important having some outline of historical material to aid in checking for omissions. The present and the two following chapters present an outline of the historical material which the physician may gather during an examination. The physician must select the emphasis to be placed on different aspects of the history. Not all topics deserve, or can possibly receive, equal attention.

## THE CHIEF COMPLAINT

The goal of the first part of the history is to obtain a full account of the entire present illness. In the course of obtaining this history one usually encounters a chief complaint, and the physician must avoid permitting this to become the only focus of future questioning. Nevertheless, there are two advantages to singling out this chief complaint for some special notice.

In the first place, the physician wants to know what troubles the patient most, even though this may not be what threatens the patient's health most. Thereby he learns something about the patient's attitudes towards health and illness. By listening carefully to the chief complaint, the physician may learn the patient's vulnerabilities, and he may learn also something of the patient's system of values, that is, what things affect him most. For example, of two patients with headaches arising from muscular tension, one may complain of unendurable pain which is "killing" him, and the other of pain which keeps him from concentrating on his work. By noting the differences in the presentation of the complaints, the physician can learn something about the different ways in which their headaches threaten these two patients.

Secondly, the chief complaint is usually the occasion for the patient's seeking medical aid at the time he does. It thus indicates the limit of his tolerance for symptoms and reveals much about his tolerance for stress in general.

The presenting complaint frequently conceals a more important complaint or disorder. The physician must seek the causes behind the complaints. And for every new causative factor turned up, he must ask another question looking for a more ulterior cause. He must behave (to himself, not to his patient) like a small boy who asks his father another question before the preceding question has been half answered. If he follows this policy, he will soon notice that the patient's first complaints often have little bearing on the nature of the main disorder. One cannot remember too often that what the patient talks about first may not be what bothers him most, or even at all. And the job of the physician includes finding out what does bother him.

In many instances the patient's complaints are really his explanations for the unusual experiences he has had in illness. Everyone tries to make sense of the world in which he lives. Sometimes the explanations which patients devise for their experiences are correct; more often they miss the mark or are totally inaccurate. The most extreme forms of incorrect explanations for experiences we find in patients with hypochondriasis and psychoses. The delusions of these patients are their best efforts to understand their strange altered perceptions. If a psychotic patient complains that his wife is poisoning him, we can understand this readily enough as an effort to explain an alteration in his perceptions of taste. But the physician should remember that many other patients besides those with psychoses devise explanations for their difficulties which they may then present to the physician as complaints. The physician should attend to these carefully, but he should always look behind the complaints to discover for what underlying experiences they may have provided an explanation to a frightened or confused patient.

In a comprehensive medical examination then, the chief complaint should be given important, but not exclusive attention. It is always the start, never the end of the physician's inquiries.

## DESCRIPTION OF THE SYMPTOMS

Many illnesses reveal no detectable abnormalities by current methods of examination. Even with repeated examinations the physician may not observe the patient during a symptomatic phase of his disorder. For example, physicians can rarely observe patients during attacks of palpitations. And in the absence of such an attack, the physical examination of a patient complaining of palpitations may reveal nothing. Yet from a detailed description of the symptoms, the physician can frequently deduce the physiological or psychological disturbance giving rise to the complaint. To illustrate further, the single complaint of "palpitations" offers several diagnostic possibilities, as follows:

(a) Sinus tachycardia
(b) Increased stroke volume
(c) One of the paroxysmal arrhythmias, e.g., extrasystoles or paroxysmal auricular tachycardia
(d) Unusual consciousness of a normal heart action with belief that this normal action is abnormal
(e) Delusions about the heart in which physical sensations play no part

From a full description of the symptoms, the physician can usually decide in which of the above categories he should place the patient's symptoms.

Similarly, with many other complaints, the physician may never have an opportunity to observe the patient at the time the patient has his symptoms. Or if he does, he may not detect any physical abnormality. Yet often he can still make an accurate diagnosis from the patient's description of the complaint. But to do this, he must draw from the patient a description of his symptoms rich in detail. When detail is lacking, distinguishing features are omitted and discrete disorders become blurred and confused with each other.

To interpret what he hears, the physician should equip himself with an extensive knowledge of symptoms through experience and reading.[5, 9, 10, 11, 12, 13] He must know the usual changes in function produced by the commonly encountered morbid processes. To understand the common disorders, he must study not only the pathogenesis of symptoms of structural disease so well described in textbooks of physical pathology; he must also study the physiological concomitants of emotions because these and their sequelae certainly account for the largest number of all symptoms.[1, 4, 6, 7, 18] More specifically, the physician should be prepared to identify:

(a) The psychological and physiological accompaniments of the common emotions, e.g., anxiety, anger, depression, etc. The physician must know the rather wide variations in such changes from person to person. For example, during anxiety most patients will show tachycardia, tachypnea, increased muscle tension, decreased salivation, increased perspiration and other changes. However, in one person the heart rate may change markedly, muscular tension rather little; in another patient, respiration may change markedly and the heart rate much less; in a third, the principal changes may occur in muscle tension.

(b) The sequelae of psychological and physiological changes accompanying emotional disorders sustained over a long period of time. For example, gastric hyperactivity accompanying resentment may give rise, over a period of time and in those otherwise predisposed, to ulceration of the gastric mucosa and its symptoms. To give another example, backache and headache are the usual effects of sustained contraction of the muscles of the back and scalp which accompanies prolonged anxiety.

(c) The physical expressions of thoughts. Symptoms of this origin usually occur most often in the motor and sensory organs served by the central nervous system (hysteria), but also arise in the internal viscera. An element of suggestion frequently contributes additional dysfunction to symptoms having other origins also. For example, a patient with palpitations accompanying anxiety may remember that his father died of heart disease and suggest to himself an increase in his original symptoms.

Nothing less than a thorough familiarity with the foregoing mechanisms of symptoms can save the physician from the erroneous and serious confusion of these symptoms with those which arise from:

(d) Functional disorders brought about by other stresses in the environment, e.g., changes in the weather.

(e) Physical symptoms of hypochondriacal mechanism, that is, those in which there is no disturbed peripheral physiological function.

The physician should collect certain essential data about every symptom. These data are outlined below under the headings of questions which the physician should usually be able to answer at the end of his history-taking interviews. Not all, but most of these questions can be answered whether the complaint is in the physical or psychological sphere.

### *What Are the Symptoms Like?*

The physician should obtain a detailed and accurate description from the patient of what he experiences during his symptoms. This should include an outline of the course of the symptoms if they come and go. Most symptoms fluctuate and their occurrence usually includes an onset with gradual increase in severity, a peak of maximal severity, and a decline.

### *Where Are theSymptoms Located?*

Often certain symptoms (e.g., fatigue, weakness, depression) cannot be located. But the majority can be located, and the location should be inquired about.

The importance of exactly locating symptoms needs no justification. We should not satisfy ourselves only with the patient's statements, but also ask him to point as nearly as he can to the site of the distress. For example, if the patient complains of difficulty in swallowing he may greatly aid the diagnosis by pointing along the path of his throat and esophagus to where he experiences the difficulty.

When a symptom is experienced over a large area of the body, a number of factors may converge to intensify it more in one part of the body than in another; or, if there are several symptoms such factors may give a special emphasis to the symptoms of one region. For example, limbs recently exercised are more apt to be the site of paralyses in poliomyelitis than others. Suggestion, often stimulated by the patent's acquaintance with another person having a similar or even quite different illness, can also lead to a focusing of the patient's attention on one organ rather than another. Such suggestions can also contribute to local dysfunctions. Thus the physician's inquiries should study not only which organ is the principal site of complaints, but other factors which might affect that organ.

### *What Is the Severity of the Symptoms?*

Whenever possible, the physician should estimate the severity of the symptoms. Some symptoms have objective components which the physician can observe. For example, a patient's coughing can be watched and his sputum measured. Whenever possible, the physician should make such direct observations, which are much more accurate and useful than the usually loose statements of patients about the severity of a cough or the quantity of sputum. Many other symptoms are entirely subjective. The severity of these may be difficult to estimate, but it is important to make the attempt. The physician should learn also to what extent the symptoms have disabled the patient by interfering with his usual life and work. Severity of symptoms and disability from them are only partly related. Wide variations in the human capacity to adapt to even severe symptoms makes almost impossible any prediction of disability from the severity of the symptoms, although this is naturally an important factor in disability.

This topic is discussed further in a section on pain (see pp. 55-57).

### When Were the Symptoms First Noticed?

Knowledge of the date of the onset of symptoms contributes in two ways. First, it tells the physician something about the total length of the illness which helps in forming an estimate of its progress and severity. Secondly, it helps to indicate the setting in which the illness began. This important subject is discussed separately in later sections of this chapter.

### What Factors Make the Symptoms Better or Worse?

The physician should seek to link the symptoms with factors which may have a causal connection with them. A complete list of all possible factors which might influence the severity of symptoms would duplicate the list of factors which act as precipitating circumstances for the original occurrence of an illness. Such a list will be given later under that heading on pages 57-58 and not repeated here. The physician should remember the more important items of this list for questioning the patient. Thus the patient may be asked whether he has noticed that the symptoms are worse during or after: exercise, eating (especially with particular foods), postural changes, sleep, fatigue, menstrual phases, and emotional disturbances.

The physician should inquire about any other physical changes which may make the symptoms better or worse, such as expectoration, vomiting, passage of stools, clots, stones, etc.

The physician should also inquire about measures that the patient himself may take to relieve his symptoms. These might include: change of posture, physical rest, drugs, applications of heat or cold, pressure (e.g., over painful areas), or removal from psychological stresses (e.g., by change of job, vacation, divorce).

The physician should not expect the patient to name easily the factors which make his symptoms better or worse. Sometimes the patient knows these; more often he does not. Often they can only be discovered by careful study of his situation at the time of changes in the symptoms. Thus the physician needs to know where the patient is when the symptoms are worse and what he is doing at the time. From the detailed study of a number of fluctuations significant relationships usually emerge. This topic receives further attention in the next section and in Chapter 10.

The drugs taken by the patient deserve special attention. Information from others (e.g., previous physicians, members of the family) should usually supplement the patient's account, which will frequently be inadequate. Sometimes the patient has taken drugs that partially or completely suppress or mask the symptoms and signs of the illness, thus making diagnosis exceedingly difficult unless the details of medication are known. Moreover, the patient may have received an appropriate drug in insufficient dosage. Failure to learn this second fact may lead the physician to assume incorrectly that some other drug should be tried or some entirely different diagnosis considered. Such detailed inquiries are equally important with regard to other treatments prescribed or tried by the patient such as diet, rest, or exercise.

### *Are the Symptoms Continuous or Episodic?*

A large number of symptoms in both physical and psychological spheres are episodic. The physician should always ask such questions as: "Do your symptoms come and go?" or "Do you always have these symptoms?"

Cycles of exacerbations and remissions characterize many diseases. The periods of such cycles vary from many years to perhaps a few hours. Many times smaller cycles of variation occur within larger cycles. Such cyclic variations derive from a wide variety of factors that occur within the patient and play upon him from his environment. Sometimes one factor influences a change in the patient's illness exclusively, but often several factors summate in producing changes. A later section of this chapter will list some of these factors under the heading of circumstances precipitating the illness.

If the symptoms are episodic, then other questions arise:

(a) What is the frequency of occurrence?
(b) What is the duration of each episode?
(c) Is the onset of each episode sudden or gradual?
(d) Is recovery from each episode sudden or gradual?
(e) With what circumstances is each episode connected, e.g., change of posture, exercise, eating, sleeping, fatigue, emotional disturbances?
(f) Are all the episodes similar or do they differ in quality or severity?

Frequently the patient will not be aware initially of the characteristics and circumstances associated with each episode. However, from a description of several episodes, the physician and patient may be able to detect factors which the episodes have in common. For episodes involving loss of consciousness, e.g., hypoglycemic attacks, fainting, or epileptic convulsions, the descriptions of reliable witnesses are usually essential and often provide decisive information.

Psychological changes furnish the most frequent factors associated with episodic illnesses. The physician needs to direct special attention to learning what thoughts and emotions were present at the time the patient noticed the symptoms. Often the patient observes himself poorly and cannot report usefully about his thoughts and emotions. For him, the symptoms "just come on all of a sudden." To supplement the patient's report, the physician needs also to know exactly what the patient was doing (and with whom) at the time the symptoms occurred. The physician should scrutinize as many of the episodes as possible for common denominators. When these are found, they may suggest or reveal the significant emotions associated with the symptoms. The important subject of psychological stresses is considered briefly later in this chapter and also in Chapter 10 under the heading of "Interviewing Patients with Psychophysiological Reactions."

The physician should remember that many episodic illnesses recur only at infrequent intervals. Thus the episodes of manic-depressive psychoses may be one, five, or twenty years apart. The patterns of some disorders remain characteristically the same in each recurrence throughout life. In other illnesses symptomatic variations occur, but the underlying disorder remains the same. For example, patients with migraine frequently report having suffered in childhood from repeated episodes of vomiting related to emotional disturbances. In adulthood, the situations provoking the attacks are usually similar, but the vomiting is joined by the characteristic severe headache, or the vomiting may cease and only the headache occur. In many patients having recurrent episodes of depression, the pattern varies from one time to another. In the early episodes, physical symptoms such as impotence, constipation and fatigue, may predominate, and the depression of mood may be little noticed. In later episodes, the depression of mood may move into the foreground, but in all of them the primary disturbance is probably the same.

*Are the Symptoms Getting Better or Worse?*

The physician should know whether the symptoms are progressive, stationary, or improving, and if they are changing he needs to know the rate of change. Certain disorders progress in a characteristic way, so that answers to this question have a bearing on diagnosis and also on prognosis.

# THE HISTORY OF THE PRESENT ILLNESS

Exactness of description again helps the physician. For example, the patient may state that he cannot walk as far as he used to walk without pain in his chest. Then the physician needs to learn just what kind of exercise the patient formerly took without discomfort and exactly how far he can now walk before the pain occurs.

Many patients come for medical aid only when their symptoms are improving. Then they feel reassured enough to tolerate the possible revelations of an examination.

## SPECIAL QUESTIONS ABOUT COMMON SYMPTOMS

This book cannot include a discussion of all symptoms. However, the following notes on some of the commonly encountered symptoms may exemplify the sort of detailed inquiry which the physician should make for every symptom. The points of inquiry given here supplement the inquiries outlined in the preceding section. Far from being inclusive, these suggestions only offer guidance in some of the preliminary questioning of the patient, especially with regard to the distinctions between physical and psychological origins of symptoms. For details of further questioning the reader should consult textbooks of medicine and psychiatry.

### *Anorexia*

Loss of appetite occurs in many general diseases, especially chronic ones such as chronic infections and prolonged carcinoma. In such conditions the loss of appetite rarely comes as an early symptom and when it does come it remains rather constantly present. Anorexia is a prominent symptom of many diseases of the liver and pancreas. It also occurs as an accompaniment of many psychological disorders, especially anxiety and depression. In these conditions the loss of appetite comes quickly with the onset of the strong emotion and fluctuates as changes in the emotions occur. The history should therefore include details of all variations in the severity of the symptoms, especially with regard to changes in the patient's life situation at the times of these variations.

### *Anxiety*

The symptoms of acute anxiety include the effects of increased sympathetic activity and increased skeletal muscular tension. Since anxiety affects many different organs, many different symptoms can result. In severe acute anxiety the patient may experience palpitations, dyspnea, anorexia, dryness of the mouth, increased sweating, especially of hands, face, and axillae, and a variety of muscular tensions. With these symptoms urinary frequency and diarrhea may combine. If the anxiety continues, insomnia and impotence occur.

Differences which are probably constitutional result in frequent variations among the organs affected most during anxiety. Some of these have been mentioned earlier. Other factors also contribute to differences in the symptoms of different patients. Elements of suggestion and anxiety about the first symptoms may direct a further focus of attention and augment particular symptoms. When anxiety becomes chronic the visceral changes may lessen somewhat, while muscular tensions continue and become worse. The patient may then have few or no visceral changes, but display signs of anxiety chiefly in tightness of his face, back or limbs. Or one viscus, e.g., stomach or bronchi, may be chiefly affected and others less so or not at all. Anxiety rarely occurs in pure form but nearly always with admixtures of other emotions, especially depression and anger. These emotions are accompanied by somewhat different visceral and muscular changes which variously neutralize or reinforce the effects of the anxiety with which they intermingle.

The result of all these factors is that patients with anxiety present to the physician's first scrutiny a wide variety of symptoms and physiological changes. One patient may complain of palpitations and shortness of breath; another of severe headaches and impotence; another of abdominal pain; still another of diminished appetite and weakness. The physician who waits for the patient to exhibit or report all of the symptoms of the acute anxiety attack will overlook and hence mistreat many cases of anxiety. The avoidance of this lies in careful questioning of the patient about other possible symptoms of anxiety whenever the patient mentions or seems to have one or a few of them. The physician will then frequently find that the patient does in fact have some of the other symptoms which have been crowded into the background by those symptoms which, for some of the reasons mentioned above, have become more prominent either in physiological changes or in the mind of the patient.

Having ascertained the presence of anxiety, the physician should additionally study what other emotions, e.g., anger or depression, join the anxiety in the production of the symptoms.

Next the physician should study the circumstances which have precipitated the anxiety or, if it is episodic, which precipitate the acute attacks. What are the stimuli for the anxiety? Here another trap awaits the uninformed physician. We know that social stresses usually provide the stimuli for anxiety attacks. If these cannot be readily identified, the physician may abandon the diagnosis of anxiety and pursue some other line of thought. For example, many patients will report the occurrence of their attacks when they are alone or during the night. In these instances the stimuli come from within the patient. He thinks or dreams some thought that brings acute anxiety. Since he may not readily recall the thought or dream he may vigorously and quite sincerely deny that it ever occurred. The patient may also report apparent anxiety attacks upon visiting some place "when nothing has happened." Here the stimuli lie in the place or people visited which evoke unconscious associations of former painful experiences. Thus the matronly and slightly forbidding wife of her husband's employer may remind the patient of her own unkind mother. She may then experience anxiety in the presence of the employer's wife before they have even exchanged opening greetings. The patient remaining unaware of the unconscious associations, it will then seem to her that her anxiety attack comes "from nowhere."

As indicated above, stimuli which produce anxiety may become generalized to other stimuli that resemble the original stimuli slightly, but incompletely. The generalization may be so extensive as to result in a pervasive anxiety in which everything seems to make the patient anxious. Moreover, the generalization of anxiety-provoking stimuli may include various aspects of the field in which the original painful conditioning experience took place.

For example, a student was unable to enter an art gallery without anxiety because, so it turned out, the art gallery resembled architecturally a university building where he had experienced an important failure accompanied by severe anxiety.

Another patient developed a phobia of buses and could not ride them to his work. Inquiry brought out the fact that he had become frightened on a bus when overhearing several loud women who reminded him of his tyrannical wife. He had had an anxiety attack while listening to these women and had left the bus to get away from them, afterwards being unable to get on any bus until treated.

Because of these complexities the physician can hardly expect the patient to provide a straightforward account of the stimuli for his anxiety at the first interview. These will usually only make sense after a number of interviews and after the physician has carefully trained the patient to notice all situations and his accompanying thoughts at the time of the anxiety attacks. And he will frequently, perhaps usually, find that what the patient first presents as the object of his anxiety is only a secondary derivative of the primary sources of his anxiety.

## Cough

The physician needs to know whether the cough is dry or productive; if productive, of what kind and amount of sputum. Does the sputum contain blood? Is the cough accompanied by pain in the chest or dyspnea? What circumstances, e.g., smoking, exercise, or postural changes, make the cough worse and what improve it?

## Diarrhea and Constipation

Since persons vary widely in their bowel functions, the physician should first inquire about what kind and frequency of bowel movements the patient usually has. Then he should ask about the details of the new pattern of bowel function of which the patient complains. How many bowel movements does he now have daily? He should ask the patient to describe his stools as to consistency, color, and the appearance of blood, mucus, parasites, or undigested food. Then the physician should study the habits of the patient with regard to diet, activity, exercise, and usual time of day for bowel movements. Have there been recent changes in these habits? Since bowel functions respond sensitively in many people to changes in personal relationships, the physician should inquire about potentially stressful events in the patient's life.

## Dyspnea

Difficulty in breathing may accompany a wide variety of physical and psychological disorders. The physician can learn most from direct observation of the patient during the dyspnea, but if he does not have this opportunity careful questioning can prove helpful and at least point towards further appropriate studies. The physician should note whether or not the patient breathes more rapidly than usual or only with subjective awareness of difficulty. Is one phase of the respiratory cycle easier for the patient than the other? Is one phase abnormally lengthened compared to the other? Is breathing accompanied by wheezing? Are dyspnea or wheezing relieved by coughing and expectoration?

The physician should try to distinguish dyspnea due to hyperventilation (or hypoventilation) accompanying emotional disturbances, usually anxiety, and dyspnea accompanying a physical disorder. Two clues may assist in making this distinction. First, dyspnea at rest occurs only as an accompaniment of emotional disturbances or of rather marked physical disease, e.g., heart failure, atelectasis, pneumonia. Consequently if the patient reports dyspnea at rest and has no signs of marked physical disorder, the dyspnea probably accompanies anxiety. Secondly, dyspnea associated with emotional disturbances fluctuates widely with changes in

# THE HISTORY OF THE PRESENT ILLNESS 53

the personal environment of the patient. People or events that induce anxiety will induce dyspnea; those that relax the patient will decrease the dyspnea.

Dyspnea can derive from both psychological and physical disorders at the same time. This commonly happens in bronchial asthma. The patient's attacks may come with changes in the pollen count, the weather, or the patient's relations with other persons.

When the physician has identified or excluded a psychological component, he should make further distinctions between mechanical difficulties in breathing, e.g., from rheumatoid arthritis or poliomyelitis, and systemic or metabolic causes of dyspnea, e.g., heart disease or pulmonary disease.

## *Insomnia*

If sleep is or seems impaired, the physician should inquire about such factors as the following: the total number of hours of sleep; the total number of hours spent in bed; the usual hours of going to bed and to sleep, and of awakening and arising; the present hours of going to bed and to sleep, and of awakening and arising; the apparent depth of sleep; exactly how the patient feels when he awakens (the patient may really be getting adequate sleep but believe he is not; this question also helps to uncover significant emotions such as depressions, which may be related to the difficulty in sleeping); other persons with whom the patient sleeps; the room in which the patient sleeps with regard to such matters as noise, heating, ventilation; the bed in which the patient sleeps; the occurrence of interruptions from other people or machines; the occurrence of dreams and nightmares; the occurrence of other associated discomforts such as gastric pain, nocturnal dyspnea, or nocturnal urinary frequency. The physician should try to learn whether some physical symptom keeps the patient from sleeping or awakens him or is merely noticed by the patient when he is awake for other reasons. For example, does the patient urinate at night because anxiety awakens him or does the urge to urinate awaken him?

The physician should ask the patient such questions as: "What seems to keep you from sleeping?" and "What do you think about while you are trying to go to sleep (or after you wake up during the night)?" The answers to such questions may indicate sleep-reducing anxieties.

## *Loss of Consciousness*

The physician's first question should inquire about the number of episodes of loss of consciousness. If only one such episode has occurred, the questioning should generally move towards possible severe cerebral disease such as cerebral thrombosis.

If repeated episodes of loss of consciousness have occurred, the physician's questions should search for data pointing towards the common causes of this symptom. These are: epilepsy, hypoglycemia, hysteria, vasodepressor syncope, and hyperventilation. Afterwards he should consider such less common disorders as orthostatic hypotension, carotid sinus syncope, and Stokes-Adams attacks.

Loss of consciousness usually provokes anxiety, which can distort the account given by the patient. In any case if he actually loses consciousness, he cannot tell much of what happens. Eyewitness accounts become invaluable in making the necessary distinctions, and sometimes are much more valuable than the laboratory studies that the preliminary inquiry will indicate. For example, many patients with epilepsy also have hysterical convulsions. An abnormal electroencephalogram may not assist in making the distinction between epilepsy and hysteria; a good eyewitness account can usually do so. The physician should not content himself with a brief account from the observer or accept the observer's label, e.g., "hysteria," "convulsions," as of adequate diagnostic value. He should insist on a minute account of everything the patient did before, during, and after the loss of consciousness.

The physician should pay special attention to two points. First, did the patient completely lose consciousness or did he remain somewhat aware of his surroundings? A patient who insists he completely lost consciousness may yet recall that frantic relatives poured water on his face and rushed to the telephone to call the doctor. Secondly, where was the patient, with whom, and what was going on immediately preceding the loss of consciousness? This information may give clues to overexertion, alcoholic consumption, or disturbances in personal relationships which could have precipitated the episode. The occurrence of the episodes at certain times of day, especially in relation to meals, will suggest hypoglycemia.

## *Nausea and Vomiting*

Patients sometimes confuse nausea and anorexia or give accounts which can lead to their confusion in the mind of the physician.

Vomiting, being an impressive symptom, may arouse anxiety in the patient which influences his account of what happened.

The accounts of relatives who have observed the patient can often aid greatly. The physician needs to know in some detail the suddenness, force and frequency of the vomiting. A detailed description of the symptom should help to distinguish regurgitation from vomiting. Did the vomiting relieve pain or other discomfort? The volume and quality of vomitus require study. What did the vomitus smell and taste like? Did the vomitus contain bile, blood, mucus, undigested food, or fecal material?

The study of nausea and vomiting should always include a careful inquiry about everything the patient has eaten during the preceding several days. However, since the patient may not recall everything he has eaten, the physician's questions should also include everything the patient has done during the previous several days. Such questioning may then disclose that the patient had been in a situation where he might have ingested contaminated food or water.

Since nausea and vomiting can sometimes accompany psychological disturbances, the history should also include an account of social events preceding the occurrence of the symptom. The physician should know what the patient was doing or planned to do when the symptom occurred. Patients sometimes become conditioned to nausea and vomiting so that exposure to the conditioning stimuli may touch off the nausea and vomiting "when nothing has happened." Thus a girl made anxious about sexuality may become nauseated and vomit on her first date and thereafter vomit whenever she plans a date.

## *Pain*

The physician should make the usual inquiries with regard to location and duration of the pain and its character. Burning pains should be distinguished from aching pains; constant ones from those which fluctuate.

The physician should especially study the severity of the pain. Unfortunately, he cannot accurately estimate the severity of a pain as a sensation from the reaction of the patient experiencing it. Reactions to pain sensations of apparently the same perceived intensity differ markedly in different people and in the same person at different times.[8, 20] Moreover, memory of pain as a sensation is usually rather weak in comparison to the memory of emotional experiences.

Apart from the foregoing distinction between pain sensation and reaction to the sensation, important variations in the actual sensation of pain may occur in different persons experiencing comparable amounts of damage to tissues. Such differences can also be related to the different attitudes of the patients to the wound or illness experienced.[2] Other factors changing the function of the central nervous system may also underlie such differences.

Anxiety focused on an organ already disturbed may further disturb its functioning. This may come about through increased muscular tension in the area and probably through other mechanisms as well. Thus a patient may develop some tension in the muscles of the scalp while watching an exciting motion picture or sport. He may then become alarmed about this initial headache. The attention focused upon his head may increase the muscle tension and the headache still further. The physician should therefore remember that the patient's complaint of pain may include the following components: *(a)* the original pain sensation and its mechanism; *(b)* the reaction, usually anxious, of the patient to the pain; and *(c)* the secondary increase in dysfunction (including more pain sensations) which accompanies the anxious reaction. Similar components occur in the experience of other symptoms besides pain.

In distinguishing the sensation of a symptom such as pain and the reaction thereto, the physician may use several clues:

1. The physician can compare the reactions of the patient under study with those usual in patients with similar disorders, and hence presumably having the same or at least similar sensations.

2. The patient or his relatives may be asked to describe the disability associated with the symptoms. The disability should be described in terms of interference with ordinary activities. In a case with pain the physician needs to know, for example, whether the patient can continue working or must pause; whether he must leave work and go home for relief; whether he must lie down; or whether only drugs relieve the pain.

3. The actual measures that the patient takes to relieve his pain (or any other discomfort), indicate more accurately the degree of suffering than do the patient's verbal reports of his sensations. Such reports may contain distortions arising from the decay of memory with time and from the unintentional influence of the physician upon the patient. The same physician (and even the same attitude) may affect the reports of different patients in different ways. For example, if a patient wishes the approval of the physician whom he perceives as admiring stoicism, he may minimize his suffering. Another patient who also perceives the same physician as stern and unsympathetic may exaggerate his suffering in order to draw greater solicitude and care from the physician.

4. The patient may be asked to compare his experience to the worst similar experience he has ever had. Giving his worst experience a rating of 100, he is asked to rate the current experience. This method is somewhat applicable to pain and also to such other symptoms as weakness, fatigue, depression, and dyspnea. By making this request of the patient, the physician obliges him to compare his sensations with previous ones, and this may have the effect of reducing the patient's distortion of the severity of his suffering. Unfortunately, most patients think that their

present sufferings are their worst. Past experience seems trivial by comparison, even though evidence suggests the contrary. This behavior is not confined to patients with physical pain. Patients with severe depressions frequently imagine that they can go no lower in mood and never have been lower than they are at present.

The physician should remember that not all patients magnify their sufferings. As indicated above, many patients minimize their discomforts. The various factors that enter into the different reactions to symptomatic discomfort form part of the inquiry into the psychological aspects of the patient. At this point in the examination, the physician should merely note any important discrepancies between the patient's apparent sensations and his reaction to them.

## *Weakness*

Generalized symptoms having no localization, such as weakness, frequently become confused with other symptoms and often require much study for their accurate identification. The physician must often question the patient incisively before he can separate "fatigue" and "weakness," or before he can distinguish either of these from various emotional states which are accompanied by some of the sensations of fatigue. Weakness is an actual loss of muscular strength usually associated with a severe physical illness. It is nearly always objectively demonstrable, although as with so many other symptoms, the physician can judge the patient's weakness better if he knows what the patient was previously able to do. Fatigue, on the other hand, is a different unpleasant sensation usually localized in the muscles, sometimes in some muscles more than in others. Fatigue is felt after muscular activity when the patient is resting; true weakness can only be noticed when the muscles are actually being used. Patients often describe fatigue with the word "tired." Weakness and fatigue can exist together. Thus a patient may complain that he cannot climb stairs as well as he could (weakness) and that after he has been out of bed for a few hours, he feels tired for the rest of the day (fatigue).

Attitudes and emotions which bring muscular tension contribute greatly to fatigue. States of depression and boredom augment fatigue, while keen interest tends to dispel it.

The physician's difficulties in making these important distinctions are often added to by the vague and self-flattering reporting of patients. Patients tend to choose descriptive language which assigns them acceptable illnesses. Thus a patient may say he feels "weak" when he is tired. Or he may state he feels "tired" when he is angry or depressed.

## Weight Changes

Fluctuations in the patient's weight deserve careful study. The physician should inquire about the patient's present weight and his weight prior to the onset of illness. In certain illnesses, e.g., obesity, the history of the patient's weight should be carried back to his early life. If possible, the physician should obtain several weights of the patient at different times during his illness to permit study of the rate of change of weight.

The inquiries should at first follow the simple principles of energy exchanges. For example, if the patient has lost weight either his intake of food for his usual needs has decreased or he has lost much of what he has taken in from excessive excretion, increased activity, or metabolism. Likewise if the patient has gained weight he has increased his intake of food over his habitual needs or has ceased to require as much as he did either from decreased metabolism or decreased activity.

The physician should inquire in some detail about the pattern of the patient's eating. If the patient overeats, does he eat excessively at three large meals a day, or does he nibble at food throughout the day and sometimes at night? Is he aware of ignoring signals of satiety when he overeats?

The kind of food preferred and actually eaten by the patient also requires study since with a poor diet he may overeat of some foodstuffs while continuing undersupplied with others.

As psychological factors frequently contribute to changes in weight these also deserve careful study. Some patients are aware that they eat excessively when anxious; others who do this are not aware of the relationship between their overeating and anxiety. Careful study of the events of the patient's life at the times of overeating may furnish suggestions or stronger evidence of such relationships. The physician can usefully ask the patient how he feels and what he thinks about at the times he eats excessively.

## CIRCUMSTANCES PRECIPITATING THE SYMPTOMS: STRESSES

Environmental factors are of such great importance in the occurrence of diseases that a history which reports no precipitating circumstances associated with an illness is necessarily incomplete. Moreover, it is correspondingly less valuable, since the factors which precipitate an illness are often precisely those which are most amenable to alteration in the patient's favor. When the physician cannot change the patient's sensitivity

# THE HISTORY OF THE PRESENT ILLNESS

to stresses, he can often help him to change his exposure to stresses. In each case, the physician should consider the common stresses to which human beings are exposed and which, by disturbing their equilibria, may act as precipitating factors for illness. These may be considered under different headings for convenience.

## *Internal Stresses*

*Exercise,* and unusual activity of various organs, e.g., the cardiovascular system in climbing stairs.

*Eating,* i.e., the process of ingestion.

*Sleeping.* Lack of sleep can be stressful. Sleep itself may be stressful if it leads to diminution in cardiac output and precipitates angina pectoris, or leads to dreams and precipitates anxiety attacks, angina pectoris, or epilepsy.

*Changes of the Menstrual Cycle.* These may include physical changes, e.g., pain, loss of blood, and alteration in electrolyte and water content of tissues; they may also include psychological changes related to attitudes towards sex and reproduction.

*Changes with Pregnancy.* These may include a wide variety of changes in the function and shape of the mother's body and also psychological changes related to these physical changes and to the presence in her body of a developing fetus soon to be a baby.

*Changes of Posture or Unusual Posture,* e.g., prolonged bed rest or sudden changes of position.

*Growth, Development and Involution.* These processes are accompanied by changes in the size of the body as a whole and of individual organs (e.g., the genitalia) and by changes in the function of various organs, e.g., the larynx or the reproductive organs.

All the stresses listed above are part of ordinary life. They become pathologically stressful according to their degree and the state of the organism at the time they occur.

## *External Stresses*

### Physical Stresses

*Meteorological Changes,* e.g., changes in temperature, barometric pressure, radiation, sunlight, etc.

*Physical Conditions of Work and Living.* These include environmental conditions to which the patient must adapt, e.g., commuting long distances to work, long hours of work, or fast machinery with which the worker must keep pace.

*Physical Trauma,* e.g., of accidents or bullets.
*Toxins, Poisons,* e.g., industrial gases or alcohol.
*Pollens,* e.g., ragweed pollen.
*Microorganisms,* e.g., viruses or bacteria.
*Parasites,* e.g., lice, pinworms, or amoebas.
*Malnutrition,* including the absence of adequate food and the ingestion of food damaging to the organism.

### Social Stresses

A list of all the social stresses to which man is exposed would fill many pages. The physician should remember the more important ones, which may be considered under the following headings:

*Adjustments to New Situations.* These would include the need to adapt to new persons and their needs, or to adopt new ways of living, or to accept new responsibilities, e.g., pregnancy, childbirth, birth of a sibling, prolonged visits of in-laws, marriage, beginning of school or college, induction in armed forces, emigration to a new country, promotion, retirement from work.

*Loss of Supportive Relationships.* This would include divorce; mental illness in a friend or relative which removes that person from the patient psychologically; deaths of close relatives and friends; geographical separation of close relatives and friends, as when the patient emigrates to another country; losses of children through their marriage; or alienations from close friends or relatives through disruption of personal relationships.

*Loss of Physical Health.* This would include actual disease and circumstances which could threaten health or even physical satisfactions, e.g., unemployment and financial losses.

*Loss of Self-Esteem.* This would include demotion, unfriendly employers, firing, failure to be promoted or to be materially successful, criminal conviction.

The complexities of stressful influences on human health require the physician to know much more about them than the foregoing list can convey. The physician can rarely obtain all the data he needs from direct questioning of the patient during the history-taking. Rather he must correlate events and symptoms and from all the information available make inferences about which events may have been stressful for the patient.

### *Correlating Symptoms and Stresses*

To correlate symptoms and stresses, the physician should first learn what events have occurred in the patient's life that might have been stressful.

Secondly, the physician should learn the temporal relationships of these events to the patient's symptoms. The strength of the evidence for causal connections depends partly on the number of temporal correlations observed. One or two correlations signify little; a dozen correlations provide strong evidence; and intermediate numbers, evidence of intermediate value, which will have to be evaluated according to other factors. The temporal correlations should be regular in occurrence, but do not need to be close in time. A reaction may follow an event which has been stressful after a latent period during which the effects were elaborated or accumulating in the patient. Also, the anticipation of some psychologically stressful event may lead to the occurrence of symptoms days, weeks, or months before the event.

Thirdly, the physician should try to establish the significance of the supposedly stressful events for the patient. This requires a study of his susceptibilities, both at physical and psychological levels. The patient's verbal statements are more valuable with regard to his physical condition than in revealing his psychological sensitivities. He is often unaware that certain social events are stressful to him. He may be aware of the symptoms he experiences without being aware of the thoughts and emotions which mediate the influence of the environmental events in producing these symptoms. However, having learned of temporal correlations between possible stresses and symptoms, the physician can then employ interviewing techniques to expose and help the patient express relevant thoughts and emotions. Later chapters will describe these techniques.

The last-mentioned step of establishing the meaning of apparently stressful events for the particular patient under study derives from the wide variation in the stressfulness of different events. The physician who assumes that only what would affect him adversely can affect others may make serious errors.

Moreover, he should not confine the search for stresses to the major calamities of life, but should remember that what would be minor events for some persons may prove exceedingly stressful to others. During periods of apparently severe stress some human beings, far from being overwhelmed, mobilize previously hidden resources of adaptation. The same persons may adapt much less well to stresses which superficially seem less disastrous, but which have become specially important to them. A man may tolerate better the burning of his house than the burning of his toast. Everard Home, in his *Life of John Hunter,* described the occurrence of Hunter's attacks of angina pectoris during "affections of the mind." Then he added: ". . . as his mind was affected by trifles these produced the most violent effects on the disease. His coachman being beyond his times, or a servant not attending to his directions, brought on the spasms, while a real misfortune produced no effect."

Sometimes no single event but the patient's whole way of life proves stressful if, for example, it deprives him of adequate rest, recreation or other needs. Also the frustration of important ambitions or expectations may prove stressful even though, or rather because, nothing has happened. In such cases physician and patient may miss important factors if they search only for special or obvious events.

Illness itself can become one of the most important of stresses, both because of its real dangers to life and livelihood and because of the meaning of these dangers to the patient. A later section discusses more fully the patient's understanding of his illness and attitude towards it.

### Precipitating and Predisposing Stresses

Stresses frequently summate and the physician's inquiry should try to identify (a) stresses which have predisposed the patient to his disorder, and (b) those which have precipitated its symptomatic expressions. The influence of stresses on seizures may illustrate these types of stress. Everyone can have a convulsive seizure if sufficiently stimulated by natural or artificial activators. In most persons the threshold for seizures remains far below that required for seizures to occur. In certain patients, certain kinds of lesions lower the seizure threshold so that convulsions occur more readily. Such lesions include tumors, scars, and vascular anomalies of the brain. A number of metabolic disorders may also affect the threshold for seizures. Persons with these disorders from time to time will have seizures. But they do not have seizures continuously. On the contrary, they often pass long intervals without seizures. Individual seizures are then precipitated by additional stresses. These include alcohol, fatigue, emotional disturbances, and changes in hydration. A similar double influence of stresses occurs in many other illnesses.

The physician should therefore learn all he can about precipitating stresses. He needs to know exactly what the patient was doing at the moment he noticed the first symptoms or on other occasions when he noticed recurrences. Was he eating, sleeping, walking, running? If he was sitting down, was he alone or with someone else? If with someone else, what was the conversation about? If there was no conversation, why not? If he was alone, what was he thinking about?

The physician should also learn about predisposing stresses. A wide variety of predisposing physical stresses may occur such as excessive work, insufficient sleep, or poor nutrition. To study predisposing social stresses the physician should examine the setting or general background of circumstances in which the last decisive or precipitating event took place. Often precipitating circumstances are set up like a golf ball on a tee, by the course of events in the days, weeks, or months preceding the onset of the illness. The ostensibly precipitating event is then much less significant than the events preceding it. Sometimes the physician will find no single precipitating event, but only a situation producing prolonged stress and gradually eroding away resistance. Social stresses especially tend to summate because each one may reduce the patient's tolerance and tend to make other previously innocuous events become stressful. For example, a patient may tolerate well enough a prolonged visit by his in-laws. However, if to this is added failure to receive an expected increase in salary, tension may mount. If then his wife announces a fourth pregnancy, he may reach the limits of endurance.

These two levels of stresses may receive different attention at different parts of the examination. For example, in the early interviews with a patient having a psychophysiological disturbance, the physician should identify the stresses associated with the first occurrence or fluctuations of the symptoms. Later he should learn more about the more serious underlying stresses which have sensitized the patient to the precipitating events. The individual episodes may occur during marital quarrels; but what lack of mutual satisfaction and shared affection do these quarrels express?

## THE REVIEW OF FUNCTIONS

Following the descriptive account of the symptoms complained of, and the search for precipitating stresses, the physician should continue his inquiry by asking about other symptoms that the patient has not mentioned. The chief complaints or symptoms sometimes jostle into the background other perhaps equally important symptoms. Patients sometimes fail to tell the physician during a medical interview about some symptom of which they were aware and had intended to report. Because of the anxiety of the interview, or perhaps because of being preoccupied with more pressing symptoms, they forget to mention the symptom. Some of these patients grumblingly say afterward that they did not mention the symptom because the physician did not ask about it. Each patient and his physician should share responsibility for reviewing all the patient's functioning. Nevertheless, the physician alone knows all the topics which they should discuss, so he has the larger share of the responsibility for comprehensiveness in the interview. When the physician focuses the patient's attention on all his organs and functions in a systematic way, the patient may then remember or become more fully aware of other important disturbances.

For the above reasons the physician should conduct a review of the entire functioning of the patient. This should not merely enumerate organs that have been diseased, but should study the ways in which their functions have been disordered.

The inquiry into functions should seek to detect the earliest and slightest disturbances. The physician should compare the patient's functioning with what is habitual for the patient and also with what is normal for similar persons. If the physician compares the patient only with other persons, he may neglect important departures from what is normal for the patient. The meaning of the patient's having a bowel movement every second day depends on whether this has been his custom or is a change from habitual function.

In searching for symptoms or evidence of disease other than those mentioned spontaneously, the physician should think of those circumstances which tax the reserves of organs and which might therefore demonstrate failing reserves. One of the earliest signs of disease is a loss of the powers ordinarily kept in reserve.[11] Such loss is best demonstrated not when the suspected organ is at rest, but when the organ must respond to extra demands for its function. Thus the inquiry should often include such matters as any change in the tolerance for exercise; an increased need for sleep; a decreased tolerance for alcohol; or a diminished capacity for sexual intercourse.

The review of functions and organs should consider every function and organ. Frequently a disorder in one organ or function becomes instantly clarified by the recognition of a disorder in some other organ or function. The physician cannot afford the risk involved in a cursory survey of the patient's functioning in areas outside the site of his chief complaints. The extreme importance of a comprehensive survey of current functioning, (and of past illnesses, which also may clarify present disorders), provides one justification for the use of a health questionnaire,[3] although such questionnaires cannot replace an interview.

The following list, far from exhaustive, includes many of the questions that should comprise the functional inquiry. A positive response from the patient on any item should immediately lead to further questions, carried into details no less fine than those outlined for the chief complaints.

*Integument:* Rashes, eruptions, hives; itching; alterations in pigment; moles, and changes in them; brittleness or other alterations in nails; loss of hair or changes in its color or texture.

# THE HISTORY OF THE PRESENT ILLNESS

*Head.* Headaches and their character; head injuries.

*Eyes.* Photophobia, unusual lachrymation; inflammation of eyes; visual acuity; diplopia; disturbances of peripheral vision.

*Ears.* Earache; discharges; deafness; tinnitus; vertigo.

*Nose.* Sense of smell; bleeding; difficulty breathing through nose; pain in nose or sinuses; excessive or unusual nasal discharges; postnasal discharge.

*Teeth, Mouth, and Throat.* Caries; pain in teeth; loss of teeth and replacement; disease of gums; sores or leukoplakia; sore throats; difficulty swallowing or speaking; swellings in area of throat.

*Respiration.* Dyspnea; chest pain; cough and sputum; hemoptysis; wheezing.

*Cardiovascular Functions.* Dyspnea; pain in the chest; orthopnea; edema; cyanosis; cough; palpitations and arrhythmias; coldness or discoloration of extremities; claudication.

*Gastrointestinal Functions.* Appetite; amount and quality of food; eating habits; belching; regurgitation; nausea and vomiting; distention or bloating; heartburn; abdominal pain; frequency of bowel movements; abnormalities of color or of other characteristics of feces; blood, parasites, or mucus in stools; hemorrhoids; jaundice.

*Urinary Functions.* Abnormalities of volume of urine; frequency or urgency of urination; dysuria; nocturia; pyuria; hematuria; pain in back, flank, or area of bladder; feebleness of stream or hesitancy; dribbling; incontinence or enuresis; urethral discharges; sores on or around the genitalia.

*Reproductive Functions.* Age at menarche; subsequent menstrual history including frequency, duration, amount, and regularity of bleeding and whether accompanied by pain or other symptoms. The date of the last menstrual period and previous menstrual period should be noted. Pregnancies and their complications; vaginal bleeding or discharge; venereal disease; frequency and kind of sexual experiences and satisfactions; frigidity or impotence.

*Hematopoietic Functions.* Occurrence of anemias or hemorrhages; use of transfusions or hematinics; abnormal bruising; enlargements or tenderness of lymph nodes.

*Metabolic and Endocrine Functions:* Abnormalities of growth and development; usual weight and important fluctuations in weight; unusual perspiration; sensitivity to extremes of temperature; unusual thirst or volume of urine; changes in voice or in hair.

*Musculoskeletal Functions:* Pain in joints or muscles; weakness of muscles; pain, stiffness, or limitations of movements of joints; fractures.

*Central Nervous System.* Headaches; syncope; vertigo; seizures; difficulty in thinking or speaking; weaknesses of limbs; incoordination; impairments of sensation; pain; insomnia; anxiety and its muscular and visceral symptoms; depression or other marked emotional states; irritability; behavioral disorders of childhood or later; unusual aspects of psychosexual development.

*Vital Functions*

The physician's inquiry should always include the so-called vital functions, e.g., eating, sleeping, sexual desire and function, bowel movements, menstruation, maintenance of weight, and muscular strength. The inquiry concerning these vital functions of the body is no less important in disorders whose origin is primarily psychological. Often when the organism is under stress, whether physical or psychological, these functions become more or less impaired. The energy of the organism is partially withdrawn from such activities and processes in the service of combating the immediate threatening stress.

As the inquiry moves towards the earliest symptoms of the illness, the physician frequently finds that an impairment of one of the vital functions was the first symptom, although this was ignored until the occurrence, some months later, of those symptoms which became the chief complaint.

Inquiries about the vital functions should survey more than the mere performance of them. The physician should know whether these functions bring pleasure or not. For a healthy person, eating, sexual experiences, and sleeping have a positively enjoyable quality. So has the use of muscles in moderate and playful exercise. In illness, pleasure in these functions diminishes or disappears before the function itself is lost. Thus a patient may state that he still eats, but that his appetite has diminished. Or he may report that he still has sexual intercourse, but with lessened pleasure than formerly. (A loss of sexual function may occur while desire remains.) Often a renewed enjoyment of eating, sleeping, or sunlight provides the first sign of a return to health in a sick person.

Conversely, when these vital functions are preserved intact and still bring full enjoyment, the illness can rarely be a severe or grave one. If a depressed patient says he still enjoys eating, he is not extremely depressed. If an anxious patient says there has been no interference with his sexual activity, his anxiety is only mild or moderate.

The inquiries should also discover the presence of any tensions associated with the vital functions. The physician needs to know not only whether the patient has a good appetite, but whether he is getting enough to eat. Similarly, enjoyment and adequate performance in sexual activities can be accompanied by considerable sexual tension. The amount of sexual activity necessary to reduce sexual tension varies widely and considerably more than the amount of food necessary to reduce hunger. The physician must inquire further to find out each patient's needs and the extent of their satisfaction.

## *Habits*

During the review of functions, the physician should inquire also about such habits as the use of coffee, tobacco, alcohol, sedatives, or special dietary cravings and avoidances.

Whenever possible, the physician should learn the quantitative details of these habits. There are important differences between one and ten cups of coffee a day, between three cigarettes and three packs of cigarettes a day. When excesses are found or suspected, the inquiry should be pushed further towards more detail. For example, if the patient consumes alcohol excessively, the physician should find out the amount consumed, the preferred alcoholic drink, the usual habits of drinking (e.g., continual or episodic, solitary or social), the usual time of day when drinking starts, what thoughts and feelings are present when the patient feels he "needs" a drink, and the way he feels after he has taken alcohol. After these questions, the inquiry can be pursued further, if necessary, towards such matters as failure to eat other food than alcohol, and episodes of pathological intoxication or alcoholic psychoses. Similar inquiries may be indicated in the study of other habits, such as the use of sedatives.

When the physician suspects a nutritional deficiency, he should not be satisfied with the patient's reassurance about his diet. Of central importance in the origin of nutritional deficiencies not caused by poverty or digestive disorders is the fact that the patient usually does not know what constitutes an adequate diet. Consequently, his assertions on the subject are often worthless. The physician must obtain from the patient an actual menu of what he eats for several days.

## THE PATIENT'S CONCEPT OF HIS ILLNESS

The history of the present illness should include an evaluation of the patient's concept of his illness. Rigidly held and incorrect opinions about the nature of illnesses interfere seriously with many patients' participation in their treatment. For example, a patient who believes firmly that a marked depression is due to the menopause may think that only estrogens will help her and may correspondingly neglect other measures proposed by the physician. The widespread dissemination of medical information and half-truths among the lay public has greatly increased the temptation to self-diagnosis while concealing its dangers and permitting patients who indulge in this to preserve an illusion of accuracy even when presented with correct information by physicians. Concealed irrational anxieties, e.g. that a cancer is present, can greatly increase suffering and probably delay recovery. The physician should therefore inquire about the patient's understanding of his illness, asking him his opinion of the nature of his illness and what causes have contributed to it.

## THE PATIENT'S ATTITUDE TOWARD HIS ILLNESS

The history of the present illness also requires for its completion some understanding of the patient's attitude toward his illness. The physician usually gains little by asking the patient "What is your attitude toward your illness?" although he may certainly offer such a question. Usually he must find the answer from observing the remarks and especially the nonverbal behavior of the patient as he tells his story, listens to the physician's explanations, or later carries out or fails to carry out recommended treatment.

The usual futility of asking direct questions about this topic obliges the physician to keep in his mind some of the factors that influence patients' attitudes toward illness as he listens to the patient and watches him. The following sections may provide some guidance for his observations.

### *Anxiety Provoked by the Disability*

The physician must estimate carefully the disability likely to be provoked by the illness. He should then compare the disability which the patient believes to exist with this standard. As mentioned earlier, patients minimize their symptoms almost as often as they exaggerate them. When the patient claims a disability that is unusually large or small for the disorder, he actually exhibits an additional psychological disorder which requires attention in itself.

Frequently anxiety about an illness takes the form of fears that an examination will reveal something worse than what is already known. This irrational attitude seems often to be a factor in delaying the arrival of the patient for proper medical care.[15]

The physician cannot understand the anxiety provoked by an illness without learning what the illness means to the patient. For example, two patients each having pneumonia may exhibit apparently equal degrees of anxiety during illnesses of comparable severity. The first patient may fear he will die, the second that his illness will lead to the promotion of another employee ahead of him.

*Apparent Gains Arising from the Illness*

Illness and disability bring with them a privileged state of dependency which, in our society, is usually acceptable to the patient and those around him. Sick children especially are given attention and privileges which are ordinarily denied them, and the same may be true of adults. It is doubtful if, as some have claimed, everyone wants to return to a state of being dependent and cared for. But undoubtedly many persons who have returned to that state find it exceedingly difficult to leave. This cannot always be considered a net gain for them, but nevertheless certain patients find certain satisfactions in the status of a sick person.

Probably recoveries are delayed less by the satisfactions of being ill than by fears of life when well. For example, if injured or incapacitated by disease, a patient may come to doubt his ability to work again as well as he worked before. As part of this fear, he may doubt his ability to support himself and his family. Moreover, he usually begins to think of such matters at a time when he has not yet fully recovered. In his still weakened condition he certainly cannot work as well as he did before he became ill. But he judges his future performance by his present sensations, forgetting that by the time he returns to work he will no longer be weak, or as weak as he is when ill. And he may come to adopt a gloomy view of his situation in which it seems better to hold on to present conditions than to risk failure by an effort beyond his imagined capacity.

The same factors need attention when the patient receives financial compensation for his disability. It often appears that the patient wants to remain ill so that he may continue to receive money without working. And certainly such compensation does often stand in the way of the patient's returning to work. Studies have shown, for example, that patients recover from so-called traumatic neuroses much more rapidly when they receive compensation in a lump sum than when they receive monthly payments while disabled. Other studies have shown that discontinuing monthly payments to unemployed psychoneurotic patients can often alter the balance of their motivations so that they return to work. However, in such instances the payments received are nearly always less than the patient's ordinary income when well. He knows that he can make more money when well than he can receive when sick. Yet he may fear to give up what he receives because he fears irrationally that he may not make even as much when well.

Psychological disorders frequently include behavior towards other persons which, while adaptive for the patient, is less than satisfactory or pleasing to those around him. Rudeness, temper tantrums, and sulks would illustrate such behavior. Such behavior is part of the main illness, not a reaction to it. Other persons may involuntarily adapt to such behavior so that the patient apparently gains through it.

In addition, as already mentioned, the status of a sick person alters what other people expect of the patient. The patient nearly always discovers this, if he does not know it from watching other sick people. He may then come to use his illness as a means of avoiding unpleasant personal and social situations. A child can learn that episodes of nausea and vomiting excuse him from school, or an adult may find that his wife is more indulgent when he has a headache and that at such times she no longer presses him to go dancing with her. The physician therefore needs to distinguish two ways in which the illness may provide gain for the patient in personal relationships:

(a) The expression, as part of the illness, of modes of behavior which although immature are partially gainful to the patient in his personal relations.

(b) The use of the status of the sick person in a gainful way to avoid unpleasant occasions and responsibilities.

In considering both of these aspects of the illness, the physician should attend to the underlying anxieties which promote such behavior.

With regard to the use of the illness by the patient to avoid unpleasant situations, the physician needs further to know whether the patient is conscious of such exploitation. He usually is not, or he may once have been and then ceased to be. Conscious exploitation of illness (malingering) nearly everyone finds hard to allow himself. Further, the physician needs to know the attitudes of the relatives towards the patient's use of his illness in this way and the extent to which they have promoted or condoned it. And he needs to know the patient's reaction to the attitude of his family towards his illness. The discussion of interviewing hypochondriacal patients in Chapter 10 includes further remarks on gains arising from illness.

In summary, it is doubtful if anyone ever wants to be ill; but many patients fear what may happen to them if they get well, or fear that their recoveries may not be complete. Such fears delay recovery through psychological and physical influences. If the physician emphasizes what the patient apparently gains from the illness the patient receives less help than if the physician tries to understand the patient's fears about his condition or about what may lie ahead after he recovers. The physician should try to understand not only what the patient may want from the illness, but what fears the illness may protect him from.

## Shame and Guilt over Illness

Large numbers of people still view many illnesses, some more than others, as shameful. The shame adheres to different aspects of illness with different disorders and patients. With regard to mental illnesses the feelings of shame often have to do with being "different" from everyone else and also with having insufficient will power and control. With physical illnesses often the thought of becoming dependent brings shame. The patient's own resentment of weak, dependent people may return with guilt when he himself becomes an invalid. In any case, some shame of illness occurs widely and can lead to denial of illness and dangerous postponement of necessary medical care.

## The Will To Recover

Experienced physicians recognize some ineffable quality in sick people which is poorly but perhaps best described as "the will to health." This may seem a vague concept, yet it must be acknowledged as an empirical fact that some such quality often brings about recoveries which are not otherwise expected. The will to recover is not always verbalized, but may merely be reflected in the behavior of the patient which indicates an enthusiastic desire to recover a former state in which life was enjoyed and lived richly. Many factors influence the patient's motivation for recovery. A happy home and stimulating, congenial work may influence him greatly by providing incentives for recovery. In contrast, where there is little to return to, there may be little wish to return.

## The Patient's Understanding of His Condition

The patient's attitude towards his condition is closely related to his understanding of it. Ignorance nourishes fear. Excessive fear, and the various means adopted for controlling it, can seriously interfere with the patient's cooperation in treatment. Among all the aspects of the patient's understanding of his condition, the physician should probably attend most to signs of the patient's sense of personal responsibility for the illness and especially for the success of treatment. Sometimes, as indicated earlier, patients respond to illness with guilt and shame which indicates an excessive sense of responsibility for what has happened. More often they lack an adequate sense of responsibility and do not see how their own behavior has contributed to illness or can aid recovery.

They look towards other people or other things for the causes and the cures of their diseases. The physician should especially notice signs of such excessive dependency for they will importantly influence his management of the case.

## WHY MEDICAL ASSISTANCE WAS SOUGHT WHEN IT WAS

The physician should try to ascertain why medical aid was sought when it was. As mentioned earlier, patients often defer seeking medical aid at the height of the symptoms, and do so only when the symptoms have somewhat abated. The physician needs to know when this happens, because the answer reveals something of the patient's attitudes toward his illness. If, on the other hand, the patient sought help during the worst suffering, this fact furnishes the physician a valuable clue to the limit of endurable suffering for the patient. The answer to this inquiry often reveals a significant stress which precipitated or exacerbated the illness.

The physician also needs to know whether the patient came voluntarily or at the insistence of his relatives and friends. Involuntary patients are usually, but not always, much less cooperative than those who come of their own initiative. An adult patient who permits himself to be brought to the physician, or sent passively and unwillingly by his family, indicates thereby his inability to accept responsibility for his health.

## HISTORY OF PREVIOUS TREATMENTS

The effects of various treatments on the illlness have already been mentioned in considering measures that have relieved the symptoms. The history of previous treatments may include nothing more than simple home remedies. In many instances, however, the patient will have engaged in much more elaborate treatments with or without expert medical advice. The physician should learn all he can about such treatments and their effect on the course of the illness. Some patients cannot prevent themselves from consulting another physician while still taking the medicines of a former one. Such medicines, e.g., analgesics, sedatives, or stimulants, may profoundly alter the appearances of the patient's disorder and deceive the new physician. Often he should ask the patient, "Are you taking any medicines at this time?" Sometimes the patient has abandoned the previously recommended treatments. The new physician should learn whether they were abandoned because of therapeutic failure, unpleasant side effects, lack of cooperation by the family, or other factors.

In some instances the present illness is simply an exacerbation of a chronic illness or a recurrence of a former illness. When the physician can be reasonably sure of this, it becomes important for him to know how the patient responded to treatments of earlier episodes of the illness. One of the best guides to the success of a treatment is a history of its previous success in a similar illness in the same patient. For example, the knowledge that electroshock therapy has helped a depressed patient in a previous depression may help the physician in deciding to use this treatment for this patient again.

Although the physician should ask for the patient's opinion on the success of a former treatment, he cannot always rely on it. To continue the above example, severely depressed patients commonly believe that nothing can help them or ever has. They may devalue a treatment that has, in fact, been quite helpful in the past.

The history of previous treatments may or may not tell something useful about the disease; it will always tell something about the diseased patient. The physician should listen especially carefully to what the patient says about previous physicians. In doing so, he will learn more about his patient than about his colleagues. For example, when a patient criticizes forcefully the treatment recommended by a former physician, the physician will not be surprised when the same patient rejects his recommendations. Thus what the patient says about former physicians and treatments may help the physician greatly in his understanding and management of the patient.

The physician should never rely solely upon the patient's statements of what happened under a previous physician or in a previous admission to a hospital. Important errors can follow from careless acceptance of the patient's reports. The physician should therefore obtain reports of previous illnesses and treatments directly from hospitals, and when indicated and feasible, from former physicians. He can often obtain additional useful information about a patient's physical and mental health from other institutions where the patient may have been examined, such as the armed services, schools and colleges, places of employment, and insurance companies.

## References and Suggestions for Further Reading

1. ALTSCHULE, M. D.: *Bodily Physiology in Mental and Emotional Disorders.* New York, Grune & Stratton, 1953.
2. BEECHER, H. K.: Relationships of significance of wound to pain experienced. *J.A.M.A. 161:*1609, 1956.
3. BRODMAN, K., ERDMAN, A. J., JR., LORGE, I., and WOLFF, H. G.: The Cornell Medical Index: An adjunct to medical interview. *J.A.M.A. 140:*530, 1949.

4. CANNON, W. B.: *Bodily Changes in Pain, Hunger, Fear and Rage.* New York and London, D. Appleton & Co., 1922.
5. CLARK-KENNEDY, A. E.: *Medicine,* Vol. I. Chapter 2, Symptoms. Edinburgh, E. & S. Livingstone, Ltd., 1947.
6. DUNBAR, H. F.: *Emotions and Bodily Changes* (4th ed.). New York, Columbia University Press, 1954.
7. GRACE, W. J., WOLF, S., and WOLFF, H. G.: *The Human Colon.* New York, Paul B. Hoeber, Inc., 1951.
8. HARDY, J. D., WOLFF, H. G., and GOODELL, H.: *Pain Sensations and Reactions.* Baltimore, Williams & Wilkins Co., 1952.
9. LEWIS, T.: *Pain.* New York, The Macmillan Company, 1942.
10. MACBRYDE, C. M. (Ed.): *Signs and Symptoms: Applied Pathologic Physiology and Clinical Interpretation* (3rd ed.). Philadelphia, J. B. Lippincott Co., 1957.
11. MACKENZIE, J.: *Symptoms and Their Interpretation* (3rd ed.). London, Shaw and Sons, 1918.
12. MEAKINS, J. C.: *Symptoms in Diagnosis* (2nd ed.). Baltimore, Williams & Wilkins Co., 1948.
13. RYLE, J. A.: *The Natural History of Disease* (2nd ed.). London, Oxford University Press, 1948.
14. SULLIVAN, H. S.: *The Psychiatric Interview.* New York, W. W. Norton & Co., 1954.
15. TITCHENER, J. L., ZWERLING, I., GOTTSCHALK, L., LEVINE, M., CULBERTSON, W., COHEN, S., and SILVER, H.: Problem of delay in seeking surgical care. *J.A.M.A. 160:*1187, 1956.
16. WEINSTEIN, E. A., and KAHN, R. L.: *Denial of Illness.* Springfield, Ill., Charles C Thomas, 1955.
17. WINN, H.: Brief psychiatric approach for the clinician. *J.A.M.A. 172:*226, 1960.
18. WOLF, S., and WOLFF, H. G.: *Human Gastric Function* (2nd ed.). New York, Oxford University Press, 1947.
19. WOLFF, H. G. (Ed.): *Life Stress and Bodily Disease.* Vol. XXIX. Proceedings of the Association for Research in Nervous and Mental Diseases. Baltimore, Williams & Wilkins Co., 1950.
20. WOLFF, H. G., and WOLF, S.: *Pain.* Springfield, Ill., Charles C Thomas, 1948.

# 4

# THE FAMILY HISTORY

**THE VALUE OF THE FAMILY HISTORY**

An understanding of its contribution to the whole examination should guide the taking of the family history. Without such understanding the physician will probably inquire into the family history in a routine and perfunctory way which may irritate the patient and waste the time of both patient and physician. The family history furnishes important information about the contributions of both heredity and environment to the growth and development of the patient, and to the origin of his illness.

The physician should know the main facts of human heredity, and particularly medical genetics.[5, 21, 24, 27] Important heredity components enter into mental as well as physical disorders.[9, 19] Predictability with respect to inheritance varies greatly, because of the imperfections of our knowledge of heredity and the great difficulty in assembling the necessary data for any given family about which we may wish to make predictions. Knowledge of genetic factors now permits prediction of inheritance rather accurately in a small number of diseases. For the great majority of diseases, however, the predictability of inheritance, although poor, is sufficiently significant to deserve careful attention. For many disorders, of which schizophrenic reactions would be an outstanding example, we can say only that a predisposition is inherited. Many persons have such a predisposition without developing a schizophrenic reaction. The play of adverse environmental factors seems necessary, in addition to the genetic factors, before an overt schizophrenic reaction occurs.

The physician should also know that in addition to the inheritance of specific diseases, a predisposition to disease of certain organs can be inherited.[1,4,22] For example, the families of patients with peptic ulcer show a higher incidence of disorders of the gastrointestinal tract than do families of patients with diseases in other organs or with no disease at all.[1] Thyroid disorders of all kinds occur more often in the families of patients with hyperthyroidism than in the families of healthy persons.[1] A similar predisposition to inferiority of the heart has been indicated by the occurrence of all types of heart disease with greater frequency in some families than in others.[22]

This kind of information about predispositions to certain diseases and diseases of certain organs forms one of the most useful contributions of the family history. Its chief value lies not in diagnosis, where it can never be entirely accurate although it may give valuable hints, but in the prevention of diseases. The family history may helpfully warn the physician of areas in which his patient will need special guidance. Obesity, for example, although never desirable, can be particularly dangerous to those predisposed by heredity to such diseases as diabetes mellitus or heart disease.

The environment in which the patient grew and developed should be studied with regard to physical components and personal or social components. The physical aspects of the environment such as important variations in the amount of heat, light, food, and other factors, are considered principally as part of the personal history. However, the family history may clarify the origins of the physical aspects of the environment. It may trace some of them (e.g., lack of food) to uncontrollable economic conditions. It may show others (e.g., dietary variations) to have arisen in attitudes that were part of the culture in which the family lived. And it may show still others (e.g., lack of light) to have arisen in special idiosyncrasies of one or both parents.

In these matters the study of the physical environment blends with the study of the personal or social environment. The family history indicates the culture or cultures in which the parents grew up. It will indicate important deviations of the parents or the patient from these cultures; these deviations can be sources of important conflicts in the patient. For example, if the parents' behavior differed markedly from that usual for the culture in which they lived, the patient's adjustment to the culture outside his family circle may have been made much more difficult. Likewise, if the patient himself grows or moves into a culture significantly different from that of his parents, conflicts may arise between the patient and his family. Even more important than the foregoing is the fact that persons may exhibit traits which differ from those of the culture in which they live at present, but which were normal in the culture of their formative years. These traits are not symptoms and do not contribute to them.

Cultural influences may modify the outward expressions of otherwise similar mental illnesses in different communities. Thus schizophrenic reactions in the United States differ somewhat from schizophrenic reactions in Brazil;[26] and in the United States schizophrenic reactions in patients of Irish extraction differ from those in patients of Italian extraction.[17] Cultural differences may importantly influence the attitude of patients towards physicians and hence, among other things, influence what information patients offer physicians easily and what information they may tend to withhold.[25]

The important contributions of cultural influences to differences in the occurrence of mental illness, to variations in the forms of mental illness, and to modifications of the physician-patient relationship makes a knowledge of different cultures necesssary, not merely useful, for the physician. He should equip himself with a wide knowledge of different cultures outside his own. He may not master the details of all cultures and subcultures from which his patients may come. But this is not so important as his being aware of cultural differences and their significance for personality development and mental health. Such an awareness can be acquired by travel and by reading. The references at the end of this chapter include a small but representative sample of books describing different cultures and the importance of cultural differences to medicine.[2, 3, 10, 11, 12, 13, 14, 15, 16, 23] However, the physician's surest method of developing awareness of cultural differences and their importance is to use each patient's family history to deepen his understanding of these differences. In this connection the patient himself is often able to tell which practices and traits in his family conflicted with the norms for the culture. Thus the physician may gradually gather information for himself with which he can improve his own evaluation of cultural traits and deviations from them.

Included in the environmental aspects of the family is the important matter of pseudo-heredity. Many disorders which occur in members of the same family are transmitted not by genetic processes but by the powerful effects of suggestion and imitation. Epilepsy in one member of a family sometimes provides a model for hysterical convulsions in another. Palpitations and pain in the chest may arise in a son's identification with a father who has the symptoms of coronary disease. Often such suggestions occur without any active promotion by the first patient; the second patient simply imitates the disorder of the first. Sometimes, however, parents covertly encourage the expression of various physical symptoms and delinquent behavior in their children. The children thus express the parents' own (usually unconscious) impulses.[6, 7, 8] Often such promotion of symptoms by the parent occurs in a subtle manner and can only be detected by the careful study of both child and parent. The occurrence of such influences, however, suggests two kinds of inquiries in taking the family history. First, the physician should know whether anyone else in the family has the patient's disorder. This will indicate hereditary or pseudo-hereditary factors. Secondly, the physician should learn, if possible, something about the parents' attitude towards the patient's disorder. This may indicate the influence of suggestion from the parents on the child, and give hints of covert encouragement of the symptoms by the parents.

## PRINCIPAL TOPICS OF THE FAMILY HISTORY

The taking of a family history again illustrates the importance of choosing certain topics for emphasis and discarding others. No physician could possibly cover all the details of family history which this chapter will mention. But any of these details may be important in any patient. As with the history of the present illness, therefore, the physician must scan the family history while prepared to enter into necessary detail on any point which seems in any way relevant to the patient's health. For one patient the inquiry will be chiefly concerned with the occurrence of a certain disease in the grandparents or cousins. For another patient the physician will wish to know if the family came from Sicily or Lombardy. For still another, the physician will scrutinize the dietary habits of the family.

The relevant information of the family history may be studied under the following headings:

(a) The relevant history of each significant member of the patient's family
(b) The social and economic background of the family
(c) The structure of the family, i.e., the genetic relationships of the family members
(d) The social habits and values of the family group
(e) The personal relationships of these people with each other and with the patient

### *Individual Members of the Family*

For each person inquired about, the following facts should be noted when the information can be obtained:

## THE FAMILY HISTORY

1. Name
2. Age
3. If dead, age at death, nature and duration of final illness (Age of patient at this person's death.)
4. Religion
5. Racial or national origin
6. Occupation. Changes of occupation and reasons for these
7. Education. Reason for terminating education
8. Marital status and children
9. Physical characteristics, including physical appearance, general health, and major diseases or dysfunctions
10. Psychological characteristics. A brief description of the person's more important habits, values, and attitudes

The foregoing data should be obtained for each member of the patient's immediate family, i.e., his spouse, his children, his parents, and his siblings. The survey should also include any member of the household in which the patient was born who had prolonged relationships with the patient in early life. It often happens that members of the patient's social family (as disinguished from his biological family) become significant persons in the patient's early life. Indeed, for adopted children or those largely assigned to the care of nurses, governesses, or "mammies," the social family may have a structure quite different from that of the biological family. Apart from these extreme situations, it not infrequently happens that a patient has a closer relationship and more interaction with some person other than his parents living in the same house. Such a situation may occur where the biological mother is a physical or psychological invalid and her role is taken over by a healthier or more dominant sister, the aunt of the patient. Similarly, a psychological vacuum created by prolonged absences of a father while working away from home (e.g., for a railroad) may be filled by an uncle who lives next door and is at home all the time.

Some information of less detail is desirable about more distant relatives. The type and quantity of detail in the information sought about all these persons will naturally vary. More time should be spent on significant persons of the patient's childhood and current life situation than upon the peripheral figures.

The physical appearance of a relative derives importance from physical similarities between him and the patient. Out of such resemblances may grow special attitudes on the part of the older person towards the younger person. Also upon such similarities identifications of the younger with the older may arise. Such attitudes and identifications depend not so much on the existence of similarities as on how they are used by the people who have them and by those who notice them. Probably such resemblances provide opportunities for the expression of already formed attitudes as often as they cause such attitudes. But this fact makes them no less deserving of the physician's attention. For example, a father may take a special liking to one child rather than another if it is pointed out to him that the child "takes after him." Then, however, the mother may express towards that same child resentful impulses displaced from the resembled father. Many times the statement "You're just like your father," starts as an observation of physical similarily and gradually, often destructively, becomes a generalization about psychological similarities. The suggestive influence of such comparisons and remarks, when often repeated, may influence the child greatly.

Special features of the physical appearance of siblings (e.g., handsomeness or ugliness) may also often influence the affection which they receive from older people and from their contemporaries. Such favoritism or prejudices can profoundly affect the patient.

The physician should inquire about physical and psychological resemblances between the patient and each of the close relatives discussed. This leads not unnaturally to inquiries about favorites on the part of the patient towards his parents, siblings, and own children, and on the part of the parents towards the patient and his siblings.

## Social and Economic Background

The physician may consider the social status and habits of the family under a number of headings. As usual, he cannot expect, and should not try to obtain, the needed information under such neat headings or by direct questioning. Rather it should emerge from the detailed discussion of the individual members of the family, including the patient himself.

### Social and Economic Status

The social and economic statuses of the family are usually revealed by the occupation of the members of the family, by the neighborhood in which they live, and by the size or quality of house they rent or own. Sometimes direct information about the income of the family and other indices of social status may be volunteered or furnished in response to questions.

With respect to residences of the family, all communities in which the family lived and reasons for moving should be noted. The transfer of small children and even of ostensibly mature adults from one community to another may be stressful. For infants, small children and many elderly people, adaptation to a new physical environment may be difficult. For persons of any age, the need to make social adaptations to the people in the new community brings an additional burden to any moving.

### Racial and Cultural Origins

As already mentioned, details of national origin often provide clues to understanding conflicts arising from cultural differences. For example, if a patient comes from Ireland, the physician should note whether he is from predominantly Protestant Northern Ireland or predominantly Catholic Eire. If he is from Italy, the physician should be aware that the Sicilians and the Northern Italians show considerable differences in their social customs. If a patient is Jewish from Eastern Europe, it is of some importance to know whether he is from Poland or Russia. If members of the family have different national origins, this should be noted.

If the family emigrated to the United States within the previous generation, the facts concerning this are relevant. Conflicts and associated emotional disturbances frequently break out between the first generation of immigrants who wish to retain "old country" habits and the second generation which strives for assimilation in the culture of the United States. Psychosomatic disorders occur more frequently in the group of the second generation after immigration than in the third; by the time of the third generation assimilation has usually been completed. Whether the family rose or fell in social or economic status after immigration should be noted. The physician may find it helpful to inquire about such matters as the reason for the family's leaving the "old country" and the current attitudes of the members towards the country of birth and towards those relatives who may still live there. During such an inquiry, noteworthy problems of adjustment to the new country will often come to light. Thus assimilation is often easier if the patient or his family were political refugees than if they left the old country for purely personal reasons, for example, to flee a scandal in the family or to make more money in the United States. In the former case ties to the old country are rather readily broken. In the latter cases nostalgia or guilt may prolong divided loyalties in the patient. However, one cannot generalize about these matters. The political refugee may believe he should have stayed at home to help his countrymen, and he may then come to idealize his homeland and compare it unfavorably to the United States. Also, success and failure in the new country may influence assimilation and the attitudes to the next generation in the new country.

Similar problems attending migrations can occur in persons who move from one state to another within the United States. Important differences in accent and customs may make difficult and even quite stressful a move from one part of the country to another.

### Religion

Formal affiliation with a church and the strength of religious practices and convictions should be noted. Changes of religion on the part of the family or its members should be noted as well as interdenominational marriages.

### Attitudes toward Social Conditions

The facts of social background achieve significance chiefly through the values and conflicts associated with them. It is towards the clarification of these values and conflicts that the discussion should move. The fact of being an Italian family of second generation in the United States need not be significant in itself. It can become significant if an issue arises between two generations over "old country" attitudes versus American social customs. And it can become significant if the family happens to live in a community many of whose members show snobbish impoliteness to persons of national groups other than their own.

Similarly, in considering the family's religion, the physician needs to know what support the members derive from it, what of themselves they give to it, and what conflicts their religion may produce in individual members, or in the relations of the whole family to the larger social group. Changes in religion derive their significance from the motives which entered into the change, from the conflicts which were aroused, and perhaps from shifts in attitudes towards a changing member on the part of the rest of the family. The gaps between professed religious convictions and practices deserve attention. Such gaps may indicate important sources of guilt or may suggest that the patient uses words loosely.

The economic status of the family indicates some of the problems which it must face, but the attitudes of members of the family towards its economic status are more significant than the status itself. A family which unambitiously accepts a humble salary and a rented three-room apartment will have quite different problems from another which, living in the same conditions, aspires to buy a large house some day.

## *The Structure of the Family: The Family Tree*

The structure of the family can be most easily recorded in the form of a family "tree." A few simple symbols add to the information given by this tree. Others may be easily devised to suit individual needs. Two examples of such trees are provided in Figures 1 and 2. Such diagrams

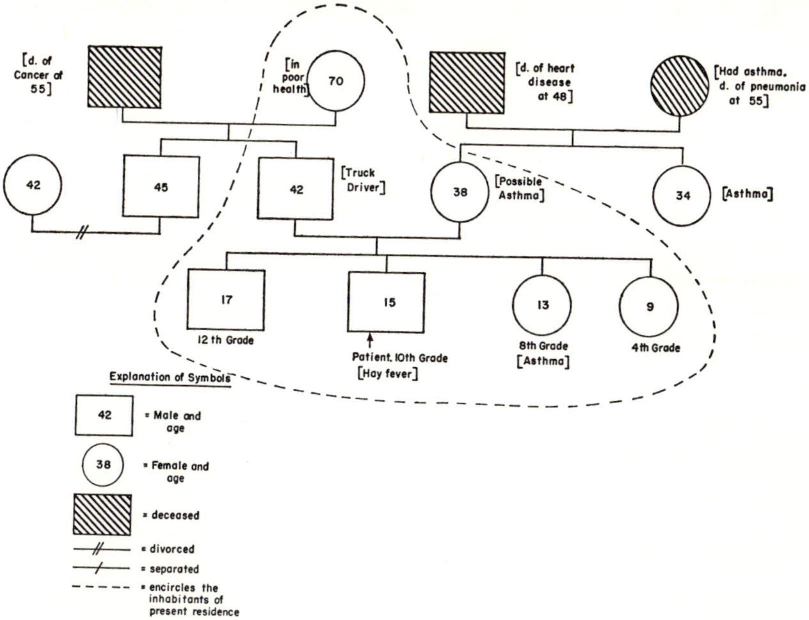

Fig. 1. Example of "family tree" useful in studying the family history, especially the relationships between the patient and significant persons in the family. A chart of this kind can assist the physician in studying and remembering the biological and social relationships of the patient.

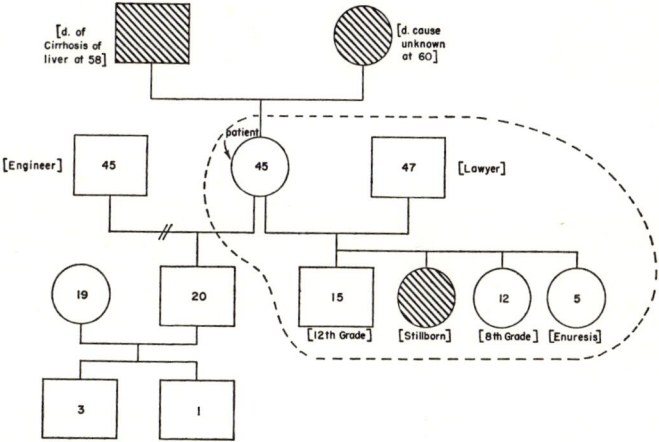

Fig. 2. Another example of a "family tree" useful in studying and remembering biological and social relationships in the patient's family. The symbols used are the same as for Figure 1.

should include significant persons of the social household, even if they are not members of the biological family. The purpose of the diagram is to emphasize relationships in the family, which it would not do adequately if it omitted any important persons.

### Age Relationships of Members of the Family

The physician should carefully note several pertinent facts of the family structure which are often overlooked. If any significant member of the family has died, his age at death and the cause of death should be noted. In addition, the age of the patient at the time of this person's death should be noted. Thus it may matter little to a patient whether his father is fifty, sixty or seventy when he died. But it does matter much to him whether the patient was two, five, ten or thirty at this time. In early childhood a difference of even a year may be significant. At six months of age an infant has usually little relationship with his father. But at eighteen months the death of the father may bring an important psychological deprivation.

The age of the parents at the birth of the patient and other siblings is significant. Sometimes a mother who starts her family at a somewhat older age than usual becomes weak or invalid before all the children have matured. She then may abdicate some or all of her maternal responsibility and authority to the oldest daughter, whose burdens become prematurely augmented.

The order of the birth of the siblings in relation to the patient should be noted. Oldest, youngest, and only children have quite different experiences from those of children in other positions of the family. Even slight differences in position may be significant. If a family has two daughters, the parents may understandably desire a boy next. If a girl arrives, their disappointment may influence their attitude towards the child. If, however, they next have a son and a third daughter comes later, they may welcome her eagerly.[28]

The number of years separating the siblings needs attention. If the patient is the youngest child in a family in which the next youngest child is ten or twelve years older, the patient may be raised in effect as an only child. Or if the patient is the oldest child in a family in which the next youngest child is ten or twelve years younger, the patient may become a kind of third parent to the younger children.

DEATH DURING THE PATIENT'S CHILDHOOD. Inquiries should also be made for siblings who may have died when the patient was a child. Although the adult patient may have largely forgotten these dead siblings, the experiences he had with them, his feelings at their birth and at their death have passed into his mental reservoirs and can remain psychologically active, even though unconscious. Likewise the experience of a mother's pregnancy, even when the announced sibling was aborted or stillborn, may have been important in the life of the patient as a child.

When a death has occurred it is important to know whether the patient was present in the home at the time and witnessed it, or was away from home and only heard of the death later. The attitudes of members of the family towards the experience of death may properly be investigated in this context.

## Social Habits and Values of the Family Group

Under this heading the physician should organize data bearing on significant habits and values of the family as a whole. The values are best derived from a study of the habits of the members of the family.

The physician should note the living habits of the family. Such questions as the following should usually be answered: How do (or did) the members of the family eat? Children with adults or separately? Hurriedly or leisurely? Are meals a social occasion for pleasant conversation or taken in front of a television set? Are any members of the family especially convivial or irritable at meal times? How do the members of the family bathe and sleep? Does each person have bathroom privacy? Do children and adults undress in front of each other? Do adults continue to sleep with and bathe children in their teens? Do adolescent children of opposite sexes bathe and sleep together? What are the habits of dress of the members of the family? Are children (and adults) dressed appropriately for their sex and age?

The physician should interest himself in the use of leisure time within the family and with other family groups. How much time in general does each parent spend with the children and with each other and doing what? Does the family favor spectator sports and entertainments or participate actively in recreations themselves? What proportion of time does the family devote to evenings at home, entertainments, or social activities with friends? Are there discrepancies between the habits of one or more members of the family and those of the majority of the family?

## Relations of Members of the Family with Each Other

The data gathered about the personalities of individual members of the patient's family have value chiefly in so far as they reveal to the physician the influence of these people on the patient and on each other. Accordingly, as the physician learns about each member of the family, he should try to build for himself an understanding of their relationships with each other and with the patient.

### References and Suggestions for Further Reading

1. BAUER, J.: *Constitution and Disease: Applied Constitutional Pathology* (2nd ed.). New York, Grune & Stratton, 1947.
2. BENEDICT, R.: *Patterns of Culture.* Boston, Houghton Mifflin Co., 1934.
3. BENEDICT, R.: *The Chrysanthemum and the Sword.* Boston, Houghton Mifflin Co., 1946.
4. DRAPER, G., DUPERTUIS, C. W., and CAUGHEY, J. L., JR.: *Human Constitution in Clinical Medicine.* New York, Paul B. Hoeber, Inc., 1944.
5. GATES, R. R.: *Human Genetics,* Vols. I and II. New York, The Macmillan Co., 1952.
6. JOHNSON, A. M., and SZUREK, S. A.: The genesis of antisocial acting out in children and adults. *Psychoanalyt. Quart. 21:*323, 1952.
7. JOHNSON, A. M., and SZUREK, S. A.: Factors in the etiology of fixation and symptom choice, *Psychoanalyt. Quart. 22:*475, 1953.
8. JOHNSON, A. M., and SZUREK, S. A.: Etiology of antisocial behavior in delinquents and psychopaths. *J.A.M.A. 154:*814, 1954.
9. KALLMANN, F. J.: *Heredity in Health and Mental Disorder.* New York, W. W. Norton & Co., Inc., 1953.
10. KARDINER, A.: *The Individual and His Society.* New York, Columbia University Press, 1949.
11. KARDINER, A.: *The Psychological Frontiers of Society.* New York, Columbia University Press, 1950.
12. KEESING, F. M.: *Cultural Anthropology.* New York, Rinehart & Co., Inc., 1958.
13. MALINOWSKI, B.: *Crime and Custom in Savage Society.* London, Routledge & Kegan Paul, Ltd., 1926.
14. MALINOWSKI, B.: *Sex and Repression in Savage Society.* London, Routledge & Kegan Paul, Ltd., 1949.
15. MEAD, M.: *Coming of Age in Samoa.* Toronto, Blue Ribbon Books Co., 1936.
16. OPLER, M. K. (Ed.): *Culture and Mental Health.* New York, The Macmillan Co., 1959.
17. OPLER, M. K.: Ethnic differences in behavior and psychopathology. *Int. J. Social Psychiat. 2:*11, 1956.
18. ORLANSKY, H.: Infant care and personality. *Psychol. Bull. 46:*1, 1949.
19. PENROSE, L. S.: *The Biology of Mental Defect* (Revised ed.). London, Sidgwick and Jackson, Ltd., 1954.
20. RICHARDSON, H. B.: *Patients Have Families.* New York, The Commonwealth Fund, 1945.
21. ROBERTS, J. A. F.: *An Introduction to Medical Genetics* (4th ed.). London, Oxford University Press, 1967.
22. ST. LAWRENCE, W.: The family association of cardiac disease, acute rheumatic fever, and chorea: A study of one hundred families. *J.A.M.A. 79:*2051, 1922.

23. SIMMONS, L. W., and WOLFF, H. G.: *Social Science in Medicine*. New York, Russell Sage Foundation, 1954.
24. SNYDER, L. H.: *Medical Genetics*. Durham, North Carolina, Duke University Press, 1941.
25. SPIEGEL, J. P.: Some Cultural Aspects of Transference and Counter-Transference, in *Individual and Familial Dynamics* (edited by J. Masserman). New York, Grune & Stratton, 1959.
26. STAINBROOK, E.: Some characteristics of the psychopathology of schizophrenic behavior in Bahian society. *Am. J. Psychiat. 109:*330, 1952.
27. STERN, C.: *Principles of Human Genetics*. (2nd ed.) San Francisco, W. H. Freeman & Co., 1960.
28. STERN, K.: Some remarks on the taking of case histories. *McGill Med. J. 18:*43, 1949.

# 5

# THE PERSONAL HISTORY

### THE VALUE OF THE PATIENT'S PERSONAL HISTORY

As with the family history, the physician should have a clear idea of the reasons for entering into the personal history of the patient.

In the first place, the personal history tells the physician about earlier factors which have influenced the patient and which may therefore be earlier causes of his present condition. Illnesses arise chiefly from stresses and the strains these produce. But the strain associated with a given stress depends, even when the stress is severe, on factors which differ with each person. Each person's ability to react to current stresses derives from the shaping of his organism by the interaction, over many years, of his genetic endowment and his previous experiences.

The physician must be cautious in ascribing causality to past events. Especially is this caution important in considering the development of the personality of the patient. It is often asserted that the events of infancy and early childhood always have a greater effect on the formation of the personality than those of later periods, but little convincing evidence has ever been brought forward to support this assumption.[32] That one event influences the response of a person to another is a matter of common observation. The events of childhood can derive importance from their temporal occurrence before later events, the response to which becomes modified by the earlier events. Nevertheless, events of adulthood may be just as important as those of childhood in altering a person's responses to current events. A full discussion of this problem is outside the scope of this book. However, insofar as possible, the physician should approach the patient's history without prejudices concerning the special importance of one group of experiences over others, or of one period of life over others. If special emphasis belongs to any part of the personal history, (considering it as a record of formative experiences), then the portions of the history which are best recalled for study deserve this emphasis. And these portions are almost invariably those nearer to the present rather than those of early childhood, the memories of which have been distorted and diminished by the erasures of time.

Secondly, the personal history is a record not only of external causes acting on the patient, but also of his responses to these stimuli. Responses to stimuli tend to become patterned and to resist changing. Hence the history of the past can clarify the present and help to predict the future. For example, the patient's record at school provides some index to his record at work in later life. A susceptibility to infections in childhood may indicate a similar weakness in adulthood. Here, however, the physician needs to use caution in interpreting the illness or behavior of one period of life as evidence of illness in another period. For example, temper tantrums, nail-biting, and enuresis in childhood indicate psychological disturbances. However, with changing circumstances of later periods of life, the psychological tensions underlying these symptoms may recede and with them the symptoms. The symptoms, therefore, indicate psychological tensions at the time of their occurrence, and not necessarily later.

A third value of taking a personal history lies in the therapeutic effect on the patient of reviewing his past life and present situation. When the physician listens to the patient's account of his present illness or to the family history, he helps the patient because of the value of his interest to the patient and the expectation of relief which his interest brings. The taking of the personal history extends these effects and adds to them. The physician's interest in the patient as a person greatly heightens the patient's attachment to the physician and confidence in him. In addition, the patient, in telling his life story, relives the important events of the past. These events were charged with emotion for him; and as he relives them, he expresses some of these emotions. This process can bring considerable relief of tension to the patient. While this is going on, the patient also clarifies some of his thoughts, feelings, and attitudes about himself and other people. The details of these therapeutic aspects of history-taking cannot be entered into here. But the physician should know that the personal history is always emotionally stirring for the patient. History-taking can be markedly therapeutic for the patient or, if mishandled, can disturb the patient and his confidence in the physician.

### Including the Positive Aspects of the Patient's Life

The physician should avoid emphasizing only negative aspects of the patient's past life and present circumstances. The inquiry into the personal history provides the physician, among other things, with some of the data that he will need in guiding the patient towards a more constructive life. But the patient's life already has many constructive aspects, and he himself has many assets. These need inclusion in the evaluation fully as much as those aspects which require modification. Often at times of illness, patients forget their own assets and the positive features of their past and present lives. When this happens, the focusing of attention on positive as well as negative aspects of the history may have a notable therapeutic effect.

## *Keeping the Personal History Relevant and Comprehensive*

Earlier chapters of this book have stressed the importance of selection in history-taking and examination. The physician can easily lose his bearings in a sea of data unless he allows the taking of the personal history to be guided somewhat by leads obtained in the earlier parts of the examination, chiefly the history of the present illness. For example, a comprehensive history of a patient's early life would be worth little if it failed to uncover the fact that the patient, now suffering from a chronic brain syndrome, had measles encephalitis as a child. Accordingly, the personal history should always be relevant to the present illness. Yet comprehensiveness also must remain a goal. Without this comprehensiveness, the physician may fall into the error of allowing the present complaints to influence the history-taking so that other unmentioned, perhaps unconscious, but nevertheless highly significant material is omitted.

## *Attitudes, Feelings, and Values of the Patient*

The patient's perception of events forms the core of the personal history. The basic facts of dates, places, and events are important; yet their importance derives chiefly from the attitudes of the patient towards them. Events shape attitudes which influence the reactions to subsequent events and so modify these. War generates hostility, and hostility leads to war.

Therefore, in listening to the personal history, the physician must constantly seek to discover the attitudes and feelings of the patient which accompanied the events described. The patient's age at the menarche matters less than the child's attitude towards menstruation. Was she prepared? Did she think she had some disease? Was she made to feel ashamed? The fact of the patient's being fired from a job is not so important as his thoughts about it and his reaction to his wife's thoughts about it. The statement that the patient belongs to a particular religious denomination tells little until it is known why he joined this group, what he gives to it, and what support he gets from it.

The exploration of attitudes and feelings should result in the discovery of those which are of chief importance to the patient. The physician must try to know the patient's hierarchy of values. Human beings differ more from each other in their values than in any other respect. One man may become violently excited about a political appointment and be indifferent to the infidelity of his wife; another may be depressed by a frown from his boss and quite apathetic about heavy debts. What terrifies one man may be high adventure for another. The reaction to a social stress is governed as much by the personality of the subject as by the nature of the stress. The physician must endeavor to find out what is stressful to a patient and how it has become so. He must listen to each patient in his own right, searching for the significance of things to the patient uninfluenced by their significance for himself.

## *The Patient's Previous Health and Diseases*

The great importance of detailed inquiries concerning previous disorders which the patient has experienced justifies a fuller discussion of this topic than will be given to the other topics of inquiry mentioned later. Physicians sometimes note the occurrence of a particular disease in the patient's history without adequately exploiting the opportunity to learn much more about the patient. Several reasons justify a careful study of the patient's previous illnesses.

First, previous disorders and diseases often provide valuable clues to the present illness. Many illnesses are recurrent and episodic, sometimes with the episodes widely separated in time. The present illness may really be one of a series of illnesses which have superficial differences, but the same underlying mechanism. Thus a patient may have a "nervous breakdown" in his late teens, then be well until a paranoid psychosis in his early forties. Details of the first "nervous breakdown" may show it to have been a schizophrenic reaction. Or a patient may have a number of spells of dizziness in his forties, followed by a period of apparent good health and then a severe cerebral hemorrhage in his late fifties. The earlier dizziness may be found to have been due to small cerebral hemorrhages. Nevertheless, the physician should not make the diagnosis of the present illness from the diagnosis of past ones. Instead, a detailed study of the former illnesses should aid in the diagnosis of the present one.

Secondly, the physician should study the patient's total behavior during the experience of an illness as an important example of his responses to stress. A severe illness can be one of the severest of all stresses experienced. If the patient has previously undergone a severe illness, his reaction to it may help the physician to estimate his probable response to the present illness, and this in turn may guide the physician's recommendations. For example, if the physician finds that the patient is disposed to prolonged invalidism and tends to drag out his convalescences, the physician can perhaps counteract this tendency before it appears in the present illness.

The physician should consider the possibility of previous illnesses when the history contains otherwise unexplained changes in the life of the patient or periods of time for which the patient can give no account. Illnesses frequently underlie changes of residence, failure of promotion in school, or changes of employment.

Commonly omitted in the remembrance of illnesses are pregnancies (which certainly are usually healthy) and accidents. The history of pregnancies is considered further in a later section of this chapter. Concerning accidents, the physician needs to remember that they frequently cause important disability and that psychological tensions often contribute to accidents. Not every accident needs to be scrutinized for such factors, but many do. One needs to consider a possible unconscious wish on the part of the patient to injure himself. Many accidents occur during intense preoccupation with highly charged thoughts and emotions which withdraw attention from the environment. The physician needs also to investigate the environmental contributions to accidents, e.g., the condition of the road and traffic in automobile accidents; dangerous machinery in industrial accidents.

## THE CONTENT OF THE PERSONAL HISTORY

Below are listed some periods of life into which the personal history may be divided for study, and the topics about which information should be sought for each person. They are discussed in further detail in the succeeding paragraphs. The predilection of the physician may readily indicate different boundaries to the epochs and topics of inquiry. As always, there should be no rigid conformity to the outline offered. Rather the physician should aim at a broad inquiry which will effectively sample the patient's experiences. Sampling is the best that can possibly be accomplished in this task. The physician should not delude himself with the idea that the creation of new divisions or subheadings will increase the accuracy of his survey.

*Periods of Life History To Be Inquired about*

Prenatal
Infancy (birth to about 1 year)
Training period (about 1 year to 2 or 3 years)
Preschool period (about 2 or 3 years to 5 years)
Early school years (6 to 12 years)
Adolescence (12 to 18 years)
Early adulthood (18 to about 45 years)
Later adulthood (45 to 65 years)
Old age (65 years and on)

*Topics of Inquiry for Each Period*

(*a*) Basic temperament, mood, energy output, dominant attitudes, chief interests, values, and activities
(*b*) Physical functions and health. This includes alimentary and eliminative functions, sexual functions, motor functions, and the occurrence of any dysfunctions or disease
(*c*) Relations with other persons
(*d*) Learning processes, school, and vocations
(*e*) Major events of the period and the patient's reactions thereto, e.g., births, deaths, separations, changes of residence, school, or employment

In the first phases of life only some of these topics are relevant. As growth and life continue, more and more areas of interest open and must be added to the list of pertinent topics of inquiry, while few are abandoned.

When the patient is a child, according to his age, some of the questions of the following pages will become relevant under the heading of the present illness or the current life situation.

Some comments on topics of special relevance in each period of life follow.

## Prenatal Period

The history of the prenatal period of the patient's life is in effect the history of a pregnancy. However, this history should comprise more than the record of physical changes or complications of the pregnancy. It should include a thorough assessment of the attitude of the mother and father towards the pregnancy and their expectations of its product.

Such information is not always or even often obtainable. But the physician should think about it and, when feasible, ask about it.

The physician should not be satisfied with simple unqualified statements with respect to whether the pregnancy was wanted or not. The patient's parents may have had mixed attitudes towards the pregnancy, wanting it for some reasons and not wanting it for others. They may also have been more or less aware of their attitudes to the pregnancy. Some pregnancies which are unexpected and even considered unpropitious are, long before the birth of the infant, accepted with eagerness and pride. If the pregnancy was unwanted, why was this so? Perhaps it came too soon after marriage before the patient's parents had come to know each other thoroughly. Perhaps his mother had barely recovered from her previous delivery before another child announced itself. Perhaps she was insecure in the possession of her husband's affection. Perhaps he objected to more children or wanted none at all. Perhaps her health was poor. Perhaps one more child further threatened a precarious livelihood. And were preventive measures taken against conception or not? All these things should be thought of when a mother appears partially or totally to reject her pregnancy.

If there are no direct evidences of the attitude of the patient's mother on this matter, sometimes the physician will find hints of troubled attitudes in a history of poor health or complications during the pregnancy. Or the mother may have noticed a vague and contentless change of mood. However, there may be many other causes of such complications and changes of mood. The father's feelings and attitudes should not be neglected. What was the impact of the pregnancy on him?

Sometimes there is a record of the activities of the fetus in the uterus. These are often the first announcements of a future temperament to be expressed later, postnatally, with the greater force of greater size.

The progress and complications of labor and delivery should be noted. These should be considered from the side of the mother. Was labor pleasant and gratifying to her, or was she injured? Did she carry off painful memories of that event, which may have influenced her attitude towards the patient or succeeding pregnancies? Labor and delivery should also be studied from the side of the infant. If labor was prolonged were there injuries to the baby? Or did damage to the mother render her incapable of caring for the patient immediately and adequately?

### Infancy[10, 22, 25]

The attitudes of the parents toward the patient after his birth become even more important than they were during the pregnancy. The nutrition of the baby is less automatic than that of the fetus, since the baby depends upon the voluntary activity of the mother for sustenance. Numerous observations attest to the capacity of newborn infants to respond sensitively to changes in the emotions of the parents as well as to changes in the physical environment.[33] The infant may perceive the emotions of the parent through changes in the parent's voice or muscular tension when the parent holds the child. Emotional disturbances probably also alter the quality of the mother's milk deleteriously (as they do in cows), and certainly such disturbances can cause changes in the quantity of milk available.

Many factors may have entered into the attitudes of the patient's parents towards him as a baby. Sometimes a baby's sex or other characteristics disappoint parents. Or some quite extraneous events may drain off attention and affection which would otherwise go to the baby. Although the details of an infant's feeding may be important, it is possible to overemphasize them, with neglect of other aspects of the infant's total functioning such as his motor function and the stimulation he receives through the skin and muscles.[25] Whether an infant is fed from a bottle or a breast is perhaps not so important as the reason for the choice. The physician should inquire whether the patient's mother was unable to nurse the baby because of inadequate milk, poor physical health, or inadequate motivation. Again more important than whether the patient was fed by breast or bottle is the total experience he had while feeding. An infant can be more disturbed when held rigidly while nursing at the breast of a tense mother than when fed out of a bottle with affectionate cuddling by a relaxed mother.

The physician should learn if he can, the amount of time the mother (or mother substitute) actually spent with the patient as an infant in giving him mothering attentions. A deprivation of such mothering may retard the child's development.[31] However, more important than what was done to and for the patient is the attitude with which the tasks were done. A contented mother, although spending little time with her infant, may give the baby better care than a tense mother who spends more time with her child.

The ages of weaning, teething, talking, and walking deserve noting together with anything unusual about these events. So does the evolution of the patient's early personality. Was he demanding or docile? Did he cry timidly or did his cry demand immediate service? When he began to crawl, how much energy and curiosity did he show?

The circumstances of the patient's parents, occupational, economic and residential, merit attention. Were the parents and patient in good health during this period? And what were their relationships with each other? A disturbance in the relations of the parents with each other may be quickly reflected in a disturbance in their child.[1]

## Training Period[10, 22, 29, 30]

In this period the patient began learning to conform to the wishes of his parents and other persons. The gradual spacing of the infant's feedings and the changes in the diet required by weaning, including the offering of different foods, had already exacted some such conformity. These restrictions, however, came in what others did to or for him. In the training period the patient had to begin exerting some control over himself in the interests of other persons. The issue of control usually occurs first and chiefly with respect to the matter of urination and bowel movements. The child is required to postpone elimination to a suitable time and place. It occurs also with respect to the child's motor activity. He finds he cannot go everywhere he pleases about the house. The issue of control arises again and again as the child goes through life. But the patterns of the infant's responses to frustrations are first clearly expressed at this time.

At this period the attitude of the mother towards the patient may have undergone a modification. A child at this age is more active and demanding than an infant and yet not able to love reciprocally as the mother would naturally wish. Later, the care she gives the child is at least partially repaid in the affection and companionship of the child. But at this period, he is not able to furnish these to her. As in no other period of the child's life, the mother must care for the child with relatively little immediate return of pleasure to herself.

The actual time of sphincter training matters less than the parent's attitude towards it. If the training is much advanced or much delayed over that customary in our society, some suggestion may thereby be given of an excessively punitive or indulgent attitude on the part of the mother. However, the suggestion must not be taken for a proof. Individual training practices of parents express quite imperfectly their overall attitudes towards children. Almost always parents have multiple and complex, rather than single and simple, attitudes. They may indulge a child in some areas of behavior, restrict and punish him in others, and remain indifferent towards still others.[29] So a parental attitude towards one matter may tell little or nothing about other deeper and more enduring attitudes of the parent towards his (or her) child, which may influence the child much more over the years. With these cautions in mind, however, the physician should try to discover whether the patient's mother was insistent, compulsive, or punitive, or able to await patiently the acquisition of sphincter control by her child. What measures did she take to promote the training? Did the patient have pleasure in his bowel movements or pleasure in thwarting his mother's wishes?

As before, the economic and social status of the family requires attention. The physical health of the members and their personal relationships with each other continue to be relevant.

To these themes must also be added others. The occurrence of a pregnancy or the birth of another sibling at this time may have provoked unfavorable reactions in the patient. Likewise the occurrence of deaths and divorces or separations from significant persons should be noted. If a mother becomes seriously ill, her child is, in effect, separated from her and the results may be comparable to those resulting from her going on a long journey.

In this period the patient moved out of his crib or playpen to his first contacts with other children and the problem of sharing arose.

From this early period patients frequently recall memories of significant events. These remembered early events often seem to be banal enough and unworthy of special notice. Nevertheless, close scrutiny of first memories usually reveals some underlying emotional significance of the remembered scenes. Such early or first memories often exemplify problems which have recurred throughout the patient's life and which accordingly deserve attention.[7, 15]

Special aptitudes of a child such as manual dexterity or speed of learning often appear clearly at this time. So also do particular drives and interests which may form the nuclei of later ambitions and strivings. Thus a child may show unusual curiosity, a tendency to take things apart, or a delight in building things up, the first buds of creativity.[9]

Speech develops at this time and the physician should inquire about the occurrence in the patient of delays or precocity in development of speech, or of abnormalities such as stuttering.

## *Preschool Period*

During this period a child's relationships with his parents and with other children become modified. At this time the patient may have developed heightened attractions to one parent and some antagonism towards the other. To what extent was this contributed to by the attitudes of the parents themselves? Did the patient become a weapon in their own rivalry or did they work together to help him mature?

Curiosity grows in a child as he explores the world around him and the world of his own body. What frustrations and prohibitions did the patient meet in this exploration? The attitudes of his parents towards his early sexual activities may have markedly influenced his later sexual behavior.

The different diseases experienced by the patient should be noted. No less important are the attitudes of the patient and his parents towards these illnesses. Were these illnesses looked upon as annoyances or did the patient's mother shower the child with unusual and unnecessary attentions? Was the patient frightened by any illness?

So, too, interest should continue in the patient's relations with other children. How much time did he spend with other children and how much time by himself? Which situations and which people did he seem to enjoy most? The patient's parents may have noticed at this period delays or difficulties in the growth of the patient's efforts at self-control, as he tried to anticipate and replace the external controls they provided.

The themes of social and economic circumstances and the relationships of the patient's parents to each other are followed in this period. The health of the family continues important. Other major events of the period should be noted, including deaths, divorces, separations, and changes of residence. When deaths and separations have occurred, it is important to know something of the attitude of the patient toward the person who died and toward the death of the person. Were there rivalries with the deceased or deep attachments to him or her? Was the death misinterpreted to the patient as a going away on a trip? Was he allowed to grieve openly or told not to cry?

The physician should inquire about the occurrence during this and the next period of such disorders as nail-biting, thumb-sucking, nightmares, enuresis, temper tantrums, or major problems in feeding and elimination. These may betray some underlying insecurity in the patient which may not otherwise have been apparent. The patient may have been described by his parents as a model, "well-behaved" child. And so he may have been in outward behavior. Yet some evidence of important psychological disturbances may be found in the various symptoms mentioned. A regression to immature behavior previously outgrown, such as a return to thumb-sucking or bed-wetting can usually be traced to some current stress. Thus the arrival of a new child or a change of residence may bring such relapses.

### *Early School Years*

During this period a child's interests begin to move away somewhat from his family towards his contemporaries outside his family. He joins and seems to live for groups and "gangs." At the same time the rudiments of altruistic behavior appear. The child becomes increasingly aware of himself as a person. This includes awareness that he is different from other people who are also persons and have their needs too. The struggle between impulses and measures of inner control becomes more manifest in the efforts of the child to conform to the standards of his group. He gradually learns that short-term pleasures can often be deferred in favor of greater pleasures later.

The patient's performance at school should engage attention. The age of starting school and, if this is later than usual, the reasons for deferment should be noted. Difficulties of both parents and the patient in separating from each other when the patient first went to school deserve notice. The age of leaving school is important too, but the reasons for leaving are even more important. Was this step regretted later? If the patient was reputedly slow in learning or retarded in school, inquiry should be made about the reasons. Often emotional disturbances or difficulty in hearing or seeing present themselves as scholastic dullness. On the other hand, genuine scholastic dullness may also evoke emotional disturbances, especially if a child is pressed by parents or teachers to keep up with work beyond his capacity.

Although many children lose their earlier interest in sexuality during this period, others do not. They retain their curiosity and continue their explorations throughout childhood.

In addition to the foregoing problems, which are somewhat special to this period, the physician should continue his interest in all the themes mentioned in connection with earlier periods. If these topics are not mentioned again this is to avoid repetition, not because they lose importance in later periods of life.

## *Puberty and Adolescence*

Puberty and adolescence widen the activity of the maturing person by bringing three new problems which have not previously been so prominent although their origins extend back many years.

First, with the welling up of sexual hormones at puberty, sexual maturity approaches. With this comes the need to modulate sexual urges and eventually direct them in satisfactory mating with a partner of the opposite sex. This process continues on into early adulthood when marriage usually takes place.

When the present illness has given hints of marital discord, the physician may need to investigate rather fully the history of the patient's first relations with members of the opposite sex outside the family. While these relationships are certainly influenced by even earlier experiences with members of the family, the early experiences outside the family may show in embryonic form the difficulties which the patient later encountered in marriage. Moreover, these experiences are usually more accessible to the patient's memory than the experiences of his earlier life. For example, later sexual anxieties and frigidity may be foreshadowed in adolescence by extreme prudishness and cautiousness in dating. Furthermore, restricted experience in dating often leaves a young girl poorly equipped to choose a mate or to adapt to one when the time comes to marry.

Secondly, the child must begin to assume complete responsibility for his own conduct. Parents loosen controls and restrictions at this time and the maturing person gradually becomes his own director. The characteristic impulsivity and mood swings of adolescence chiefly derive from the struggles associated with this process of winning freedom by demonstration of the capacity to use it. This period tests the maturity of the parents also. Some parents seek to relive their own lives vicariously through their children, others can accept the children as individual persons with their own right to self-determination. Some parents cannot allow the child to become an adult and need to hold him a captive in the family. Parents may have most reluctance to let an only child or a youngest child grow up.

Thirdly, the adolescent moves closer to the selection of a life work. The final choice of vocation may occur in childhood or not until far into adulthood if extensive college preparation is undertaken. But the young person must usually face the problem in some form at this period. He must accept the need to become economically independent even if he does not decide the manner of accomplishing this immediately. Decisions taken in this matter, e.g., the leaving of school or college, may have a later influence which a young person rarely anticipates at the time. The physician should inquire into the events and motivations behind such decisions.

## *Early Adulthood*

In this period, the problems posed by adolescence are usually restored in one way or another. Sexual impulses find satisfactory outlets in marriage, or perhaps less satisfactory ones elsewhere. However, marriage involves much more than sexuality. It signals the willingness of the maturing person to accept responsibility for the welfare of others, first that of the spouse and then that of the children. It taxes the adaptability of the participants, since each must learn to live in close contact with

# THE PERSONAL HISTORY

someone brought up in a more or less different environment. When the couple cannot compromise, the marriage becomes strained and may break.

Since the marital and parental relationships provide the principal immediate sources of pleasure or tension in adult life, the physician can hardly afford to pass over them lightly. He should study more than the outer facts that the patient married at a certain age and now has a certain number of children. He will need to enter into such details as the following: occasion of meeting the marital partner; length of courtship; qualities which attracted him to the partner; special circumstances, e.g., financial hardships or opposition of parents, at the time of the marriage; religious aspects of the marriage; early relations of the couple; sexual relationships; planning of parenthood; pregnancies and their complications, both physical and psychological; childbirth and its complications; pleasures and problems of rearing children, e.g., breast feeding and training; and later relationships of the couple, including increase or decrease in intimacy and companionship with passing years.

A previous section considered some aspects of pregnancies and child rearing, but then chiefly from the point of view of the patient as an infant and child. Now the physician must consider pregnancies and child rearing from the point of view of the patient as a spouse and parent.

Allied to the demands made by marriage are those arising from the participation of the family and its members in larger social groups. Perhaps a person reaches the highest level of maturity when he proves himself capable of participating in the goals of groups larger than his immediate family. The family presumably shares most of his interests and values; but the larger groups always demand more unselfishness since the community of immediate interest is less, or less apparent, in larger groups than in smaller ones. Thus the physician can learn much of the important values of a patient by inquiring into his attitudes towards such groups as unions, professional organizations, schools, local and national governments, and religious organizations. The patient's actual participation signifies more than his verbal statements on the subject.

### Occupational History

The physician should learn about the various past employments of the patient, his enjoyment of them and the reasons for changing jobs or vocations. The vocational history tells much about the interests and satisfactions of the patient and also about important qualities of character such as perseverance, which the pursuit of distant goals requires. The physician should distinguish between vocational and personal reasons for changing jobs. Frequent changes of job suggest that the patient encountered personal difficulties with fellow employees or supervisors which he could not handle except by leaving.

The occupational history should include mention of the patient's military service and what he experienced then, including his attitudes then and at present to these experiences.

The discussion of the current life situation in a later section includes further remarks about occupation.

*Later Adulthood*

In later adulthood some decline in physical power often appears, although intellectual power and emotional maturity reach their peak. Problems related to the decline in sexual capacity and reproductive capacity often arise in this epoch. Women especially may encounter difficulties, although most women pass through this period without turbulence or even uneasiness. Physiological disturbances may occur with associated psychological effects. But most of the psychological problems of the involutional period arise not so much from physical changes as from the way in which the patient views these physical changes. If he has strongly associated sexual and reproductive capacity with youth, power and prestige, the threat to these values may bring more difficulty than the simple decline of physical potency. A woman may find the decline in her sexual attractiveness especially distressing when contrasted with a daughter's growing success in the same arena. Regrets and bitterness over unfulfilled aspirations or attempts to revive the past by imitations of youth inevitably lead to difficulties.

Moreover, the growing independence of the children forewarns the parents that they will eventually leave the home for jobs or marriage. The first difficulties of later adulthood often coincide with the first signs of loss of companionship from children and the demands for new adaptations which this entails.

Later adulthood also brings a certain quality of finality to the decisions of a person's life. Age gradually squeezes out the element of choice in such matters as vocation, place of residence, and indeed, with respect to nearly all material goals. The patient may need to adjust himself to the fact of not realizing all his desires and aspirations. Failure to accept with equanimity the course of events may bring tension and discomfort.

*Old Age*

The onset of old age depends much more upon attitudes than upon reaching a particular year of life. The remarkable achievements of such men as Verdi, Titian, and Goethe in advanced age illustrate the skill and creativity which elderly persons can have. However, certain experiences come to all elderly people sooner or later, and these pose new psychological and physical problems to which they must adapt.

Physical power declines and usually with it the ability to earn a livelihood. This may bring economic dependence upon other persons or upon the state, something not experienced since childhood. A person who has in the interim proven himself capable of economic self-support usually finds this a distasteful and humiliating experience when it recurs.

Retirement from active employment may do more than threaten an older person with economic dependence. It can disturb his sense of usefulness and his satisfactions in contributing to common goals. Retirement may threaten a man who has found his only enjoyment in working and none in other areas of living. He resembles an investor with all his money in one stock.

The deaths of friends expose the older person to isolation unless he practices the art of winning new ones. And since a social separation of the generations seems to be increasing in our society, the older person must often make his new friends from the depleted ranks of his own contemporaries. He may have to live alone if there is no place in the homes or the hearts of his children for him, or if he chooses to reject such a place.

*The Patient's Opinion of His Past Life*

As mentioned earlier, the events of the patient's life derive their chief importance from the meaning they have for the patient. The physician may find it helpful to ask the patient at some time to tell his thoughts about his past life as a whole. Does he consider it to have been satisfactory or has he a sense of failure about it? What was his best time and what his most unhappy time? What would he have done differently?

## CURRENT LIFE SITUATION OF THE PATIENT

The physician should learn as much as he can about the patient's current life situation. The importance of this topic may exceed that of the past personal history. In the first place, the physician needs to know the environmental forces which act upon the patient and to which he must respond. The physician cannot possibly understand the psychological state of the patient, and often the physical state, without knowledge of the stimuli which the patient receives from his environment. Such a knowledge bears not only upon the origin of the patient's illness, but equally upon measures taken for his rehabilitation. Too often in the past, patients enduring some life stress have been admitted to a hospital and have there recovered sufficiently to be discharged, only to re-enter the unchanged noxious environment which originally sent them to the hospital.

Secondly, the details of the patient's life situation, and especially those of his occupation, may influence decisions made about medication or recommendations concerning employment. The physician needs to avoid giving a machinist large doses of sedatives which might dangerously reduce the patient's attention. His advice to a patient with epilepsy who drives a truck will differ from his advice to another patient with epilepsy who works as a salesman.

Thirdly, the life situation of a patient, like his clothes, reveals further important data about himself. For the environment, inflexible as it may be in part, is also in part the product of the person who inhabits it. The patient himself has to a varying extent created his own environment, and the kind of environment he inhabits tells something of the kind of person he is.

In inquiring into the current life situation of the patient, the physician should consider the following topics.

*Physical Residence*

The actual location of the patient's house tells much about his economic status and his social position. So does the quality of the residence he occupies and whether he rents or owns it. Are there enough bedrooms, adequate plumbing, ventilation, and heating?

The physical condition of the house and the furnishings tell something of the economic status and also of the values of the patient. And, as indicated above, they also influence his psychological state by providing him with a certain structured physical environment for much of his time. Of importance also is whether the patient and his family live in the same type of residence and community as those of the previous generation, or whether they have bettered themselves or declined in status.

The physician's inquiry about the home address of the patient supposes a detailed knowledge of the area in which the patient lives. The physician gains nothing by learning that his patient lives on 1328 Eusapia Street unless he also knows something about the part of the town through which Eusapia Street runs. It makes a great deal of difference to the patient, and may make a great deal of difference to his health, whether he lives next to a freight yard, in an elegant residential section of the suburbs, in a swamp, in a warehouse district, or beside a chemical plant.

When the patient's illness has its principal origins in disturbed personal relationships, the physician can helpfully ask for details of the living arrangements in the home. A plan of the patient's house with notes on such matters as sleeping arrangements, bathrooms, and provision for privacy can often clarify obscure tensions. Do children see nude adults habitually? Do adults and children sleep or bathe together?

The inquiry about the residence should include questions about the presence of pets or farm animals which may carry important illnesses.

### Community of the Residence and Group Affiliations

The community in which the patient lives influences the resources of employment and recreation available to him. A patient living in a small market town serving an entirely agricultural community has fewer opportunities for change of work than a resident of a large city. But he may have more friends and acquaintances interested in helping him find work than his urban counterpart.

The patient's life is influenced by the demands made on him by the larger social group in which his family lives. In turn, this larger group provides him with recreational opportunities and psychological supports which the family alone cannot give. Thus the patient's membership in clubs, unions, lodges, and religious organizations is relevant to the understanding of his total situation.

### Inhabitants of the Residence

The question, "Who lives at home besides you?" always opens important topics. In addition to members of the patient's immediate family, there may be in-laws, uncles, aunts, parents, boarders, or friends who just dropped in and stayed. These are the people with whom the patient must live daily. Other persons, such as those he meets at work, he can get away from, at least on some days. His relationships with the other residents of his home are cardinal factors in his contentment and an important object of the physician's curiosity.

The occupations of the family need attention. Are the children at school and the adults at work? Or is the house continually crowded so that privacy and adequate rest are impossible?

A middle-aged woman with a paranoid personality developed an acute paranoid psychosis early one summer. The family lived in a two-room apartment. There was no solid partition between the rooms. Only a curtain separated the room where the patient and her husband slept and the adjoining room occupied by their fourteen year old son. Sexual relations between the parents usually took place during the day when the boy was at school. In June of this year, when school closed, the boy began to spend most of the day at home. This led to severe sexual frustration which seems to have been one of the significant precipitating factors in the patient's psychosis.

### Social Habits

The physician should inquire about the social habits of the patient's marital family along the lines indicated for inquiries about his biological family in Chapter 4.

### Occupation[17, 23, 27]

The physician needs to know more than the general type of occupation of the patient. He needs to know whether the patient is self-employed or works for others. If he works in a factory, at what factory is he employed? What does he do there? Of far greater importance than the business of his employment are the exact details of what the patient himself does at this employment. It is not enough to know that the patient works at a sugar refinery. He may be president, tend cane grinders, watch gauges on the evaporators, pack sugar, or do any of many other tasks. Each different task requires different responses from him. The patient may be able to meet the demands of some tasks; others may impose a significantly deleterious strain on him. For example, many machines operate at speeds which induce tensions in some of the men who tend them. A man may be unable to keep up with such a machine, but work quite well at some other task. This other job may actually require more skill or more output of energy, but may make different demands on him which he is equipped to meet. And so the physician should let every patient transport him mentally to his place of work. In his imagination the physician should stand behind the counter with the salesman, climb on girders with the riveter, or look over the shoulder of the bank teller.

Housewives no less than those who work outside the home have different jobs to do in different circumstances which need as much study as those of any other occupation.

At managerial levels of employment, tensions arise not from the demands of machinery, but from the complex personal relationships between the employees. However, personal relationships at work are scarcely less significant for artisans and laborers.

Personal relationships especially require attention in the employees of large companies and factories. Often the employee comes to think of "the company" as a benign entity full of maternal solicitude for the employees. Negative aspects of the situation he then attributes to some person or persons, such as foremen or supervisors who irritate him. These people are not considered part of "the company." Or the reverse pattern may occur in which the patient derives much support from some fellow-employees or supervisors, but entertains a diffuse hostility for "the company." Only careful detailed inquiries can permit an accurate dissection of the rational and irrational elements in attitudes towards companies and the individual people who compose them.

Many other details of the patient's employment deserve attention as possible sources of conflict and tension. The physician needs to know the number of hours the patient works and whether he has suitable rest periods. Of relevance often is the distance of work from home. Long distances usually require long hours of commuting which add to the total fatigue of the day. The patient is nearly always concerned about promotions and increases in salary. The physician should inquire about these and also learn the patient's attitudes towards them.

The meaning of his work for the patient deserves attention. Does the patient work for money only, or does he work for the pleasure of expressing a skill or improving a talent? To what extent does good work on his part derive from the satisfactions of exercising a skill usefully and to what extent does it depend upon praise and approval from those around him? Does the patient go about his work in a relaxed way or does he work in a rush or with tension?

Different occupations will indicate different questions the physician should ask. In every instance, however, the physician should try to learn as much as he can about the balance of tensions and satisfactions which the patient finds in his work.

## *Economic Status and Security*

Occupation reflects economic status to a limited extent only. The patient's economic security depends not only on his income but on the relation of his income and expenditure, and also upon his prospects for continued income and for accumulating reserves. Thus the permanence of his job becomes important. So does the frugality or extravagance of his family. His ability to save in the past and the future means much. His physical health, on which depends his ability to work, also influences economic security.

Among the middle and upper classes differences in wealth affect chiefly the gaining of luxuries and prestige and have nothing to do with the physical necessities of life such as food and shelter. On the other hand, among the poorer classes the connection between money and the basic essentials of living remains extremely close. Consequently, "financial difficulties" have entirely different meanings in these two groups. The conflicts engendered by them belong to different aspects of human living.

The physician should not hesitate to inquire frankly into the details of the patient's financial condition. A study of the exact relations between income and expenditures may often clarify tensions within the family and within the patient. No patient resents this when it is done in the context of a medical history and in the interests of understanding the patient's circumstances. Indeed, many patients welcome the physician's interest in such matters.

The more superficial facts will rarely suffice. The physician must attend to fine detail. For example, it is not enough to know that a widow receives a check for $75.00 a month from the Department of Public Welfare. Her financial position may be relatively secure or quite precarious according to such factors as the number of children she has, the rent she must pay, her ability to supplement this check with some outside work, and the cost of medicines which have been prescribed for her.

*Attitudes toward the Current Life Situation*

As in every other area of inquiry the patient's attitude merits attention no less than the situation itself. The physician should elicit the answers to such questions as: "Do you like your job?" "Would you rather be doing some other work?" "Do these living arrangements suit you?" "Would you like to move to another house?" The questions themselves need not be asked directly, and should not be, if the needed information can be obtained without them.

## BASIC PERSONALITY OF THE PATIENT

The personal history should also include a survey of the patient's personality before the present illness. Illness affects personality as much as personality affects illness. Patients frequently complain: "I was never this way before, irritable with the children and inconsiderate," or "When I get this pain I get depressed and just don't want to see anyone." Information about the patient's usual personality assists the physician in estimating the severity of the psychological changes associated with the illness, and in estimating also the influence of psychological factors in the origin of the symptoms.

The changes wrought by illness in the personality of the patient vary greatly among different illnesses and different patients. When the illness affects the personality only slightly, the patient himself can usually furnish reliable information about his basic personality. But when the illness brings great changes to the personality the patient is usually a poor witness of these changes and the physician must turn to his relatives.

When the relatives talk about the patient, the physician should discourage generalities such as: "He was always kind," or "He was always worrying." These statements tell something, but not enough. The physician needs more specific data. He needs to know, for example, to whom the patient was kind and in what ways. He needs to know what the patient worried about and how much. He should also try to keep the descriptions provided by his informants purified of their interpretations. This he can best do by pressing the informants to furnish examples with which to document their statements. When a patient becomes ill, his relatives usually feel guilty, solicitous, and anxious. Such attitudes may contaminate their evaluation of the patient's personality. The physician will hear comments like: "Sure he worried, but he had lots to worry about." The physician should remain alert to possible distortions in the statements of relatives.

The following topics deserve attention in evaluating the basic personality of the patient.

## *Intelligence*

The level of formal education attained reflects imperfectly the level of intelligence, but this information does give some hint of intelligence. The quality of work performed in the levels reached provides a more accurate index of intelligence. Some further indication is provided by the pursuit of learning after leaving school. But intellectual interests must not be confused with intelligence.

The relatives of the patient are usually poorly equipped to evaluate his intelligence, but they may make pertinent remarks indicating a change in intellectual functions. For example, they may comment upon the patient's having had an acute memory or a special skill with names or figures which the illness has diminished.

## *Satisfactions and Pleasures*

What enjoyment did the patient get from eating, sex, exercise, and sleeping? How much time did he spend in the pursuit of these activities? What other activities did he enjoy? What did he most enjoy doing? How did he spend his spare time? To what extent did the patient derive enjoyment from primary or immediate experiences with his body or in the practice of skills? In contrast, to what extent did his satisfactions come from secondary sources, e.g., expectations of later reward, or the approval and admiration of other people?

*Special Skills*

It is helpful to know what skills the patient has developed in different areas of living, both of work and play. The existence of such skills not only indicates a source of pleasure for the patient, but tells much about his main interests in life and about certain fundamental traits of character. For example, a skill, although perhaps based upon a genetically endowed talent, can never be fully developed without special interest on the part of the patient. For a successful farmer, life has different interests than it offers a skillful musician or an expert engineer. And for the development of the skill the person must add to interest patience and perseverance in the practice and improvement of his talent. So the existence of a skill always suggests these important qualities of character, at least in their application to this one skill, and hence potentially to other areas of living.

*Habits and Use of Time*

A study of what patients do during a typical day often provides much insight into their personalities. Everyone has time to do the things he wants to do within his physical resources. What a person actually does with his time is therefore a good index of his desires, although not the only one. Moreover, this investigation frequently has the most practical results because, as already mentioned in Chapter 3, many physical and psychological tensions result simply from the abuse of mind and body by violations of the principles of hygiene. Many patients work unnecessarily long hours or hold two or more jobs at the same time. Others permit themselves no rest during weekends or vacations. Often patients do not work particularly long hours, but adhere to a rigid schedule, deviations from which bring painful tensions. Sometimes personal ways of living do not harm the patient, but greatly annoy the people around him and hence become the source of obscure tensions between him and the members of his family or other persons. Often the patient remains quite unaware of the harmfulness to himself and others of the way he lives. Because the patient often remains unaware of the destructive effect of certain aspects of his daily living, the physician may not learn about these as complaints. But he can often uncover such harmful behavior by detailed inquiries into exactly how the patient spends his time.

The physician can ask the patient or other informant to outline exactly

# THE PERSONAL HISTORY

what the patient does throughout a typical 24-hour period. Such an outline may show that the patient spends all his time in fretful activity or work, sparing none for quiet repose or leisurely recreation. Or the reverse may be true. Relaxation may blend into idleness so that the patient accomplishes nothing of what he plans. The account of the day's activities should indicate the amount of time which the patient spends working, traveling, playing, and sleeping. It should note how much time he spends alone and with others. And it should note the regularity and rigidity of the patient's habits, and the variations he practices on weekends or holidays.

## *Habitual Mood or Emotions*

The physician should identify, if possible, the usual mood of the patient's premorbid personality. The patient himself often cannot say whether he is habitually slightly depressed, or slightly elated, or "just right" because this is the way he feels all the time, unless he is liable to shifting moods. He may be able to report about such a tendency to mood swings. His family and friends, however, can usually report his habitual mood which they judge from his expression, remarks, and behavior. They will also note lability of mood.

The physician should learn also about the patient's susceptibility to the arousal of strong emotions. What kinds of events stir him? Does he show a characteristic response to stress or frustration, e.g., blaming himself, blaming others, or blaming no one? Does he return to equilibrium readily or do strong emotions linger after a stress?

## *Dominant Attitudes*

The physician should interest himself in certain traits of character which, although not often apparent over a short period of observation, nevertheless strongly influence the course of the patient's life and his satisfactions in it. Under this heading the physician should consider such qualities as perseverance (the ability to pursue a distant goal), curiosity (the love of new knowledge), and adventurousness (the love of new experiences).

## *Relations with Other Persons*

The physician can derive much information about the patient's relations with other people from the data already obtained in the personal history. This he can supplement by questions directed to clarify particular points.

In connection with the patient's previous relations with other persons, the physician should especially note important differences in the patient's behavior with different persons. For example, was the patient gay at home and shy at parties? Was he a tyrant at home and meek at work? The physician should learn about the patient's maturity along the axis of dependence and independence. To what extent does the patient manufacture his own confidence by real skills and accomplishments? To what extent does he depend for confidence upon supplies of approval trucked in by his family and friends? Important accompaniments of excessive dependency are indecisiveness and efforts to attribute unwise decisions to others, or to blame others for mistakes and misfortunes.

## *Goals and Aspirations*

No account of the patient's personality is complete without some mention of the goals towards which the patient was moving before he became ill. Humans are not merely products of the past; they are also moving towards a future which is at least partially shaped by their desires. Moreover, much of the tension felt in the present derives from the gap between present satisfactions and future goals. There is no frustration without desire. Many of the patient's problems may be illuminated by learning in what ways his life is not turning out as he wished.

The relationship between aspirations and efforts toward their fulfillment deserves attention. Many patients have quite sensible ambitions associated with the fantasy that they can achieve their ambitions without effort. Only a careful comparison of the patient's aspirations and his behavior can inform the physician of the extent to which such a fantasy hinders the patient's satisfactions.

The most important of all the patient's goals is what he wants to become himself. Physicians can become excessively preoccupied with the patient's past to the neglect of the direction in which he is moving. For we shape our behavior not only by the experiences through which we have passed, but also by what we want to make of ourselves. In what a man wants to become are found some of the most important foreshadowings of what he will become.

## *Ideals and Religion*

The ideals of the patient influence his conduct in attaining his aspirations. For a maturing person, whether adult or child, ideals guide psychological expansion. Clashes between the desires and ideals of a person may bring as many conflicts as do those between these desires and the needs of other persons.

The patient's ideals may be connected more or less firmly with a formal religion, but the strength of such connections varies widely. Little can be inferred from the name of a religious denomination about the ideals which actually influence behavior.

The physician should try to learn to what extent the patient's system of ideals constitutes only a set of proscriptions of immoral behavior and to what extent it includes guidance for positive action. In brief, how many of the ideals are "donts" and how many are "do's"? Something should be known also about the rigidity with which ideals have been and are held. Some persons adopt the values of their parents and find no reason afterwards to change. Other persons can shed those parental attitudes which prove meaningless or destructive and adopt new values and ideals which serve them better.

## *Changes in the Patient's Memories and Presentations of His Personal History*

At one time it was thought that memories of previous experiences were accurate and unvarying. Investigations of memories have shown them to be much less stable.[1, 14] They are much more influenced by current stresses and recent experiences than was previously realized. Thus a person may give one account of his past under one set of circumstances and a somewhat different or even completely different account of it under other circumstances.[35] Moreover, certain kinds of experiences are remembered more accurately than others.[12, 24] And finally, the physician himself by his behavior or merely by his evocation of other persons in the patient's past experiences may variously facilitate or inhibit the recall and the expression of different memories. These factors account for very considerable variations in personal histories (as well as in the histories of the present illness and the family histories) given by the same patient to different interviewers.

## References and Suggestions for Further Reading

1. BARTLETT, F.: *Remembering: A Study in Experimental and Social Psychology.* Cambridge, England, Cambridge University Press, 1954.
2. CAMERON, D. E.: Frontiers of social psychiatry. *Psychiatric Quart.* 20:638, 1946.
3. COBB, S.: Technique of interviewing a patient with psychosomatic disorder. *Med. Clin. North America* 28:1210, 1944.
4. COBB, S.: *Borderlands of Psychiatry.* Cambridge, Mass., Harvard University Press, 1943.
5. DRAPER, G., DUPERTUIS, C. W., and CAUGHEY, J. L.: *Human Constitution in Clinical Medicine.* New York, Paul B. Hoeber, Inc., 1944.

6. Erikson, E. H.: *Childhood and Society* (2d ed.). New York, W. W. Norton & Co., Inc., 1963.
7. Freud, S.: A childhood recollection from "Dichtung und Wahrheit." *Collected Papers,* Volume IV. London, The Hogarth Press and the Institute of Psychoanalysis, 1950, p. 357.
8. Fromm-Reichmann, F.: *Principles of Intensive Psychotherapy.* Chicago, The University of Chicago Press, 1950.
9. Gesell, A.: Early evidences of individuality in the human infant. *Scient. Month. 45:*217, 1937.
10. Gesell, A., and Ilg, F. L.: *Infant and Child in the Culture of Today.* New York, Harper & Brothers, 1943.
11. Gesell, A., and Ilg, F. L.: *The Child From Five to Ten.* New York, Harper & Brothers, 1946.
12. Haggard, E. A., Brekstad, A., and Skard, A. G.: On the reliability of the anamnestic interview. *J. Abnorm. Soc. Psychol. 61:*311, 1960.
13. Heath, C. W.: An interview method for obtaining personal histories. *New England J. Med. 234:*251, 1946.
14. Hunter, I. M. L.: *Memory: Facts and Fallacies.* Harmondsworth, England, Penguin Books, Ltd., 1957.
15. Kahana, R. J., Weiland, I. H., Snyder, B., and Rosenbaum, M.: The value of early memories in psychotherapy. *Psychiatric Quart. 27:*73, 1953.
16. Masserman, J. H.: Psychiatric supplementation of the medical history and physical examination. *Dis. Nerv. System 13:*1, 1952.
17. Mayo, E.: *Human Problems of an Industrial Civilization* (2d ed.). Boston, Harvard University. Graduate School of Business Administration, Division of Research, 1946.
18. Menninger, W. C.: The psychiatric evaluation of the sick person. *Dis. Nerv. System 1:*324, 1940.
19. Meyer, A.: The Life Chart and the Oligation of Specifying Positive Data in Psychopathological Diagnosis. *Collected Papers of Adolf Meyer,* Volume III, (edited by Eunice Winters). Baltimore, Johns Hopkins Press, 1951, pp. 52-56.
20. Meyer, A.: Outlines of Examinations. *Collected Papers of Adolf Meyer,* Volume III (edited by Eunice Winters). Baltimore, Johns Hopkins Press, 1951, pp. 224-258.
21. Minks, J. P.: Human and social factors in caring for patients. *Med. Clin. North America 23:*1401, 1939.
22. Orlanski, H.: Infant care and personality. *Psychol. Bull. 49:*1, 1948.
23. Pederson-Krag, G., *Personality Factors in Work and Employment.* New York, Funk & Wagnalls Company, 1955.
24. Pyles, M. L., Stolz, H. R., and Macfarlane, J. W.: The Accuracy of Mothers' Reports on Birth and Developmental Data. *Child Develop. 6:*165, 1935.
25. Ribble, M. A.: *The Rights of Infants.* New York, Columbia University Press, 1957.
26. Robinson, G. C.: *The Patient as a Person: A Study of the Social Aspects of Illness.* New York, The Commonwealth Fund, 1939.
27. Roethlisberger, F. M., and Dickson, W. J.: *Management and the Worker.* Cambridge, Mass., Harvard University Press, 1939.
28. Saslow, G. and Chapple, E. D.: A new life history form with instructions for its use. *Applied Anthropol. 4:*1, 1945.

29. SEWELL, W. H., MUSSEN, P. H., and HARRIS, C. W.: Relationships among child training practices. *Am. Sociol. Rev. 20:*137, 1955.
30. SILVERBERG, W. H.: *Childhood Experience and Personal Destiny.* New York, Springer Publishing Co., Inc., 1952.
31. SPITZ, R.: Hospitalism: an inquiry into the genesis of psychiatric conditions in early childhood. *Psychoanalyt. Study of the Child 1:*45, 1945.
32. STEVENSON, I.: Is the human personality more plastic in infancy and childhood? *Am. J. Psychiat. 114:*152, 1957.
33. STEWART, A. H., WEILAND, I. H., LEIDER, A. R., MANGHAM, C. A., HOLMES, T. H., and RIPLEY, H. S.: Excessive infant crying (colic) in relation to parent behavior. *Am. J. Psychiat. 110:*687 1954.
34. SULLIVAN, H. S.: *The Interpersonal Theory of Psychiatry.* New York, W. W. Norton & Co., Inc., 1953.
35. TOBIN, S. S., and ETIGSON, E.: Effect of stress on earliest memory. *Arch. Gen. Psychiat. 19:*435, 1968.

# 6

# TOPICS FOR FULLER DISCUSSION

The physician's study of the physical aspects of a patient's illness moves from the history, guided by its data, towards the physical examination and clarifying laboratory examinations. His study of the psychological aspects of the illness moves from the history towards a fuller discussion of topics which will clarify the patient's disorder. On this side of the examination the interview corresponds to the physical examination on the other side.

So that his interviews may not spread out diffusely the physician needs to give them some direction towards topics of significance. Subsequent chapters will offer suggestions on the technique of interviewing. This one will consider the major objectives of interviewing in the psychological area and how the physician can detect the principal areas of psychological disturbance.

## *Limitations in Communication of Experiences*

The limitations to communication about all experiences require mention at this point. The patient can say in words only a small fraction of what it may be helpful to know about him. Much of importance about him must be inferred from his nonverbal communications and much can never be known. The factors limiting communication include the following:

1. Unconscious processes. Large areas of important mental functioning remain outside the patient's awareness. He cannot possibly report these to another person because he does not know them himself.
2. Conscious guarding by the patient. Much of what the patient does know about himself he does not like or thinks other people will not like if they see it in him. He therefore avoids as much as possible presenting these aspects of himself to the physician.

# TOPICS FOR FULLER DISCUSSION

3. Limitations of language and other media of communication. Even when patient and physician come from the same geographical area and speak the same dialect, serious defects may remain in their communication with each other due to special meanings and connotations which one or another has attributed to certain words. Moreover, the best words often fail to communicate to other persons much of the richest and most important experiences of life. Who can describe to another what he feels during a symphony, when seeing a sunset, or while in a storm of rage?
4. The magnitude of experiences. The enormous volume of experience which comes to any human far transcends his ability to communicate even a small portion of it with the crude means at his disposal.

These limitations provide severe handicaps for the interviewer. He gains nothing by thinking of the interview as a sharp tool. In its field it is often no better than the physical examination in its area. But these limitations require all the more that the physician focus the interview towards certain data and neglect others. The data sought should include the following:

1. The subjects of greatest psychological significance for the patient. These include major sources of anxiety and important life stresses. The following sections of this chapter will discuss the detection of these subjects
2. Relationships between events, e.g., *(a)* the relation of life stresses to thoughts and emotions; and *(b)* the relations of thoughts and emotions to each other and to symptoms

    These topics are taken up in later sections of this chapter, and in Chapter 10 under the heading of Interviewing Patients with Psychophysiological Disorders.
3. Signs of psychological disorders in the patient

## DISCOVERING THE TOPICS OF MAJOR SIGNIFICANCE

Wide variations occur in the reactions of different people to similar events. What follows from this of importance here is that the physician should not intrude his own personal interests and preconceptions of the significance of different topics. Certainly his experience of illnesses and of human behavior will provide some guide to topics likely to be important to his patient.

The physician's selection of topics should derive from his past medical experience and judgment and not from his own biases, curiosities, and wishes. It nearly always requires some effort to give up the pursuit of special interests in favor of letting the patient himself tell and show which subjects have most importance for him. Yet whatever effort the physician makes in this respect will find adequate rewards in much more useful interviews.

The physician has three means of discovering the subjects of greatest significance to the patient. First, he can ask the patient direct questions. Secondly, he can study the patient's goals and aspirations to discover the points of frustration. Thirdly, he can stimulate the patient to talk freely with some covert guidance, and as the patient talks can try to detect the important subjects by signs shown by the patient.

### *Direct Questions*

Of the methods mentioned, the first has the least value, but is not to be rejected completely. The physician may ask the patient quite simply and directly to tell him what bothers him. He may say, for example, "Do you have any worries?" "Is anything bothering you?" or "You know, headaches are often caused by emotional upsets. Do you think anything could be upsetting you?"

To such questions the patient sometimes replies with useful information. More often he does not. In fact, he usually cannot, because he himself is not aware of what troubles him most. He may have more or less successfully denied his difficulties or any painful feelings. If the patient could answer these simple confronting questions and tell the physician what his chief difficulties are, he would usually be glad to do so, because he also wants to know. To help him find out what they are is one of the chief goals of the interviews. The physician should accept the fact that the patient usually cannot tell him directly where the trouble lies. Then he can turn to the techniques of indirection which will yield data from which he can often make useful inferences about the patient's difficulties.

Such confronting questions usually carry a further disadvantage. They alert the patient to the fact that his personal life is being investigated. He may partly believe that this would be helpful to him, but he may also think that it might be unpleasant or even quite painful. So he may fend off such questions with bland denials. Such questions almost invariably evoke replies designed to present the patient to the physician as the normal, healthy person he wishes the physician to think him.

# TOPICS FOR FULLER DISCUSSION

## *Scanning for Frustrated Aspirations and Life Goals*

The physician may reach some of the patient's major psychological difficulties by asking him about his goals, his aspirations, his satisfactions and his frustrations. (This important topic has been mentioned in Chapter 3 as a significant aspect of the Personal History). The patient does not usually see himself as a product of his past. Instead he views himself as moving towards or away from a desired future. Tensions arise, according to the patient, not because his past experiences influence his conduct in the present. From his point of view, trouble arises from current frustrations to the attainment of future goals. This simple principle often permits the physician to reach rapidly the areas of tension by searching for the gaps between desire and fulfillment. For example:

PHYSICIAN: What would you like to be doing five years from now?
PATIENT: *(an unmarried girl of 30)*: I guess I'd like to be working at what I am doing. But then I had always planned on getting married.
PHYSICIAN: Naturally, that would be understandable.
PATIENT: Yes, really I guess one of the things I think of most is how to avoid being lonely.

Other questions of a similar type are the following: "Are you doing what you want to do with your life?" "Have things turned out the way you would wish them?" and "What would you do if you had three wishes (a million dollars)?"

This approach undoubtedly offers one of the shortest ways of scanning the significant difficulties of the patient. But it also has important limitations. Many patients are defensive even when talking about their aspirations and their goals. Many are not even aware of having any clearly defined ones. Yet such people also have anxieties and sources of tension which need study.

## *Detection of Significant Topics during a Free-Flowing Interview*

The fact that much of the patient's psychological functioning is unconscious and much of the remainder guarded from exposure to other people make a simple question and answer method of interviewing unsatisfactory with regard to psychological difficulties. Almost always the physician must use an indirect method of detecting important difficulties. He must supplement his skills in questioning with those which facilitate the patient's talking freely about a wide variety of topics so that gradually the patient will reveal some at least of what is important.

As the patient talks he will nearly always allude to other people. Emotional disturbances usually arise from the patient's relations with other people, or are brought to expression through those relationships. Accordingly, the physician should especially note significant references to people in the remarks of the patient. Such references to people may occur at any time during the conversation and should be followed when possible. They may occur as early as the first few minutes of the history of the present illness. For example:

PHYSICIAN: Do your headaches seem worse at some time of the day or week?

PATIENT: *(a housewife)*: Why, yes, they do. I seem to have them worse on Saturdays.

PHYSICIAN: Saturdays? Why then?

PATIENT: I don't know, but my mother-in-law comes over then, so I guess I am a bit busier. She usually stays to supper. *(Pause)*

PHYSICIAN: She stays to supper?

PATIENT: Yes, in fact she comes so regularly I could set the clock by her. It's quite a nuisance. Saturday afternoon is one time I might have with my husband....

The physician should endeavor to focus the patient's thoughts on the person mentioned. This can be done so casually that the patient does not realize that the conversation has been shifted, for example, from her symptoms to her relationships with her mother-in-law.

## CLUES TO THE SIGNIFICANCE OF A TOPIC

During the conversation the patient will certainly mention many people and other topics. Limitations of time oblige the physician to focus on the more significant matters. This poses the problem of picking out the more significant references which the patient makes. He finds clues to significance in the content of the patient's remarks, and in the emotional changes shown by the patient as he talks.

### *The Content of the Patient's Remarks*

#### What the Patient Talks about Most

Among any group of people each member will have a favorite topic of interest and conversation. One will perhaps talk about clothes much of the time. Another often seems to bring the conversation around to food. Still another wants to know the value in money of everything he sees. The amount of time each spends talking about his favorite topic gives some indication of the amount of time he spends thinking about it. This provides a rough estimate of the importance these things have for these people in contrast to other subjects of less importance to them. The physician can similarly note what subjects his patient talks most about. If the patient consumes thirty minutes out of sixty in a recital of grievances against his father, his father is important to him. If not, he would be talking about something else.

The physician should note not only the volume of talk on a given subject, but its time of occurrence in an interview. The topic chosen by the patient in response to an opening general question by the physician often touches on his most important difficulties. This may remain true even if the patient does not refer again to the same topic for several interviews. Similarly, the physician should note the first responses of the patient to other general questions offered later in the interviews.

The physician should also note the topics to which the patient recurs repeatedly. Even though the patient may say little in volume about the topic each time, if he returns to it again and again he must have something more to say about it. This recurrent touching on a topic may indicate anxiety in the mind of the patient about the physician's response to this particular topic. He goes back each time, as it were, to feel out the physician's responses to his offering. When finally he feels sure that this response will not be unfavorable, then he permits himself to open the topic for fuller discussion.

The tendency of people to talk first and most about what is most on their minds, provides the physician with the single most important reason for allowing patients as much freedom as possible in the selection of the topics of interviews. If he does this, then these important topics usually rise to the surface like cream on milk. But they do not always so rise, and the physician must also watch for other clues.

### What the Patient Avoids Talking about

What the patient does not want to talk about should be noted as much as what he wants to talk about. When a patient fails to mention a person or an area of living which is significant for most persons, the physician should suspect some reason for the avoidance. The patient may remain quite unconscious of the reason and even of the concealment itself; nevertheless, the fact of avoidance deserves noting. For example, if a patient describes in detail his childhood, his brothers, sisters, mother, uncles, and aunts, and fails to mention his father more than casually, the physician needs to know much more about the patient's relations with his father.

Avoidance of a topic may be manifested by failure to mention it at all, as if a complete erasure had been achieved. This is somewhat unusual. Denial of the importance of a topic is more common. The patient may simply say: "I don't see what my mother has to do with my pain," or "We don't need to talk about my father since he was never around when I was a boy."

Simple denial of the importance of a topic does not necessarily prove its importance. The patient may not understand why the physician interests himself in the people he inquires about. Denial of the importance of a topic has therefore more significance when the patient already understands the value of the personal and family histories, or after these have been explained by the physician.

The emotional emphasis with which importance is denied should receive more attention than the denial itself. When the patient shows irritation or anxiety as he minimizes the importance of a topic which has been broached, the strength of his reaction confirms the importance of the topic.

Even more common than complete avoidance or verbal denial of a topic are such maneuvers as changing the subject of conversation when significant subjects are encountered. As if he had been touched by fire, the patient hurries off to something cooler.

### Confusion and Distortions of Thinking

The significance of a topic may be revealed by retractions of previous statements, by slips of the tongue, and by inconsistent statements on the same subject. Difficulty in organizing thoughts on a subject often indicates its importance. Important gaps in memories of persons or events often betray underlying difficulties needing exploration.

### The Importance of Noting Associations

Patients frequently reveal important relationships by linking one topic with another as they talk. They frequently make such remarks as: "My palpitations were bad this week; and to make matters worse, my little girl has been sick, too," or "I had another asthma attack, and I want you to tell my husband that I'm not able to sleep with him." One can usually find a reason for the patient's making such paired statements or other seemingly irrelevant interpolations. An association of two items, especially when either arouses strong emotions, usually indicates an important connection between them. Together they make a complex which deserves further investigation. As a general rule, the more seemingly irrelevant the association, the greater the probability of a significant connection between the two items associated. Topics which are not pressing towards expression keep their silence, as it were, until an appropriate outlet appears. But topics under great pressure will appear at any time whether the context warrants their expression or not.

The physician should especially note recurrent words and phrases which run through the patient's remarks like a leit-motiv. Such repetitive words and phrases nearly always reveal important topics which need discussion.

**Dreams**

Among other types of communication of significant topics, dreams are often especially valuable. Fortunately, however, we have also many simpler pathways to the significant contents of the patient's mind. For the physician to ask for dreams during simple diagnostic interviews is not always helpful, often distracting and sometimes even alarming. If the patient spontaneously mentions dreams the physician should note them, together with any comments or associations the patient may offer. The characters in a dream are often pertinent to the chief difficulties of the patient. The main theme of a dream usually exemplifies an important conflict. Recurrent dreams especially point to significant, unresolved psychological problems.

## Emotional Changes in the Patient

The physician derives many valuable clues to the significant problems of a patient from the emotional changes in the patient. Emotions express major values and interests. When important interests are affected, emotions change. The surgeon palpating the abdomen first gently feels the whole surface, often starting away from areas known to be painful. As he presses the abdomen the patient tells him where he feels the pain and the surgeon gradually focuses his examination on that area. Emotions betray mental pain and tell the interviewing physician where to explore further. The physician watching the play of emotions in the patient can usually pick out the more significant topics discussed. But this requires that he know and recognize the signs of emotional changes in other people.

Anyone can tell when someone else experiences the grosser emotions. This we learn to do in childhood. The infant and child gradually associate certain patterns of behavior (e.g., words, tone of voice, gestures) on the part of the mother and father with other types of behavior (i.e., more or less helpful and comforting activity on the part of the parents in the care of the child). The child then learns to make predictions of the parents' behavior from signs such as those mentioned. The child himself develops similar patterned responses to situations which consist partly of signs and expressions communicated to others. These patterns of behavior in the child become differentiated into a number of more or less discrete states for which the child learns the verbal labels applied by the adults around him. In this way he comes to know what anger, fear, and joy are in himself and others.

Unfortunately, the various verbal symbols for these constellations may come to be applied in an individual or eccentric way by the growing person. Experiences may teach him to keep various portions of his emotional experiences out of awareness. Or he may come to deny the label usually applied to persons undergoing the experience which he seems to be having, according to his observed behavior. A common example of this occurs in persons who have been taught by parents never to show anger or even to be angry. In situations ordinarily evoking anger in most persons, these persons usually show one of two responses. They may actually have a different inner experience, one which is, compared to that of most persons in such a situation, a relatively impoverished one; that is, they may really feel little or no anger and hence show little or none. Or they may have the experience usually labeled anger, but suppress its expression. If it shows nevertheless, they may insist that they are not really angry. They protest that they are merely "hurt" or "upset," but not angry. Other persons cannot admit they are frightened, but find it acceptable to be "nervous." Such distortions of emotional experiences and their communication to others occur almost universally and greatly increase the difficulty of correctly detecting emotions in patients.

Accordingly, the physician needs to be humble about his capacity to know what emotions the patient is expressing either in words or behavior. Major emotions he can usually estimate with reasonable accuracy. Yet he cannot expect his patient to fly into a rage; he must learn to notice signs of mild anger or irritation. He will rarely see abject terror in his patients; instead he must learn to detect slight anxiety. For such tasks he therefore needs to employ a variety of means, frequently checking them against each other. Emotions are communicated in many different ways, some of which the following sections discuss.

### Verbalized Indications of Emotions

Patients may make direct statements about emotional feelings just as they sometimes make verbal evaluations of the importance of topics discussed. Thus they may say: "I get angry when I talk about my mother."

or "It makes me sad just to think about my brother." In such comments patients do not always name the emotion they are experiencing or describe it clearly. Rather they more often refer to fragments of an emotional complex or to generalized discomfort poorly localized and vaguely communicated. They use such phrases as "upset," "nervous," "weary," or "heavy" to describe these sensations. From such words and phrases and their contexts the physician may learn to identify the emotions to which the patient refers. In this task he can help himself by asking questions from time to time to clarify the feelings and emotions experienced by the patient. He can say, for example, "How do you feel about all this?" or "It seems to bother you a bit to talk about your family. Can you tell me how?" Because the patient usually observes and describes his emotions poorly, however, the physician must rely heavily upon other clues to the presence of emotions in the patient.

**Vocal Changes**

Vocal changes refer to the manner of speaking as contrasted with the verbal content. Vocal changes often tell more about emotions than verbal content. Changes in the rate of speech may indicate emotions. Speech may become slow or blocked entirely as the patient reaches some topic of importance; whatever a patient needs help in expressing usually means much to him. Or the patient may talk rapidly as if hurrying away from the topic. Changes in the timbre or pitch of the voice also reveal emotions. Most people recognize the "cracked voice" of tense persons. Laughter in all its forms, and whether it is forced or natural, should be noted. The accent of words and the rhythm of sentences may also change. Strong emotions may peel away an accent acquired in later life. Then an accent learned in earlier and sometimes less sophisticated surroundings may appear beneath.

**Muscular Activity**

The physician should study the expression of emotion in the patient's face. Other skeletal muscles express emotions as much as those of the face. The hands and feet especially expose feelings. The grip of the handshake at the beginning of the interview, and during the interview the hands in their movements, may talk as much as the lips. The whole posture of the body and the gait also indicate something of the prevailing emotion. Many psychotic patients express themselves almost entirely by bodily postures and gestures, but other persons also say much with their bodies. The speed of bodily movement reflects depression when it slows, and elation and excitement when it increases. The physician should note whether the patient sits on the edge of the chair with legs straight and without supporting his back or whether he can relax deep in the chair and cross his legs. Frequent, restless movements of the extremities indicate a high level of prevailing tension. So do tremors of the extremities unless these are found to arise from some neurological disorder.

Many patients have characteristic mannerisms which anxiety evokes. For example, some people rub their hands over their eyes when anxious, others stroke their hair or scratch their scalps. Still others light a cigarette or pipe. When the physician has connected such actions to anxiety he thereafter has useful guides to the occurrence of further significant topics during the interviews.

### Changes in Visceral Activity

The internal viscera are probably more sensitive to emotional changes than any other part of the body. Physiological changes with emotion have been observed and studied in every organ of the body. Such visceral changes during emotion may be the only expression of an emotional disturbance, since patients can learn (often unconsciously) to control the expression of emotions in word and skeletal musculature. They may present an appearance of calm during visceral turmoil. The hospital bed, the office, and the clinic do not provide facilities for the detailed study of visceral changes with emotion. Nevertheless, the alert physician may often note such changes. He can observe changes in the color of the skin such as pallor or flushing. He can often notice increased sweating. He can notice changes in respiration, and quite often in the heart rate. Sometimes he can count or estimate the heart rate at the carotid artery or as the heart forcefully beats against the clothes over the chest. The physician may see the patient lick the dryness off his lips, and can observe tears glistening in the eyes. From tears alone the physician cannot tell the nature of the emotion experienced, since people cry in grief, in anger, in loneliness, in joy, and in love, but he can tell that something important has been touched in the patient.

Sometimes physiological changes accompanying emotions aroused during interviews evoke the patient's actual symptoms, e.g., headache, palpitations, dyspnea, fainting, etc. A patient with asthma may wheeze when the interview touches on some significant stress (see Figure 11). Or a patient with dermatitis may scratch his skin when the interview evokes a relevant emotion. Such occurrences provide especially useful opportunities for both patient and physician to learn about the connections between stresses, emotions and symptoms.

# TOPICS FOR FULLER DISCUSSION

## THOUGHTS, EMOTIONS, AND OTHER BEHAVIOR

Thoughts and emotions link together and reinforce each other (Figure 3). Throughout the interview the physician should try to notice linkages between the patient's words (thoughts) and his emotions or other behavior. Emotional changes show that something important has been touched, but they alone rarely show in what way this topic is important. For this the physician must turn back to the patient's remarks or thoughts which tell something of the meaning of the emotion.

Sometimes the meaning of the emotion stands out clearly enough from the context in which it occurs. At other times the physician must inquire more specifically. He must ask such questions as:

"Why does talking about this make you anxious?"

"What were you thinking about when you were crying just now?"

"Can you tell me why this makes you angry?"

When the patient does not exhibit emotions during the interview but describes having them at other times, similar questions may be useful, for example:

"What do you think about when you're nervous (angry)?"

"What thoughts do you have when you feel depressed?"

Sometimes patients deny all thought content at the time of important emotions, or they may generalize about an attitude or feeling state without relating these to other events. The physician can often train such patients to notice their thoughts and link them to emotions. For example, he can say:

"When these depressed feelings come over you, try to notice what you are doing and what thoughts come into your mind."

"The next time you have the feeling you're a bad mother, notice what has just happened between you and your children and then try to remember what thoughts you have about it."

Many laymen (and some physicians) confuse thoughts and feelings. Often the word "feeling" refers to a mixture of thoughts and emotions. When a person says: "I feel bad about leaving college," he means: "I have certain thoughts about leaving college and these thoughts are accompanied by unpleasant feelings." If he says: "I feel my wife is wrong about the house we should buy," he probably means: "My wife and I disagree (have different thoughts) about the house, and I think her opinion is incorrect." If he says: "I have feelings of inadequacy," he probably means: "I have thoughts about being less adequate than other people and these thoughts are accompanied by unpleasant feelings."

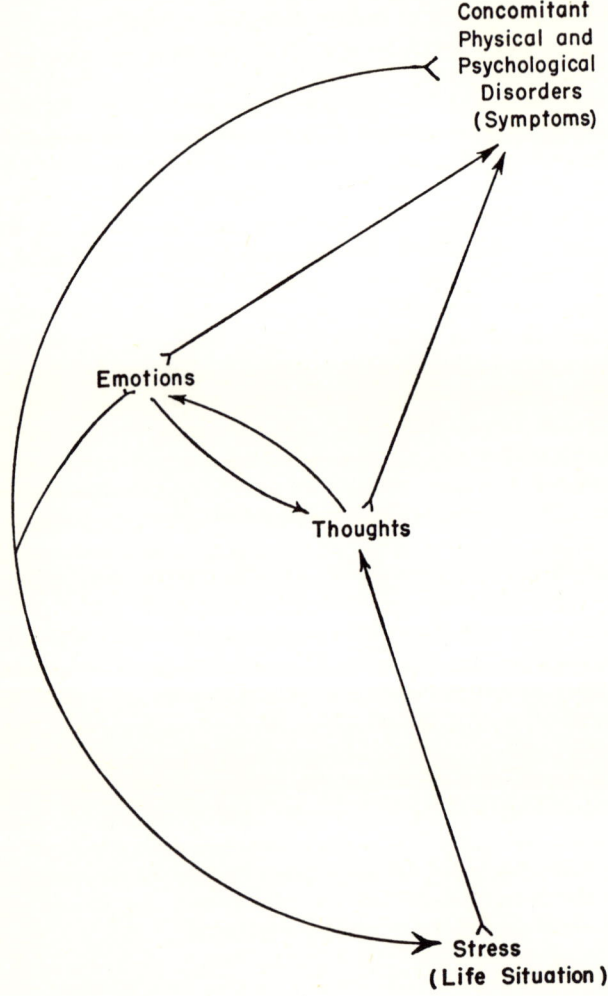

Fig. 3. Relationships between stresses, thoughts and emotions, and symptoms. The stress becomes meaningful, i.e. arouses emotions, through the thoughts of the patient about it. Hence thoughts are shown lying between stresses and emotions. Emotions influence thoughts, so the arrows between thoughts and emotions run in both directions. Emotions and thoughts can both bring symptoms. Symptoms and unpleasant emotions can both lead to efforts to modify the life situation so as to reduce the stress.

Since patients frequently confuse thoughts and emotions, the physician should particularly avoid doing so. If the physician asks the patient only such questions as: "How did you feel about that?", he may never hear much that he should learn. The same or very similar feelings may be associated with quite different thoughts and particular thoughts give the significant specificity to the experience of the patient. Moreover, the patient may offer quite different thoughts and feelings under the same label. He may say: "I felt guilty about this," when in fact he had no remorse at all. He may have had fear of detection which is quite different, or he may have had no unpleasant feelings whatever; he may merely have served up a conventional formula to suit, so he believed, the expectations of the physician. In response to such a statement, if the physician doubts the presence of genuine guilt, he might say: "Exactly what thoughts did you have about what you did?" or "Tell me what thoughts were in your mind when you felt guilty."

Feelings are difficult to communicate for the following reasons. First, feelings are by their nature less definite and less describable than thoughts. Secondly, feelings often seem to bring more guilt and shame than thoughts. Most people cannot readily admit to certain feelings which indicate for them unpopular psychological states. Thus if the physician asks the patient, "How did you feel when the boss scolded you?", the patient may not be able to say, "I felt angry." But if the physician asks, "What went through your mind while the boss was talking?" the patient may reply: "Well, I did think of choking him." Asking for thoughts leaves the patient a much wider range of possible answers than asking about feelings. For example, one could expect only a limited number of replies to the question, "How do you feel about your daughter's marriage?" Many more different responses might be heard to such a question as, "What thoughts do you have about your daughter's marriage?"

Many times the physician will hear what he needs to know by inquiring about feelings. Sometimes he will not. He should ask about thoughts when he wants to hear about thoughts.

### *The Patient's Words and His Emotions and Other Behavior*

The physician should notice both the patient's words and his emotions and other behavior. He must attend to the patient's words for they show how the world appears to the patient, or more accurately, they show as much of that appearance as the patient can confide in the physician. On the other hand, the patient's words tell only a part of what the physician can learn about him. His display of emotions may tell the physician as much as his words or more. The extent to which nonverbal communications modify and add to the patient's remarks varies greatly from one patient to another and in the same patient at different times. The value of the patient's verbal reporting usually fluctuates with the topic and situation. Sometimes what the patient says may be taken at face value. Then the physician should accept and react to the content of the patient's remarks. At other times, the physician will find the actual content of the patient's remarks less important than the underlying emotions connected with them. Such occasions are usually indicated to the physician by the physical signs of strong emotion in the patient, or by other clues to the strong personal significance of a topic for the patient. So the physician must attend to these also.

Many of the attitudes and values of the patients which thus influence his remarks and behavior lie outside his awareness, although the amount of awareness of these qualities also varies greatly from one person to another. Patients are more often aware of their emotions than they are of the connections of these emotions with thoughts, people, and events, and of the extent to which emotions influence their words and behavior. Thus a patient may be conscious of anger felt towards his employer, but unaware of why the boss angers him and of the extent to which his anger influences what he says about the employer to the physician. Or a patient may be aware of delaying the narration of certain events to the physician, but only slightly or not at all aware of why he cannot tell the physician what he has censored. In medical interviewing the physician has very rarely to deal with conscious deception or insincerity. But he must often help the patient to overcome involuntary defensiveness which keeps the patient from confiding freely.

The physician should remember that the cliché, "actions speak louder than words," gives only half the truth. We cannot usually evaluate motivations accurately from either the patient's actions or his acknowledged motives alone. The same action may be driven by quite different motives. A woman may go to the polls to vote because she wants to please her husband, because she has strong convictions about democracy, or for any of a number of reasons. Watching her casually at the polls, one could hardly tell why she was there. One could only assume that it was more important for her to be there than to stay at home on election day. Nor would her own words give a much more reliable indication of her motives. She would be tempted to select for reporting the motive which would make her appear most rational and most worthy in the eyes of the person to whom she was talking. "We judge other people by their actions, ourselves by our intentions." But we are always trying to persuade other people to judge us by our intentions and to persuade them that these intentions are rational and praiseworthy.

When action directly contradicts words, the physician may then conclude that the stronger motivations underlie the actions, the weaker ones being expressed in words only.

The complexities of evaluating motives should not deter the physician from making the attempt. He may be helped if he remembers the following points:

(a) The same behavior in different persons may arise from different motives.

(b) Any given piece of behavior may be driven by more than one motivation. Especially forceful behavior occurs when several motives converge, e.g., patriotism, self-preservation, and love of prestige may contribute to make a soldier courageous.

(c) Action indicates a higher intensity of motivation than words, but reveals little about the nature of the motivations in play.

(d) Much of human motivation is irrational and unconscious. The awareness of motivation varies greatly from one person to another.

(e) Persons reporting their intentions tend to report motives or explain their behavior so that they will appear rational and praiseworthy.

(f) Statements by other observers about the motivations of any person usually tell more about the observers than about the person whose motivations they apparently describe.

These matters deserve attention because of temptations to neglect one or another aspect of what the patient presents. Internists and surgeons, for example, accustomed as they are to dealing with concrete physical events, may attend only to the patient's words and overlook the patient's manner of saying them. Some psychiatrists, on the other hand, attend only to covert implications in the patient's words and seemingly do not hear what the patient says with these words. One can come away from an interview with a good deal of data about the patient's psychological defenses while ignoring, because one did not hear, the statement of the patient that his mortgage is about to be foreclosed.

In summary, the physician should avoid the opposite errors of disbelieving or ignoring what the patient says and accepting as literal truth everything he says. The physician should not devalue the patient's words. He should listen respectfully to what the patient says. But he should also interpret and assess the significance of what the patient says in the light of those values and attitudes of the patient which are chiefly revealed in his emotions. Sometimes the emotions will contradict the patient's words; more often they will emphasize his words. What the patient says is important; how he acts as he speaks is equally important. The physician should always attend to both.

## LIMITATIONS TO FOLLOWING LEADS TO SIGNIFICANT TOPICS

The previous sections of this chapter have presented suggestions for the detection of important topics of which the physician wishes to encourage a fuller discussion. Later chapters on technique will suggest how the physician can do this. Here will be added only some cautionary remarks on the immediate expansion of topics as soon as their significance has been detected. The physician cannot immediately follow all of the clues to even the significant topics. Three factors prevent this.

First, significant topics are usually far too numerous to be pursued immediately or at the same time. The effort to do this would make the interview resemble a hunt with many foxes spreading scent.

Secondly, the spontaneity of the patient's talk must be retained as much as possible. As mentioned before, this spontaneity aids the patient to bring to the surface all the important problems troubling him. If the physician promotes too many digressions or frequently diverts the patient from the main stream of his talk, the patient may never reach the most important things of all, or he may become irritated or defensive, and hence less talkative. Accordingly, the physician should channel the patient's talk only when he can do this smoothly without damming the patient's flow.

Thirdly, the patient touches lightly or briefly many topics of emotional significance before he can discuss them fully and comfortably with the physician. Typical of such subjects are sexual experiences and hostile feelings towards loved relatives like parents and spouses. The patient may refer to such a topic in the first interview, but may then drop the subject and not return to it for several interviews. We should never force him to talk of something which he does not wish to discuss.

The physician needs time to explore the various topics suggested by the clues which occur during the first interview or first few interviews. Many times he will follow false leads and gain little, but he must often spend the time necessary to do this before he can pursue other leads to more helpful results. And the patient needs time to become used to talking about his difficulties and often to make sure that he can trust the physician.

## References and Suggestions for Further Reading

1. Darwin, C.: *Expression of the Emotions in Man and Animals.* New York, Philosophical Library, Inc., 1955.
2. Deutsch, F.: The associative anamnesis. *Psychoanalyt. Quart. 8:*354, 1939.
3. Dunbar, F.: Psychosomatic histories and techniques of examination. *Am. J. Psychiat. 95:*1277, 1939.
4. Gill, M., Newman, R., and Redlich, F. C.: *The Initial Interview in Psychiatric Practice.* New York, International Universities Press, 1954.
5. Meares, A.: *The Medical Interview.* Springfield, Ill., Charles C Thomas, 1957.
6. Ruesch, J., and Kees, W.: *Non-Verbal Communication.* Berkeley, University of California Press, 1956.
7. Sainsbury, P.: Gestural movement during psychiatric interview. *Psychosom. Med. 17:*459, 1955.
8. Saul, L. J.: The psychoanalytic diagnostic interview. *Psychoanalyt. Quart. 26:*76, 1957.
9. Stevenson, I., and Matthews, R. A.: The art of interviewing. *GP 2:*59, 1950.
10. Sullivan, H. S.: *The Psychiatric Interview.* New York, W. W. Norton Co., Inc., 1954.
11. Whitehorn, J. C.: Guide to interviewing and clinical personality study. *Arch. Neurol. & Psychiat. 52:*197, 1944.

# PART III

# THE TECHNIQUE OF HISTORY-TAKING

# 7

# HOW TO TAKE THE HISTORY

## THE HISTORY OF THE PRESENT ILLNESS

The art of history-taking consists in skillfully blending the encouragement of the patient's spontaneous talk with enough guidance to elicit the essential data. In starting, the physician should first encourage the patient to tell the story of his illness in his own way, listening with as few interruptions as possible. He will usually hear a disjointed and incomplete account. He nevertheless obtains valuable information from noting what the patient emphasizes and how he tells the story. If the physician interrupts prematurely, he often disturbs the patient's spontaneity without adding to the information obtained.

This suggestion can be illustrated by considering the effects upon a patient of different responses to his opening remark. When the physician invites the patient to tell him about his illness, the patient may begin by saying, "Doctor, I have terrible headaches." To this the physician might reply by saying immediately, "Where do you feel them?" or "When did they start?" A much better reply would be simply, "Tell me about them." This remark leaves to the patient the choice of what he will talk about first and what he will emphasize. From observing these elements of the patient's story, the physician can learn about the patient as well as about the symptom. Questions can and should come later when the patient's initial flow has dried up.

Some patients cannot provide spontaneously flowing accounts of their illnesses. Anxiety, a poor memory, or lack of organization of thoughts may prevent this. Awkward silences may occur if the physician allows the patient to struggle by himself. As soon as (but not until) he notices that the patient cannot tell the story unaided he should relieve the patient by asking questions.

Many patients can give systematic and chronological accounts of their illnesses if given cues to do this. When a patient does not start at the beginning, the physician should let him talk freely about the symptoms he first mentions. Then when the patient stops, the physician can say, "How did it begin?" And after he has heard this, he can add, "What happened next?" Such minor promptings often suffice to elicit a chronological account of the illness.

Eventually the physican must ask questions even of those patients who have talked freely, systematically and coherently. For what the patient says spontaneously never answers all the questions in the physician's mind. The patient, for example, will not mention significant factors or events which were absent or which did not occur. He will not say that the pain in his chest is not brought on by exercise, if this has not happened. Yet a physician who closed a history of chest pain without discovering that the pain was not made worse by exercise would have a poor understanding of the pain. A patient with hysterical convulsions may not comment that she never has her convulsions during sleep or when she is alone, yet the discovery of such facts may help the physician in excluding epilepsy from the diagnoses considered. Thus using the information the patient has already given, the physician asks further questions or provides further guidance to the interviews so that he can test the various diagnostic hypotheses which arise in his mind until he can find the most satisfactory one. This he then tentatively accepts until he can test it with other examinations. Of the many questions which the physician may need to ask, the following paragraphs can mention a few only of the more important ones.

Initial descriptions of symptoms usually need clarification. For example, of a pain the physican needs to know whether it is aching or burning or has some other quality. If the patient complains of "nervousness," the physician must ask the patient for details of the actual physical sensations (and thoughts) during the symptom.

The patient may say, "I can't swallow," but the physician should not accept this statement as sufficient. He should ask, "Tell me exactly what happens when you try to swallow." He should try to learn whether the patient gags and does not actually swallow; whether he regurgitates liquid through his nose, whether he actually swallows well enough, but experiences discomfort or pain after the food has passed into the esophagus; whether he can swallow liquids, but not solids; and at what part of his throat or esophagus he experiences the most discomfort. He should ask the patient to point to this place.

The physician should not content himself with the simple labels which the patient may apply to the symptoms. Rather he should obtain a detailed account of everything the patient experiences during the occurrence of his symptoms. Only in this way can subtle but significant distinctions he made. For example, to a question about sleeping flat in bed, the patient may reply that he frequently has to sit up in bed to breathe. The physician may consider this evidence of "orthopnea" and leave the matter there. Orthopnea may arise from several causes. Two which need clear distinction are heart failure and anxiety attacks which often occur at night, during both waking and dream states. These can be distinguished readily enough by asking the patient for a moment to moment account of his activities, thoughts, and sensations before and during the time he feels it necessary to sit up in order to breathe. And they cannot be distinguished in any other way, since anxiety attacks and cardiac failure can occur in the same person.

As mentioned earlier, the location of a symptom should not be assumed from the patient's words alone. Many errors have been made through accepting a patient's statement that his pain was in his "stomach," when in fact it was significant inches away in the area of his appendix. The physician should ask the patient to point to the site of his distress when he can do so.

The patient's first account of his illness may begin halfway through the illness with some symptom or symptoms that especially aroused his anxiety and attention. This may occur even when the physician has asked, "How did it begin?" Often he can stimulate further memories of earlier changes by asking a further question such as: "What did you notice first?" "When did you first think you were ill?" and "When were you last perfectly well?"

### *Clarifying the Patient's Terms*

During an interview the physician is primarily responsible for maintaining effective communication, which requires that the patient and physician attach the same meanings to the words they use. Many of the physician's questions must therefore be directed towards the clarification of meanings. The physician may need to help the patient define words, as in the following example:

PATIENT:    When I was eighteen I had a bad attack of nerves and I don't want that to happen again.
PHYSICIAN:    What do you mean by an "attack of nerves?"

Or the physician may need to help the patient substitute a description for a name given to an illness.

PATIENT: Five years ago I had a "nervous breakdown."
PHYSICIAN: What was the nature of your "nervous breakdown?"
PATIENT: I was just very nervous then. Just terrible.
PHYSICIAN: Well, can you tell me exactly how you felt and what you did and how you were treated during that period?
PATIENT: I was weak all over, and my heart used to race. I thought I was going to die and used to go to bed for days at a time, and . . . .

No label, even when physician and patient seem to agree on its meaning, surpasses in value a description of actual symptoms and events. If the physician accepts a phrase instead of a description, he may think he understands the patient's meaning without actually doing so.

Some commonly confusing lay expressions are given below with an accompanying list of medical disorders which they may indicate:

| *Lay Expressions* | | *Possible Equivalents in Medical Terms* |
|---|---|---|
| Spells<br>Blackouts<br>Falling out<br>Faint<br>Stroke<br>Convulsions | may indicate | Cerebrovascular accident<br>Hysterical convulsions<br>Hyperventilation<br>Epilepsy<br>Vasodepressor syncope<br>Orthostatic hypotension<br>Carotid sinus syncope, etc. |
| Headaches | may indicate | Headaches<br>Difficulty concentrating<br>States of deficient mental functioning where there is impaired attention, etc. |
| Nervous breakdown | may indicate | Physical exhaustion<br>Hysteria<br>Various psychoses<br>Reactive depression<br>"Temper tantrum" or other immature reaction to stress, etc. |
| Nervousness | may indicate | Anxiety state<br>Restlessness<br>Insomnia<br>Psychoses<br>Irritability, etc. |

| Lay Expressions | | Possible Equivalents in Medical Terms |
|---|---|---|
| Shortness of breath<br>Can't breathe<br>Have to breathe fast<br>Breathing heavily | may indicate | Anxiety state with hyperventilation<br>Emphysema<br>Cardiac failure<br>Diabetic acidosis<br>Sighing respiration, etc. |
| Blue<br>Moody<br>Unhappy<br>Low spirits<br>Sad<br>No energy<br>No pep | may indicate | Unhappiness<br>Mild depression<br>Psychotic depression<br>Physical exhaustion or fatigue, etc. |

Other terms which nearly always need clarification are "dizziness," "weakness," "tension," "fatigue," and "noises in the head." Terms used to describe the qualities of emotional feeling require definition especially often. Everyone attaches private connotations to such words as "love," "anger," and "guilt," even more than to the labels of physical symptoms. The private meanings to a patient of words describing psychological states can rarely be reached by asking him to define his terms or describe his experiences. The physician can usually only deduce the meaning of these terms for the patient by repeatedly noting the contexts in which the patient uses the words.

The foregoing emphasis on clarifying the meanings of terms should not lead the physician to reject the patient's language and insist upon his own. The patient usually knows little of exact medical terminology, and he will be more at ease using language with which he is familiar. All that is required is that the physician try to understand exactly what the patient means by what he says.

## Inquiring about Stresses

In inquiring about stresses which may act as precipitating factors in the illness, or as exacerbating causes in episodes of the illness, the physician should at first avoid suggestive or leading questions. If possible, he should begin with the most general questions and move toward more specific ones. For example, he can say, "Your symptoms seem to fluctuate a good deal. Do you have any idea why?" or "You said you were perfectly well until June. I wonder why you got ill then? What do you think?" A somewhat more suggestive question would be the following: "Was anything going on in your life when you first got sick?" Still more suggestive questions would be: "Do you get these symptoms at any special time such as when you are tired, hungry, or nervous?" or "Do changes in the weather make your asthma worse?"

In evaluating the responses to such questions, the physician should remember that patients are usually more reliable in their reports of physical stresses than in remembering and telling about social stresses. The physician must constantly remember the human tendency to ignore, overlook, and conceal stresses and disturbances in the social sphere. Thus, a negative response to a query about social stresses by no means excludes such stresses. Often the physician can deduce the operation of such stresses only from other data, chiefly the repeated temporal correlation of the symptoms with the suspected stress. Chapter 10 includes further remarks on the use of questions appropriate for demonstrating stresses. The physician can often obtain useful information about stresses and also about the patient's attitude towards his symptoms from inquiring of the patient why he sought treatment when he did. He can say, for example, "What led you to come for treatment at this time?" or "Tell me why you came to me (the hospital) just at this time although you had been feeling bad for some time before."

The physician should avoid asking questions lying beyond the patient's probable understanding. For example, the physician usually gains little and can unnecessarily offend by asking an alcoholic patient "Why do you drink?" The question is much too general since many factors enter into the why of the patient's drinking. Moreover, the patient may hear in such a question implications of moral judgment by the physician. On the other hand, the alcoholic patient should be able to furnish answers to such questions as, "What thoughts do you have when you want a drink badly?" "What leads up to your drinking excessively?" and "How do you feel different after you have had a few drinks?" From the answers to these and other questions the physician may also learn much about the patient's ideas about his illness. Similarly, it is unhelpful to ask the patient: "Why are you nervous?" More useful questions are: "What sort of things make you nervous?" "When do you get nervous?" and "How do you feel when you are nervous?"

## Symptoms Other Than the Chief Complaint

Several symptoms can arise from one or two physiological or psychological disturbances. Accordingly, symptoms usually appear in patterns or groups called syndromes. The recognition of these syndromes through the identification of their principal symptoms greatly shortens the work of history-taking and examination. These syndromes must not be considered "entities," or confused with the patient. Nevertheless, their recognition often brings a more rapid understanding of the whole illness. This justifies the physician in following his study of the chief complaint with an inquiry about other symptoms which could arise from a disorder of the same system as that of the chief complaint. Thus, if chest pain is the principal complaint, the physician should first investigate the characteristics of this pain and then inquire about such symptoms as dyspnea, weakness, swelling of the legs, palpitations, or other symptoms of cardiovascular diseases. After he has investigated the occurrence of these symptoms, he can widen his survey to include other symptoms.

In asking about other symptoms, the physician should avoid leading questions as long as possible. He should proceed from the general to the specific. If he obtains a positive answer only in response to a highly specific question, he should consider to what extent his suggestion may have influenced the reply. For example, he may proceed as follows:

PHYSICIAN: Has anything else been troubling you in addition to the things you have mentioned?
PATIENT: No, nothing I can think of right now.
PHYSICIAN: How about your sleeping?
PATIENT: No, I don't think there's anything unusual about that.
PHYSICIAN: What time do you awaken in the morning?
PATIENT: Well, now that you mention it, I do wake up a little earlier than I used to. I think I awake around 5:00 A.M. now and my alarm doesn't go off until 6:00.

## The Patient's Understanding of His Illness

During the taking of the history, the physician should ask the patient at an appropriate time for his opinion about the nature of his illness. He can say, for example, "What do you think is the nature of your illness?" or "In what way do you think you are ill?" The patient may also be asked about his ideas of the causes of the illness with a question such as, "What do you think has caused your illness?" Frequently patients will rebuff such inquiries on the grounds that they are mere laymen and defer to medical authority on such matters. These patients the physician should usually press rather firmly for their opinions, since such diffidence may conceal some dangerous misinformation which the patient does not wish exposed and possibly challenged. The physician may reasonably tell such patients: "Perhaps you don't know everything about your condition, but you must have had some thoughts about its nature even if you haven't worked out a full explanation. I'd like to hear what your thoughts about it are. Then I can see what explanations I can offer to help further."

The physician should especially attend to anxiety which arises when the illness is discussed, all the more so if the patient does not verbalize such anxiety. He should try to encourage the patient's expression of his fears with some comment such as: "You seem frightened. Is it about your condition? Do you have some frightening ideas about it?"

### Recording the History of the Present Illness

In medical histories the chief complaint is often written in brief telegraphic style, e.g.:

> Anorexia, 3 months' duration
> Weakness, 3 weeks' duration
> Nervousness, 3 days' duration

This style has only the merit of brevity to set against the disadvantages of not telling a story completely. The physician does better if he devotes a brief paragraph to a sketch of the presenting problem which should include what the patient noticed and complained of, perhaps what others noticed in his appearance or behavior, and why medical aid was sought at the time of consultation. As much as possible of this material should be recorded in the patient's own words.

After this introductory paragraph should come a chronological account of the illness reconstructed from the patient's (usually unchronological) account. The story should begin at the time of the patient's first deviation from health, often earlier than the first notice of the chief complaint or complaints.

The recorded history should again include liberal use of the patient's own words in quotation marks. Organization and dignity of language should characterize it. Humorous or derisive expressions and psychiatric diagnoses used as epithets have no place in the history. The physician should recall that what he writes may strongly influence treatment of the patient at some future date in the same or perhaps a distant hospital or clinic. And it becomes a legal document which can be brought into courts of law. Conciseness should be aimed at, but not a brevity with important omissions.

### Reviewing the History of the Present Illness

Although the initial history should always be as thorough as possible, circumstances often make it incomplete. Several factors may contribute to such incompleteness. In the first place, although lack of time is rarely

## HOW TO TAKE THE HISTORY

a permissible excuse, some real urgency may force the physician to close the first history-taking sooner than he would otherwise wish.

Secondly, the patient's anxiety or other psychological distress often interferes with his memory and thinking so that he omits important data during the initial interviews. This happens so frequently that the physician will often find it helpful to start a second interview by saying something like: "No doubt after our last talk you remembered some things you didn't tell me about. Perhaps we could start with those today."

Thirdly, the patient's desire for quick relief may lead him to try to foreshorten the initial history on the grounds that, in his opinion, details are unnecessary, since the cause of his illness is clear. If the physician fails to detect this attitude, he may unwittingly cooperate in the patient's negligence.

Fourthly, the preliminary examinations nearly always turn up data which suggest possible diagnoses. These may lead the inquiry back to the history of the present illness, further questions about which can help to eliminate or confirm the possibilities.

For these ample reasons, the physician should review the history of the present illness from time to time with the patient. He should remember, however, that repeated reviews and especially questioning may introduce and fix errors in the history. Although questions are often necessary it is better to ask the patient to give his account again from the beginning and then let him talk freely.

## THE REVIEW OF FUNCTIONS AND OF PAST SYMPTOMS AND ILLNESS

After a thorough study of the present illness, the physician should turn to a review of the patient's functioning apart from the areas of his complaints. This survey can begin with inquiries about the vital functions, e.g., eating, sleeping, bowel movements, menstruations, etc., and then move towards inquiries about specific symptoms.

The inquiry should review functions rather than organs. This approach actually reproduces the patient's own thinking about his body. If the patient experiences some unusual discomfort, for example, in his breath he never thinks first, "There is something the matter with my heart." Such a thought must always be preceded by some reflection as, "I used to run up these stairs; I wonder why I don't do it any more," or "I never used to get short of breath when just walking." Although patients frequently connect functional disturbances with a particular organ, they do not always do so. Consequently, if the physician asks a patient, "Have you ever had any heart trouble?" he may receive a sincere negative reply. But if he asks the same patient, "Have you ever noticed any change in your breathing?" the patient may remember his dyspnea.

Moreover, the conventional review of symptoms is often too suggestive for many patients, and also too frightening. It may leave them with an expectation of soon experiencing the mentioned symptoms. Questions about symptoms in a context of inquiry concerning normal function, however, rarely frighten the patient. So the physician can best start the questioning by asking about the function of each organ as if it were normal. Questions about specific symptoms which may have occurred can then follow. For example:

PHYSICIAN: Have you noticed any change in your breathing?
PATIENT: No, none at all.
PHYSICIAN: Do you have any difficulty with breathing when you exercise?
PATIENT: Well, that does remind me that I do get a little short-winded when I walk the six blocks to the bus in the morning, but I have put on some weight recently, and I thought that might account for it.

Not all functions and organs can be considered in this way. There is no need to ask the patient how the muscles and blood vessels of his head function. Instead he can be asked quite simply if he has headaches. But the physician should think in terms of processes and functions rather than of organs alone, and he should avoid suggesting to the patient symptoms which the patient does not have.

Attention to the phrasing of questions may help the physician stimulate the patient to recall changes which he may only have noticed slightly and perhaps has since half-forgotten. Thus it may be more helpful to say: "How do your clothes fit now?" than "Have you gained or lost weight?" And more helpful to say, "Do your rings seem tight on your fingers?" than "Have your hands become larger?"

The physician may find convenient and helpful the grouping together of inquiries about present symptoms (the review of systems) and past illnesses. As mentioned in Chapter 5, past illnesses frequently clarify the present one. A history of enuresis in childhood may illuminate one of current impotence. A history of arthritis and fever which kept the patient in bed for many months as a child can modify the interpretation of a cardiac murmur. The physician can fuse the two inquiries readily enough by asking each question about an organ or function twice, once for the present and once with reference to the past, e.g., "Do you have any headaches?" and "Have you ever suffered from headaches?"

The physician should remember the limitations of questions slanted

## HOW TO TAKE THE HISTORY

in a particular direction. He should learn that clues and more definite information about previous illnesses may come in different ways. For example, many patients do not recall the particular symptoms of an illness, although they may vaguely recall the illness as a whole and its name. If the physician asks them only about the symptoms he may learn nothing about the occurrence of the illness. Other patients may not know the name of an illness, but remember the symptoms quite well. If the physician asks such a patient only about particular illnesses he may again miss some important disease. Another example is provided by a woman who does not recall severe complications of pregnancy in connection with any symptoms named or even as a "previous illness," but who remembers them when discussing her pregnancies.

Some illnesses the patient may remember only because of other changes which the illness occasioned. For example, as a child the patient may have been kept in bed for months on the advice of a physician or because of the anxiety of his mother. The patient may not have been ill at all. Or if he was, he may himself have noticed nothing but a mild fever, not being aware of other evidence of illness which a physician found. Such a patient may have the memory for the illness filed under the heading of a grade missed at school, or restrictions placed on his playing games.

The physician should certainly look for previous illnesses during the functional inquiry. But he should also supplement this information by other inquiries. He should ask each patient direct questions about previous illnesses, accidents, and admissions to hospitals, e.g., "Have you ever had any severe or long illnesses, or any severe accidents?" "Have you ever been in a hospital before?" After the patient has had a chance to answer spontaneously, the physician can offer him a list of diseases for his consideration. The list should include the common childhood infectious diseases, any disease known to occur in the patient's family, and any disease possibly relevant to the patient's present illness. Sometimes the physician will find it useful to return to the subject of previous illnesses during each division of the personal history. Thus in connection with the period of infancy, the physician should ask a question such as: "Were you told of having any illnesses when you were an infant?" When the questions are repeated in different contexts, the correct associations for eliciting the memories may eventually be touched.

In inquiries about past illnesses the physician should prefer "open" questions to those which suggest the expected reply or permit the selection of alternatives. For example, in asking about a previous treatment, the physician should at first avoid direct questions such as: "Did the treatment help you?" He should start with questions such as: "You apparently got much better for a time. How did that come about?" or

"What helped you to get well the last time?" If the patient does not mention the treatment about which a physician wishes to hear, he may next ask: "How did you feel after such and such a treatment?" This question still does not prompt the patient to say whether or not the treatment benefitted him. Finally, the physician may say, "Do you think that such and such a treatment helped you?"

### Adapting Questions to the Readiness of the Patient

Every disturbance of a function should prompt a detailed inquiry. But the time for this may not always come in the first interview. The physician suspecting or learning about sexual tensions needs to know many details about the patient's sexual life, e.g., such matters as modes and frequency of sexual activity; the partners involved and the patient's relations with them; the emotions aroused and the satisfactions obtained; the patient's attitude towards his sexual experiences. However, premature attempts to elicit such data may merely arouse the patient's anxiety or anger and disturb his growing attachment to the physician. The physician must judge in each instance the correct place for such important questions as "Do you have any sexual tensions?" and "How are your sexual relations?"

The physician may coax, but must never force the patient to talk about such a subject. For example:

PATIENT: Whenever I talk about sex or when anyone else talks about it, I get all upset and nervous.
PHYSICIAN: That may mean that it would be a good idea to talk about it here with me.
PATIENT (*becoming more tense*): Not for me, it wouldn't. I'd just rather leave that alone.
PHYSICIAN: Well, you can try and perhaps it will be easier than you think. Or we can leave it today and perhaps you'll want to come back to it later.
PATIENT: Let's talk about something else today, if that's all right with you.
PHYSICIAN: Perfectly all right. You were saying before that you thought getting into a larger apartment would help the whole family.
PATIENT: That's right. I know it would. . . .

### The Order of the History after the History of the Present Illness

After he has obtained the history of the present illness, the physician may obtain other parts of the history in various orders without interfering with the result. One common order is: history of the present illness, family history, personal history, current life situation. But sometimes the following order may provide smoother transitions: history of the present illness, current life situation, personal history, family history. This last order would suit especially well when the current life situation bears importantly on the present illness. As already mentioned, the physician should flexibly modify the order of the parts of the history if strong needs and sensitivities of the patient seem to require this. Some patients talk easily about their families, reluctantly of themselves; other patients show opposite preferences. If the physician finds such strong biases he will do well to let the patient talk first of what he can tell easily and afterwards guide him onto the more difficult terrain.

## THE FAMILY HISTORY

As with the history of the present illness, the physician will not obtain the data of the family history in an orderly manner neatly organized under appropriate headings. On the contrary he must often work even harder to obtain the information he needs. The patient nearly always wants to talk about his present illness. In contrast he frequently sees no relevance of the family history to his present illness and has no natural wish to talk about it. His reluctance may go further. He may think the physician needlessly intrudes into private matters tearing open cupboards with imaginary skeletons in them. These attitudes the physician must tactfully ignore or try to modify.

The physician can find a number of different avenues to the family history each of which may suit more than the others on different occasions. Frequently the physician can make an unnoticed transition from the history of the present illness to the family history. During the patient's account of his current illness, he almost always makes some passing, or perhaps lengthy, references to members of his family. If it seems natural, the physician may simply pick up these references and draw the patient into an expression of greater detail about the persons mentioned. The physician may then fill any gaps with questions. In this way the physician can sometimes learn all he needs to know about members of the patient's family.

Another approach lies through inquiries about other persons who may have an illness similar to that of the patient. For example, the physician should always ask such questions as: "Does anyone in your family have an illness like yours?" "Has anyone in your family ever had an illness like yours?" and "Do you know anyone (Have you ever known anyone) with an illness like yours?" Such questions aid in studying the influence of heredity, contagion, and suggestion. Following such questions, the physician can naturally continue with: "Well, tell me some more about the health of the members of your family. What (other) illnesses have any of them had?" After the patient has answered this, the physician may ask further questions about members of the patient's family whom the patient has not mentioned.

In such an inquiry, the physician may mention various diseases, especially those of special relevance to the patient's disorder. However, questions of the form: "Has anyone in your family ever had . . . ?" may furnish unreliable data or, worse still, make the data appear more complete than they are. For the patient may not associate the physician's phrase for a particular illness, e.g., "mental illness" with a disorder which he remembers, but has always thought of under a different name, e.g., "nervousness." Also the files of memory open best through visual images of persons and places. The patient may not remember that anyone in the family had a mental disorder until he is asked about his grandmother, and then recalls the time she went away to the hospital for six months and seemed somewhat strange and different when she returned. Consequently, the physician will obtain the most reliable data about illnesses in the patient's family when he asks the patient about each individual member in turn.

This forms a third approach to the family history, that of asking the patient to tell something about each member of his family. The physician can ask the patient first for the names and ages of the members of the family and arrange these in a list or family tree. Then he can ask the patient questions about the physical health, occupation, marital status, and similar "neutral" topics before inquiring about the personalities of the persons mentioned. In discussing other matters, however, the patient may at any time refer to psychological aspects of these persons. Indeed, he can scarcely avoid doing so, and the physician should usually follow the lead thus offered and then return to further questions. The following fragment of an interview may illustrate this approach:

PHYSICIAN: Will you tell me something about the members of your family?
PATIENT: Sure, what would you like to know?
PHYSICIAN: Well, I'm interested in who's at home with you.
PATIENT: There's my wife and I and our two children.
PHYSICIAN: Tell me something about them. Let's start with your wife. Is she in good health?

PATIENT: Excellent. She's never sick.
PHYSICIAN: Good. How about your children? How old are they and how is their health?
PATIENT: Well, my little girl who is three has bad bronchitis. My wife worries about her a lot.
PHYSICIAN: Does she? What about it makes her worry?
PATIENT: Well, I'm not sure. I think she really exaggerates. In other words, I don't think the kid is as sick as my wife makes out.
PHYSICIAN: Is that so? Tell me about that.

In this example the physician has slid the conversation from the physical health of the family to an important anxiety in the patient's wife. After the patient has talked about this topic, the physician can continue with his questioning and listening until he has obtained whatever he needs of required information about each member of the family mentioned earlier.

After the physician has inquired about the patient's marital family, he may turn the patient's memory back to his biological family as in the following example:

PHYSICIAN: You probably have some brothers and sisters.
PATIENT: Sure, do you want to know about them?
PHYSICIAN: Yes, the same sort of things you told me about your children and wife.

After these people have been described, the physician may continue:

PHYSICIAN: Are your mother and father still living?
PATIENT: Mother is, but Dad died twenty years ago.
PHYSICIAN: *(taking the opportunity to learn about the patient's relations with his father)*: Do you remember his death?
PATIENT: Sure, I remember it well. I was just ten then and it happened suddenly one day when I was just coming home from school. . . .

And after this has been talked out:

PHYSICIAN: How old was your father when he died?
PATIENT: Forty-five, but he looked much younger. It was his heart.
PHYSICIAN: What else do you remember about him?
PATIENT: Why, he was always a big strong man and, as far as I know, never had a bit of ill health his whole life. He used to like hunting and we would go out into the woods together. . . .

In this way, by alternately listening and gently questioning, the physician can help the patient deliver all the pertinent data about the members of his family and also much about his relationships to them.

## *The Psychological Characteristics of Relatives*

As indicated above, the patient will frequently refer in passing to the personalities of relatives when he discusses such matters as their ages, occupations and physical health. The physician can often pursue these references further to elicit data about the psychological aspects of the relatives. In many instances, however, the patient will make few or no such references and then the physician must resort to questioning. A fuller discussion of questioning in Chapter 9 supplements the following remarks.

In questioning about each person, the physician should start with "neutral" data such as no one wishes to conceal and work towards topics about which the patient may have anxiety. If the physician plunges in with such remarks as: "Was your father ever mentally ill?" he immediately makes the patient defensive. If, however, he asks a number of questions about the father's health and inquires after various physical illnesses, a subsequent inquiry about mental disorders seems natural enough. The question is thus half-hidden by the other questions and will usually be answered readily. So when possible, the physician should first accustom the patient to talking about some of the basic facts of the father's life, e.g., his age at death, his last illness, and his occupation. Then, when the patient has talked some about his father, the physician can usually make an easy transition to questions about the father's personality. For example:

PHYSICIAN: Did anyone else tell you anything about your father's health which you didn't see yourself?

PATIENT: My mother said he had tuberculosis when he was young. He was supposed to have caught it from his father. But he had quite gotten over that by the time I knew him.

PHYSICIAN: Did you ever have any idea that he had anything like a stroke, cancer, arthritis or any such serious disease?

PATIENT: No, I'm sure he never had anything but the heart attack I mentioned and that old tuberculosis.

PHYSICIAN: Well, tell me some more about him. What was his occupation?

PATIENT: He was a plumber just like me, and just like me he said he wished he'd given it up.

PHYSICIAN: Why did he say that?

## HOW TO TAKE THE HISTORY

PATIENT: Well, I guess like me, he figured he would have been further ahead if he had done something else.
PHYSICIAN: Like what?

After such a discussion has been pursued for a short period, the physician can move towards more details of the personality of the relative discussed:

PHYSICIAN: Well, tell me some more about what your father was like.
PATIENT: Well, he was tall and well built, as I said. He had rather long arms. Is that what you mean?
PHYSICIAN: Yes, I'm interested in that and I'd also be interested in the sort of person he was, I mean his personality.
PATIENT: Oh, that. That's hard to describe. You see, he would change a lot. Sometimes, like when we were fishing, he was all smiles and really nice to me. Then at other times . . . .

As in all history-taking, questions should be kept general at first and then made more specific with leading questions used only as a last resort. A general question such as "What was your father like?" gives the patient the choice of describing him physically or as a personality. The patient's choice of what to say first tells something of the way he perceived his father and hence of his father's influence on him.

The descriptive portraits of their relatives provided by patients tell much about the patients themselves. Sometimes patients realize that in their remarks about others they reveal themselves. Or they may have notions that it is bad to criticize one's parents. Or they may think the physician will not believe their version of events and will criticize them. In such instances the anxiety aroused may block the patient from describing his parents freely as he saw them. The physician may sometimes flank such anxiety by asking the patient questions about what other people thought of the relative in question. For example:

PHYSICIAN: Can you tell me what your father was like as a person?
PATIENT (*becoming anxious*): Why, he was just ordinary. There was nothing unusual about him. I wouldn't know what to say about him.
PHYSICIAN (*coaxing*): You must remember him pretty well. How did he seem to you?
PATIENT (*still anxious*): Not much different from other fathers as far as I could tell.
PHYSICIAN: Well, how was he thought of in the community? What did other people think of him?

PATIENT: Well, he seemed to be respected. But I think he didn't seem friendly to many people. I remember overhearing people say he was stuck-up. I heard some of his own brothers, my uncles, say that once when they didn't know I was listening.

An ability on the part of the patient to answer direct questions with reliable answers about his relatives would greatly aid the history-taking. For example, the physician may often wish to ask such direct questions as the following: "Who was the dominant member of the family?" "Was anyone considered a black sheep in your family?" "Did your mother respect your father?" "Did your father respect your mother?" "In whose company did your father (mother) seem happiest?" "Which of your parents made the major decisions in your family?" "Did one member of the family dominate the others by sickness, by greater forcefulness, by excessive demands, by superior intelligence, or by displays of temper and sulking?" "If so, how did the other members of the family react to his maneuvers?" "Were you at any time ashamed of any of the members of your family, and if so, why?" "Were there any favorites among the children or the parents?" Unfortunately, such questions when posed directly usually evoke defensive denials or routine, conventional answers designed to preserve, so the patient believes, the physician's approval. Occasionally, the physician may find such direct questions useful. Much more often he will learn more by leaving them unspoken and listening for the answers hidden among what the patient tells spontaneously. If he succeeds in encouraging the patient to talk freely about the members of the family, he can finally assemble a much more accurate account of the personal relationships within the family than he can obtain from asking direct questions about these relationships.

The limitations of questions should not prevent the physician from asking questions which help the patient document his statements. The physician should ask for anecdotal examples in support of generalizations the patient may make about his relatives. For example:

PHYSICIAN: What sort of a person was your mother?
PATIENT: Oh, she was pretty mean to us kids.
PHYSICIAN: You remember that well? What do you remember?
PATIENT: Well, I never forget how she would get angry and go without talking to us for three or four days at a time. We'd have our meals without saying a word because everyone else would feel down on account of her. Then, at other times, she could be sweet and kind. . . .

The example asked for explained the patient's use of the expression "mean" and also helped the patient to clarify his thoughts of his mother by bringing back memories of another side of the mother.

In obtaining a characterization of a relative, just as for the patient himself, the physican can obtain valuable information by inquiring about specific habits, values and attitudes. This helps him then to form his own estimate of the character of the relative independently of the opinion of the informant.

The physician should avoid questions which can be answered with a simple "Yes" or "No," or one word, in favor of those which demand a sentence and, if possible, some thought for reply. The following lists of possible questions in this area illustrate the difference:

| *Less helpful or useless questions* | *More helpful questions* |
|---|---|
| Was your father good (or bad) to you? | What did your father do in his spare time? |
| How much time did your father spend with you? | What sorts of things did your father do with you? |
| Were your parents sociable? | What kinds of friends did your parents have? |
| Did your parents have many friends? | What did your parents do when they were with their friends? |
| Did your father like sports? | What did your father like to do most? |

## *Attitudes toward the Family and Its Situation*

The patient's attitudes toward the members of his family and toward its social and economic situation usually become exposed as he talks. To learn about these the physician should attend both to what the patient says and also to his manner of saying it, as outlined in Chapter 6. Sometimes these fail to convey adequate information about the patient's attitudes. Then the physician can interject such questions as: "What did you think about that?" "Did that seem to make a difference to you?" "Did you wish things were different?" or "It seems to trouble you to tell about that. Can you say in what way it was important to you?"

As he notes the topics which the patient chooses for emphasis or omission, those he glides over and those which affect him deeply, the physician may come to learn more about the patient than about the family. However, he should not object to this, since increased knowledge of the patient is the principal goal of the entire examination.

The psychological state of the patient influences his attitude towards the members of his family, and his attitude towards them will influence the selection of what he tells the physician about them. Often in early interviews the patient will describe members of his family as if they were unusually honest and gentle. Later the physician will hear about the villainies of these people. Or conversely, the patient will at first reproach his family with all kinds of sordid actions towards him and only later tell how much he owes to them. Such variations in portraiture remind the physician not to take what the patient says at first for the final version of the family history.

## Supplementing the Patient's Account of His Family

If information about members of the family is obtained from different informants, the different accounts should be separately identified. It is unnecessary and unwise to attempt a fusion in the hope of arriving at "the truth." The physician needs the patient's account of his family because this tells how they appear to him. The patient acts according to his perceptions, not those of someone else. On the other hand, the physician also needs any other available accounts of the family to serve as a guide to distortions in the patient's report of his family. But a fusion of the two accounts might abolish the usefulness of both.

# THE PERSONAL HISTORY

## Following the Patient's Own References to His Personal History

The easiest entrance for exploring the patient's personal history, current life situation, and psychological difficulties is provided by the patient's almost invariable references to these subjects during earlier parts of the history, notably the history of the present illness and the family history which usually follows.

In the context of a comprehensive examination the physician can readily notice allusions of the patient to the past, to his environment, or to his own thoughts and emotions. If the physician picks up these references, the patient will often talk more readily along these lines than if asked directly to talk about the same topics. This may be illustrated by the following example occurring during the history of the present illness:

PHYSICIAN: Have you noticed anything which brings the asthma on?
PATIENT: Well, yes, I have. It seems I get an attack whenever we're going out to a party or to visit people we don't know well. That's one thing that does it. I guess I never did grow up.
PHYSICIAN (*focusing on patient's reference to his early life*): Is that what you think?

PATIENT: Yes, sometimes I do. You know my mother always wanted me around her and I never got out much when I was a kid. She was sick herself.
PHYSICIAN: Tell me about that.
PATIENT: I can remember it all very well, we never knew when she might have one of her spells. She often . . . .

In the above example, the patient referred to his personal life himself. The physician had only to show interest in the topic and the patient went into further details. This kind of digression may temporarily lead the interview away from the pursuit of other data. But the digression itself serves to collect important data of a kind which do not come so easily in response to direct questions as they do with the indirect method illustrated. The answers to direct questions such as: "What was your mother like?" are rarely as useful as the products of such digressions, because the directness of the question nearly always makes the patient slightly (or perhaps much) guarded in his responses.

The physician will have to judge repeatedly to what extent he will enter openings for such digressions at the time they arise. He will be influenced by the time at his disposal, the nature of the patient's chief complaints, and the readiness of the patient he is talking with. Sometimes he can merely note the patient's reference with the intention of returning to it later. At other times he may pick up the patient's remark at the time. Some other occasions for useful digressions are illustrated in the further examples which follow.

Opportunities for exploring the personal history may arise from questions about past health and physical functions. For example, in the ordinary survey of past health the physician can naturally ask about menstruation and its onset. When the patient has mentioned her age at the menarche, the physician can ask quite casually questions such as: "Were you expecting it?" and "What did you think about it?" These questions almost always carry the subject beyond the physical aspects of menstruation into the topic of the patient's early sexual education and experiences and hence into the even more important topic of her relations with her mother. The patient usually needs only the physician's interest to encourage a full account of these subjects. Inquiries about particular past illnesses may also be followed by the question: "How did you feel about being sick then?" And again the patient will usually start telling the physician part of his personal history.

Tangents leading to the personal history and psychological difficulties may also lead out of the patient's account of his current life situation. For example:

PATIENT (*describing his work*): Yes, I like my work all right. Only the machines are fast and you have to keep watching them all the time or they get stuck. Can't take your eyes off them for a minute. The other day something went wrong with my machine. Before I could do anything, the whole thing stopped on me.
PHYSICIAN: It did? What happened?
PATIENT: Well, the foreman came over and started to blame me.
PHYSICIAN: That made you feel pretty bad?
PATIENT: Sure it did. He had no business blaming me. It wasn't my fault. Suppose I did forget to tell him about the loose switch.
PHYSICIAN: I see. Have you had this sort of treatment from other foremen?
PATIENT: Yes, from a lot of them. All the foremen in my trade seem to be the same.
PHYSICIAN: Does this particular boss remind you of anyone else you've worked with or known?
PATIENT: No, I don't think so. At least . . . Well, he sure does remind me of a school teacher I had once. She used to pick on me too, just the way he does.
PHYSICIAN: She did? What do you remember about her?

In this example the physician has been more directive than in the preceding one. However, if the patient picks up the lead, it should be followed in an exploration of significant life experiences and recurrent patterns of behavior.

The discussion of the family history often provides easy access to the patient's personal history. The route starts from the questions about the physical health of a member of the family. The patient can usually talk about this topic easily. From there a transition is made to the personality of the relative under discussion. Then a short step leads to reminiscences of the patient's own experiences with this person. For example:

PHYSICIAN: You told me about your mother's physical health. I was wondering what she was like as a person.
PATIENT: Mother? Well, she's rather hard to describe. I hardly know what to say. I guess the chief thing I remember now was the way she'd get mad at Dad.

| | |
|---|---|
| PHYSICIAN: | You remember that well? |
| PATIENT: | Yes, I sure do. My brother and I would just disappear into the back room until they'd cool off. |
| PHYSICIAN: | Do you mean you were frightened? |
| PATIENT: | I was indeed. They looked fearsome then, though I suppose I wouldn't be so afraid now. |

Thus as many tangents as possible should be followed out of the history of the present illness, the current life situation, or the family history. These will usually provide a sampling of the patient's personal history. But the physician will almost certainly wish some more detailed information. To obtain this, he must often direct the patient more specifically.

## *Approaching the Personal History Directly*

The physician can ask the patient to tell him something of his personal life with a simple, direct request. The physician should ask a general question and then note what topic the patient chooses to talk about first. For example:

| | |
|---|---|
| PHYSICIAN: | Can you tell me something of your very early life, what you remember from way back as a child, your school life and all that? |
| PATIENT: | I hardly know where to begin. There wasn't anything unusual about my early life. Mother was always kind to us. She had arthritis but she never punished us. |

After such an opening the physician can help the patient to talk about his mother and, incidentally, about his experiences with her. After that topic has been explored as much as possible for the time, the physician can guide the patient by means of other general questions to talk of other aspects of his personal history.

It is possible but unwise to jerk the patient abruptly back towards the past. Some patients will fail to see the relevance of the past to their present illnesses and may think the physician wastes precious time in trivial and remote occurrences of the past. Other patients may interpret inquiries about the past to mean that the physician thinks the illness extends far back and therefore, according to their fantasies, it must be severe and irremediable. Still other patients, familiar with certain psychological theories, may go off into the past in hot pursuit of some single traumatic event or, worse still, of some malignant person who supposedly warped the patient's developing personality. Some patients become anxious when they (correctly or incorrectly) imply that the physician wants to uncover some shameful or otherwise painful event of the past. The physician must therefore note the patient's responses to inquiries about his past. He must be prepared with necessary explanations to reduce the patient's confusion or anxiety. Often a brief statement will suffice such as, for example, "It's quite possible, although we don't know yet, that some of your trouble extends back further than you think. I'll have a better understanding of your illness and your health if I know more about your early life." When the patient shows great anxiety in discussing the past it is often wise to let him defer this for a time or talk only a little about it at each interview.

## *Meanings of Events in the Personal History*

The personal history will include the record of many events such as previous illnesses, changes of job, marriages, and deaths, which have profoundly influenced the patient's life afterwards. But many of these events have acquired their importance through the special meaning they had for the patient. For other people the same events might have mattered less or not at all. This obliges the physician to attend, as he listens to the patient, not only to the recital of factual events but to the evidences of the meaning these events had for the patient. (Chaper 6 has discussed the detection of such evidences). Thus the personal history should provide:

(*a*) a history of outward events in the patient's life
(*b*) the meaning of these events to the patient
(*c*) the history of how the patient came to attach such meanings to events

## *The Limitations of Direct Questions*

In the personal history even more than in other parts of the history, direct questions have limited value in revealing personal relationships. The physician nearly always learns more when he succeeds in getting the patient to talk freely than when he asks questions directly. If the patient talks freely he gives the answers to the necessary but unspoken questions much more readily than in response to the same questions asked directly. These nearly always evoke defensive or conventional answers. For example, if the physician wishes to know how the patient got along with other people he may ask the patient directly, but he should not expect a reliable answer. The patient knows that the ability to get along with other persons is highly valued in our society and, to preserve his own esteem, he must believe that he conforms to this ideal.

Thus the physician must fall back on other data to evaluate the patient's relationships with other people. He must rely chiefly on the evidence of other informants and on his own inferences from the anecdotal material furnished by the patient. Useful clues may be obtained from the patient's current relationship with the physician, although this will sometimes so differ from the patient's former behavior that it may be a quite unreliable index.

## *Recording the Personal History*

The personal history is, in effect, a biography of the patient. It extends from his conception to the present, so it has a temporal dimension. At the same time it creates the image of a living person at each epoch of his life. The physician can take cross-sectional views, as it were, of the whole patient at different periods of his life. Or he can follow one interest or activity, e.g., sexuality, as it threads through the other activities over the entire life span. In talking to the patient he may use now one, now the other approach. Sometimes he may say: "Tell me all about what you remember of your early childhood." Then he hopes the patient will give a survey of all those activities which he can recall of that period of life. At other times he may say: "Tell me something about your sexual experiences." Then he hopes the patient will offer a more or less chronological account of all his sexual activities.

However, in recording the history, the portrayal of all the patient's experiences at different periods of his life seems preferable. Of the two methods, this one more closely represents life as it is lived—as a series of related experiences. In arbitrarily dividing the patient's life into temporal periods, the physician should remember that there is nothing discrete or natural about such divisions. He makes the divisions for convenience in studying the patient's life, not because such divisions occur in the life itself.

### The Use of Dates

In recording the personal history, figures should be given for the age of the patient *and* for dates when these are known. The age of the patient immediately permits a comparison of events in the lives of other persons of his age group. If the physician notes only that the patient finished the eighth grade of school twenty years ago, he may forget that the patient is now thirty-eight and therefore was eighteen when in the eighth grade. Why was the patient behind his peers? To say a patient married thirty-three years ago may suggest someone who has ripened and matured. But if he is now only fifty, then he married at seventeen. Was he mature then? Why did he get married when he was only seventeen?

Relating events to definite dates assists the physician in the correlation of symptoms and possible stresses. Such expressions as "one year prior to admission . . . ," "three weeks before this clinic visit . . . ," have little value except in reviewing the march of events of an acute illness. Phrases such as "in April the patient noticed . . . ," "in June he began to feel . . . ," are preferable because they help to relate the symptoms to possibly influential external events. Perhaps in April there were heavy storms. Or in June schools closed and the patient's children were at home all day every day.

Giving the calendrical date also illuminates the patient's history by providing ready reference to national and international events which impinged on the patient's life at different times.

A girl recalled many memories of her father sitting at home in his underwear for days at a time. Occasionally he would sally from the apartment in a futile search for work. His presence in the home during the years of the patient's childhood was an unpleasant experience because he dispensed advice freely and irritably to the other members of the family who were so much more active than he was. The picture of a disgruntled failure evoked by these memories was somewhat modified when it was learned that the events took place during the period of the great economic depression of 1930 to 1935. The father, although not lacking in imperfections, was no more often unemployed at this time than other members of his trade.

A thirty-nine-year-old man attributed his difficulty in finding work to lack of training which in turn was related to his having left school at an early age. This step was forced upon him by the unpleasantness of his teachers and fellow students towards him.

This patient was born in Texas, the child of a German father and a French mother. The patient spent his early childhood among German-speaking people in a Texas town almost entirely settled by Germans. His parents had emigrated from Alsace-Lorraine. They were unhappily married and their personal quarrels were often expressed in the issues of Franco-German rivalry. Indeed, they continued the Franco-Prussian War as a sort of private feud in Texas. When the patient was twelve, the family moved to a new town where the patient attended a school at which only English was spoken. Here the patient's clumsy English became a subject for derisive comments by teachers and fellow students. Significantly the move from the German-speaking community to the new town took place in 1917 at the height of the anti-German feeling in this country. Of this he was made only too conscious. Life became so uncomfortable for the patient in his new school that he decided to leave it and never returned. Later he used the fact of having left school so early as an oversimplified explanation of his difficulties in finding work. An understanding of his life against the background of the larger events of his time showed how the events lent themselves to the rationalization which he adopted to explain his failure.

### Use of a Life Chart

A chronological chart provides in simple form a panoramic view of the significant events of the patient's life.[2, 3, 16] Such a chart also helps in arranging the data for the fuller written record. Figures 4 and 5 illustrate charts which the physician can easily include in the record of the patient.

Such a form may sometimes be shown profitably to patients, who will often cooperate eagerly in filling it out and thereby achieve new insights into the relationships between life situations and symptoms. The patient should not be asked to fill it out alone, however, as the physician thus deprives himself of the opportunity of studying the patient's reactions to the events described.

The same disadvantage greatly reduces the value of having a patient write out his life history rather than talk it out. Nevertheless, some physicians find that asking the patient to write his own history saves time and proves otherwise helpful. When the physician receives the history from the patient, he should ask, "With which parts of the history did you have the most difficulty?" or "Were you aware of any unpleasant feelings as you wrote about different events of your past life?" The answers to such questions may partially substitute for the opportuntiy of watching the patient's emotional changes as he recounts the story directly to the physician.

### Adequate Documentation

Only a small amount of the material can be recorded verbatim. The remainder should be carefully documented with details. The charm and the success of great biographies like Boswell's *Life of Dr. Johnson* lie not in any subtlety of psychological penetration of the subject's personality by the author. Rather they derive from the clever assembling of exquisitely descriptive anecdotes about the subject's life. From this material the reader can construct his own appraisal of the subject's personality. A good medical history should offer the reader the same opportunity. The history should be sprinkled with anecdotes and illustrative examples. The patient should be asked for these whenever he does not furnish them spontaneously. He should hear often from the interviewer such remarks as, "Do you remember that? What exactly

| NAME: | | | OFFICE OR HOSPITAL NUMBER: | |
|---|---|---|---|---|
| YEAR | AGE | LIFE EVENTS | PSYCHOLOGICAL REACTIONS OR SYMPTOMS | PHYSICAL SYMPTOMS OR ILLNESSES |
| 1929 | 1 | | | |
| 1930 | 2 | | | |
| 1931 | 3 | | | |
| 1932 | 4 | | | |
| 1933 | 5 | | | |
| 1934 | 6 | Started to School. Used left hand. | | |
| 1935 | 7 | | | |
| 1936 | 8 | Accident to left thumb. Obliged to write with right hand. | Resented parents pressure to return to school and write with other hand. | Onset of Stuttering |
| 1937 | 9 | | | |
| 1938 | 10 | | | |
| 1939 | 11 | | | |
| 1940 | 12 | Changed Schools | Constantly embarrassed by his impediment. | Stuttering continued throughout childhood |
| 1941 | 13 | To High School | Resented mother's impatience when he tried to speak slowly. | |
| 1942 | 14 | | | |
| 1943 | 15 | | | |
| 1944 | 16 | | | |
| 1945 | 17 | | | Stuttering diminished at about this time |
| 1946 | 18 | To College. Failed Freshman year | Humiliated by failure | |
| 1947 | 19 | Left home | Angry with mother. Felt better when away | Able to speak easily |
| 1948 | 20 | Joined army. Became corporal. | Lonely. Antagonism to officers. | Recurrence of stuttering |
| 1949 | 21 | | Tense, hostile. | |
| 1950 | 22 | Discharged from army for "nervousness" | Incensed over treatment and discharge. | Severe stuttering |
| 1951 | 23 | Back to college briefly | | |
| 1952 | 24 | Tried going to sea in merchant service | Contented | Again able to speak easily. |
| 1953 | 25 | Marriage. New job. | Contented with marriage and job | |
| 1954 | 26 | Failure to advance in work. Trouble with in-laws | Moderately depressed | Return of severe stuttering |
| 1955 | 27 | Psycho-therapy | Much less tension | Speaking freely again |

Fig. 4. A type of life history form useful in correlating life stresses and symptoms. This one has been filled in with the data, somewhat compressed chronologically, from a patient with stuttering. The heavy line indicates the periods of symptoms and their approximate severity. Arranging the data in a form of this type often makes clear correlations not otherwise so apparent.

NAME:                             OFFICE OR HOSPITAL NUMBER:

| YEAR | AGE | LIFE EVENTS | PSYCHOLOGICAL REACTIONS OR SYMPTOMS | PHYSICAL SYMPTOMS OR ILLNESSES |
|---|---|---|---|---|
| 1918 | 1 | Difficult delivery. Mother almost died | | |
| 1919 | 2 | Birth of younger brother | | |
| 1920 | 3 | | | |
| 1921 | 4 | | Recalls early fear of father and concern over mother's frequent illnesses | |
| 1922 | 5 | | | |
| 1923 | 6 | To Grade School | | Frequent vomiting when anxious |
| 1924 | 7 | | | Also dizziness and nausea |
| 1925 | 8 | | | |
| 1926 | 9 | | | |
| 1927 | 10 | | | |
| 1928 | 11 | | | |
| 1929 | 12 | To High School | | Onset of headaches |
| 1930 | 13 | | | |
| 1931 | 14 | | | |
| 1932 | 15 | | | |
| 1933 | 16 | | | |
| 1934 | 17 | | | |
| 1935 | 18 | To College | Disappointment about fraternity. Resentment at father. Withdrew socially from other students. | Severe headaches |
| 1936 | 19 | | | |
| 1937 | 20 | | | |
| 1938 | 21 | Graduated from College | | |
| 1939 | 22 | Death of favorite aunt | Depressed for several months | |
| 1940 | 23 | Post-Graduate studies away from home | Happiest time of his life | No headaches |
| 1941 | 24 | Began working in store; difficulties with employer | | Most severe headaches |
| 1942 | 25 | | | |
| 1943 | 26 | Changed jobs | Much relieved | Some improvement in headaches |
| 1944 | 27 | | | |

Fig. 5. Another example of a life history form which facilitates correlations of life stresses and symptoms. The heavy line indicates the periods of symptoms and their approximate severity. The data, derived from the history of a patient with migraine, have been somewhat compressed chronologically. Systematic organization of the data from the history of the present illness in a form of this type will often demonstrate correlations not otherwise so apparent.

do you remember?" "For example?" "Can you give me an example of that?" and "What happened?" Such comments always encourage the patient to offer more of the always necessary details.

In description, all vague and general terms should be omitted or defined. Such statements as: "In childhood the patient was unsociable" are valueless, because they do not define either the areas of social difficulty or the degree of deviation from the customary behavior of the patient's group. The child was presumably not unsociable with all members of his family. He almost certainly counted someone a friend. Yet perhaps he did lack social ease in some situations. Then with whom precisely was he uncomfortable and during what periods of childhood? How much time did he spend alone and how much with other children or adults?

The story as it unfolds should be set down in natural strength without, so far as this is possible, either dilution or concentration by the recorder. Interpretations and formulations should appear, but at the end where they can be disregarded or used profitably according to their merits. The use of such general terms as "unsociable," "withdrawn," "introverted," "submissive," and "passive" often arises from the confusion of labels with description. Too often the patient becomes tagged with a label based on scanty or inaccurate data. And the attachment of a label to the patient can then interfere with further interviewing and examination which it seems to make superfluous. If the physician can become aware of this danger, he will wisely extend his study of the patient into further detail. Then he may find that labels often distort perceptions in a subtle way which tends to reinforce the conviction that the label fits. These difficulties he can only combat by rigid adherence to documentation. The physician may find useful a life history form which facilitates the recording of the actual amount of time the patient spent in interaction with significant persons during each period of his life.[18] While the use of such a form may be excellent training, it can be replaced by careful attention to the documentation of the history with exact data. When the physician can discipline himself to this task, he will not need forms to remind him of the difference between data and interpretations of data.

### The Reliability of the Informant

The physician needs a reliable informant for the patient's personal history as much as for the history of the illness and the family history.

When doubt exists about the reliability of the patient, the physician should consult another, and perhaps a third informant, until he can be sure of the basic facts and dates. But however many stories the physician obtains, he can never dispense with that of the patient. He should seek the psychological truth rather than the "absolute" truth. This means that the physician tries to know how things seemed to the patient. People act according to how things appear to them, not according to how they appear to others, or according to how they really are. Yet the physician should also estimate distortion in the patient's perception of events. That is, he should study to what extent the patient's perceptions differed from those of other persons who participated in the same events. For this he often needs other informants to aid in estimating the distortion in the patient's account.

The physician can also watch for clues to distortion in that account himself. When the patient's memory falters, when he shows signs of evasiveness, or when his story contradicts itself, the physician may suspect distortion. Major discrepancies between the patient's words and his reported actions should alert the physician to question the reliability of other data furnished by the patient. The physician should also note the plausibility of the patient's avowed reasons for his actions. Much rationalization of behavior may indicate defensiveness and an accompanying tendency to distort events.

A patient may exhibit marked distortions in one part of his story, but give a rather accurate and objective account of other matters. This happens because distortion occurs chiefly with respect to events which affect him deeply; the patient needs to edit less in considering unimportant events.

The patient's current relationship to the physician also influences markedly the amount of distortion in the patient's history. When the patient feels accepted, he will modify the story less than when he thinks himself on trial.

## THE CURRENT LIFE SITUATION

The physician can approach the patient's current life situation in a number of different ways, choosing the most convenient entry for each patient. Some aspects of the current life situation may be reached through following spontaneous references which the patient will almost certainly make to his environment during the recital of the other parts of the history. For example, he can hardly give a full account of his present illness without at some point mentioning his work. The patient's work is nearly always either causally related to the illness or interfered with by the illness. When the patient mentions his work, or at a suitable time later, the physician can simply return to the subject and ask the patient for more details. For example, he can say, "You mentioned that your symptoms are worse at work. Can you tell me something about your work?" Similarly, the physician can nearly always exploit references the patient makes to his home or other aspects of his current living. In this way physician and patient may explore rather fully the patient's environment without ever taking this up as a separate topic.

Important gaps may remain in the data obtained in the above manner and in that case, the physician needs to make direct inquiries about the patient's life situation. These may precede the past personal history or follow it. Some patients are rather defensive about their current living, believing that they may be blamed for its defects. They can talk much more readily about earlier events of their lives. Other patients willingly talk about the present, and are more reluctant to review the past. The physician can often obtain some clues to these different attitudes during the earlier parts of the history. For example, he may detect a definite defensiveness on the part of the patient when the conversation touches his wife and children. Such a patient may then be led to talk first of his past life. As he does this he becomes somewhat more accustomed to the physician and also to talking about himself. When he has finished talking about his past personal history, he may be ready to talk more freely about his current life situation.

The physician may introduce this subject by some such remark as: "Will you tell me something about your life now, such as your work and home and what you do with your time?"

As this inquiry progresses, the physician should not hesitate to question the patient about even minute details of his living. The physician must, as it were, enter the world of the patient and, as nearly as possible, try to see how that world appears to him. If the questions are directed in this spirit, the patient will respond readily to the interest of the physician and his confidence in the physician will increase. The usual rules of questioning, discussed more fully in Chapter 9, apply here and no patient should be nagged with questions when he is reluctant to talk about the topics under study. But usually the interest of the physician in the details of the patient's current life attaches the patient to him as much as anything else he does. Such an impression on the part of the patient, it should hardly need saying, must be warranted by the genuine interest of the physician. Patients can readily tell a genuine from a spurious interest on the part of the physician.

The exploration of the current life situation frequently clarifies the contribution of social and physical stresses to the illness. But to elicit information about social stresses and accompanying emotional disturbances the physician must take time to let the patient talk freely about whatever is troubling him. A few direct questions such as: "Is anything bothering you?" will rarely suffice. Table 1 summarizes four series of cases with

Table 1. Four Studies of the Significance of Emotions in the Precipitation of Congestive Heart Failure

| Source | No. of patients studied | No. of patients in whom emotions were found to be significant | Percentage of patients studied in whom emotions were found to be significant | Type of interview |
|---|---|---|---|---|
| Sodeman, W. A., and Burch, G. E.: *Am. Heart J. 15:*22, 1938 | 100 | 2 | 2 | Not stated Apparently brief direct questions |
| Boyer, N. H., Leach, C. E., and White, P. D.: *Blood, Heart and Circulation*, 1940, Lancaster, Pa., Science Press, pp. 203–212 | 1000 | 1 | 0.1 | Not stated Apparently brief direct questions |
| Chambers, W. N., and Reiser, M. F.: *Psychosom. Med. 15:*38, 1953 | 25 | 19 | 76 | Lengthy interviews, indirect techniques |
| Vernon, C. R., Martin, D. A., and White, K. L.: *J.A.M.A. 171:*1947, 1959 | 30 | 26 Indirect causes–14 Direct causes–19 | 83 | Lengthy interviews, indirect techniques |

markedly different results in eliciting a history of emotions as precipitating factors in congestive heart failure. In two of the series an extremely low incidence of emotions as precipitating factors was found[1, 19] and in two other (much smaller) series the incidence was found to be quite high.[2, 24] How can we account for such marked differences? Surely not by a real difference in the incidences of emotions as precipitating factors in congestive heart failure in different cities. More likely the differences arose from the use of different techniques of interviewing. Chambers and Reiser[2] and also Vernon, Martin, and White[24] all used lengthy interviews with indirect techniques for eliciting information about emotions in the patients interviewed. Sodeman and Burch[19] and Boyer, Leach, and White[1] did not describe their techniques of interviewing and it may be unfair to say what they were. It seems very likely, however, that they confined themselves to a few short questions and were easily satisfied with negative answers. This comparison may be open to the objection that the interviewers who reported a higher frequency of emotions as precipitating factors may have guided their patients to furnish them with the histories they were seeking. Since they were trained interviewers it seems unlikely that their data would result only from such crude influences. But even if this were the case the comparison between the two series with high incidences of emotions as precipitating factors and the two with low incidences would still support my contention that the interviewer is the most potent factor in the development of the history. He may cause the patient to minimize or to amplify various details or even the main events of the history. This being so, one of the interviewer's most important tasks is to observe his influence on patients and make modifications in his behavior whenever he can so as to facilitate the aims of his interviews.

## References and Suggestions for Further Reading

1. BOYER, N. H., LEACH, C. E., and WHITE, P. D.: *Blood, Heart and Circulation. Underlying Causes and Precipitating Factors of Congestive Heart Failure.* American Association for the Advancement of Science Publication 13. Lancaster, Pa., Science Press, 1940, pp. 203-212.
2. CHAMBERS, W. N., and REISER, M. F.: Emotional stress in the precipitation of congestive heart failure. *Psychosom. Med. 15:38,* 1953.
3. COBB, S.: Technic of interviewing a patient with psychosomatic disorder. *Med. Clin. North America 28:*1210, 1944.
4. COBB, S.: *Borderlands of Psychiatry.* Cambridge, Mass., Harvard University Press, 1943.
5. DEUTSCH, F.: The associative anamnesis. *Psychoanalyt. Quart. 8:*354, 1939.
6. DEUTSCH, F., *Applied Psychoanalysis.* New York, Grune & Stratton, 1949.
7. DEUTSCH, F., and MURPHY, W. F.: *The Clinical Interview,* Volumes I and II. New York, International Universities Press, Inc., 1955.
8. DUNBAR, F.: Psychosomatic histories and techniques of examination. *Am. J. Psychiat. 95:*1277, 1939.
9. FINESINGER, J. E.: Psychiatric interviewing. 1. Some principles and procedures in insight therapy. *Am. J. Psychiat. 105:*187, 1948.
10. FROMM-REICHMANN, F.: *Principles of Intensive Psychotherapy.* Chapter V, The Initial Interview. Chicago, University of Chicago Press, 1950.
11. GARRETT, A. M.: *Interviewing: Its Principles and Methods.* New York, Family Welfare Association of America, 1951.
12. GILL, M., NEWMAN, R., and REDLICH, F. C.: *The Initial Interview in Psychiatric Practice.* New York, International Universities Press, 1954.
13. HENDRICKSON, W. J., COFFER, R. H., JR., and CROSS, T. N.: The initial interview. *A.M.A. Arch. Neurol. & Psychiat. 71:*24, 1954.
14. MENNINGER, K. A. (with MAYMAN, M., and PRUYSER, P. W.): *A Manual for Psychiatric Case Study* (2d ed.). New York, Grune & Stratton, 1962.

15. MENNINGER, W. C.: The psychiatric evaluation of the sick person. *Dis. Nerv. System 1*:324, 1940.
16. MEYER, A.: The Life Chart and the Obligation of Specifying Positive Data in Psychopathological Diagnosis. *Collected Papers of Adolf Meyer*, Volume III. (edited by Eunice Winters). Baltimore, Johns Hopkins Press, 1951, pp. 52-56.
17. ROETHLISBERGER, F. J., and DICKSON, W. J.: *Management and the Worker.* Chapter XIII, The Interviewing Method. Cambridge, Mass., Harvard University Press, 1939.
18. SASLOW, G., and CHAPPLE, E. D.: A new life history form with instructions for its use. *Applied Anthropol. 4:*1, 1945.
19. SODEMAN, W. A., and BURCH, G. E.: Precipitating causes of congestive heart failure. *Am. Heart J. 15:*22, 1938.
20. STEVENSON, I., and MATTHEWS, R. A.: The art of interviewing. *GP 2:*59, 1950
21. STEVENSON, I.: *The American Handbook of Psychiatry* Vol. I. (edited by S. Arieti), Ch. 9, The Psychiatric Interview. New York, Basic Books, 1959.
22. STEVENSON, I.: *The Psychiatric Examination.* Boston, Little, Brown and Company, 1969.
23. SULLIVAN, H. S.: *The Psychiatric Interview.* New York, W. W. Norton & Co., Inc., 1954
24. VERNON, C. R., MARTIN, D. A., and WHITE, K. L.: Psychophysiological approach to management of patients with congestive heart failure. *J.A.M.A. 171:*1947, 1959.
25. WHITEHORN, J. C.: Guide to interviewing and clinical personality study. *Arch. Neurol. & Psychiat. 52:*197, 1944.
26. WITMER, H. L. (ed.): *Teaching Psychotherapeutic Medicine.* Chapter I, History-Taking. New York, Commonwealth Fund, 1947.

# 8

# HOW TO HELP PATIENTS TALK FREELY

Previous chapters have emphasized the importance of the physician's attitude in promoting successful history-taking and interviews. If the patient can experience the interest of the physician his usually strong desire to tell his story impels him to do so. Attentive listening certainly forms the physician's chief contribution to the success of the interviews. But in addition he must help the patient to talk freely, and he must guide the interviews towards the important topics. The present chapter will discuss the first of these tasks and the next will discuss the second.

## THE IMPORTANCE OF MINIMAL ACTIVITY

Experienced interviewers find that in general the less they say the more the patient will say. They try to accomplish the tasks of guiding and encouraging the patient's talk with the minimal activity which will accomplish them.[3] Several sound reasons support this practice.

First, the physician's interruptions may be unintentionally irrelevant. This tends to force the patient's thoughts into a new channel so that he never develops the old topic. The interruptions often ask for material which is soon forthcoming anyway. The patient often misconstrues them as lack of interest in the topic on the part of the physician, or pressure to talk of something else, the patient knows not what. When the patient makes such deductions (and they may be gross errors), he may be annoyed and his flow of talk disturbed.

Secondly, interruptions bring the physician's personality into the foreground. It is no part of good interviewing to have the physician remain a shadowy figure without substance for the patient. On the contrary, the patient must believe he is confiding in a definite person. However, the detailed qualities of this person should not be pressed forward. If they are, the patient may start reacting to them in ways which obstruct his spontaneous expression. For example, if a physician asks a great many questions about trivial points, the patient may associate him with his mother who was always asking him details of where he had been, what he had been doing, and with whom. Thereafter in the interview, the patient may quite unconsciously use towards the physician the same defenses he adopted for evading his mother's questions. In fact, he may stop talking altogether. Some reactions on the part of the patient to the physician both in his role as a physician and as a person cannot be avoided. But they should be reduced as much as possible so that they do not hinder the patient's talking. The patient should be occupied in telling his story, not in reacting to the audience. An experienced physician can remain unobtrusive while the patient talks, without erasing himself as a person worth talking to.

Here we need to mention again the fact that the patient responds not only to what the physician does, but also to what he is, both in fact and in the imagination of the patient. The patient responds not only to the physician's planned activity, but also to his incidental or unintentional behavior. Moreover, the patient may misinterpret the physician's activity along quite different lines from those expected or hoped for by the physician. For example, the patient may misinterpret the physician's practice of minimal activity. He may think that the physician's long silences, meant to be encouraging, mean disapproval. This interpretation may inhibit the patient's revelations of himself. Or the patient may react in the opposite manner. To overcome the physician's supposed disapproval the patient may pour out torrents of self-justifying remarks perhaps quite irrelevant to the previous theme. The physician should constantly observe such reactions on the part of the patient in order to modify his own intentional activity. And he should remember that this activity provides only some of the stimuli to which the patient responds in the interview.

The foregoing should make clear that minimal activity is not an end in itself, but only a means to the end of the patient's talking more freely. Whenever that end is not served by silence or slight activity on the part of the physician, his activity must be increased or changed. Successful interviewing may be compared to helping an infant learn to walk. So long as he does well, stay out of his way; when he stumbles, help him to his feet. Similarly the physician's activity should be the minimal consistent with the desirable movement of the interview. Accordingly, we shall next consider a number of situations which require greater or different activity from the physician.

## WHEN THE PHYSICIAN SHOULD BECOME MORE ACTIVE

The physician should generally restrict his interventions to the following purposes:
1. To change the topic of conversation.
2. To elicit information not brought out spontaneously.
3. To reduce irrelevance and circumstantiality.
4. To interrupt unhelpful silences.
5. To reduce the patient's anxiety and offer reassurance.
6. To encourage the patient's emotional expression.
7. To channel the interview towards significant topics. (This is discussed in Chapter 9.)

### *Opening a New Topic for Exploration*

In opening a new topic for discussion, the physician may get results by simply saying, for example: "I thought perhaps you could tell me about your early life." Occasionally the patient will not find this enough. He may stumble or he may query the physician about why he asked this question. Then the physician must provide the needed explanations. The physician should watch for signs of confusion and puzzlement in the patient. These often indicate uncertainty or anxiety about the reasons for the topics chosen by the physician. The patient is always entitled to know what the physician is trying to get at. Physicians who think that the patient should go along blindly without explanations frequently obstruct their own progress. These remarks do not mean the physician should flood the patient with explanations for everything he does, but that he should help the patient to understand the purpose of what is going on whenever the patient does not understand spontaneously.

### *Eliciting Relevant Information Not Brought Out Spontaneously*

If the patient does not mention places, dates, ages, or other factual data, the physician may ask for this information. Such questions are asked because the information is pertinent, not in order to fill in a form. The questions should usually come after the patient's flow of talk on a subject has temporarily ceased.

Especially in the beginning of his experience, the physician may interrupt the patient to shrink his own anxiety during an awkward pause or even while the patient is still talking. The physician's interruption may be more or less relevant to the topic, but is really motivated by his own anxiety. He wants to relieve a silence or perfectionistically to complete a record. In this way, the physician may break up a pause in the conversation by asking the exact date or place of a certain event which the patient is describing. The time and place of the event may be important, but if so, they can always be ascertained by a question later. But the insertion of a question about time and place in the middle of the patient's recital can interrupt the patient's thoughts and even make the patient think the physician is more interested in external events than in how the patient felt about these events.

Nevertheless, the patient's account always will omit some important facts the physician must know, and he should ask for them at the right place.

The physician nearly always needs to ask many questions designed to clarify the patient's symptoms. Chapter 7 offers examples of such questions. And when the patient's reaction to some event remains unclear or when he fails to communicate his attitudes, thoughts and feelings sufficiently, the physician should invite him to do so with such questions as: "How did that make you feel?" "What did that mean to you?" or "How did that affect you?"

The physician may also ask the patient to be more specific by asking such questions as: "Can you give me an example of that?" "Do you recall any incidents of that?" "What do you remember?" or "What happened?"

When the patient recounts some exchange between himself and other people he will usually include adequate detail if the physician has facilitated the patient's emotional expression. When the patient relives an episode with full emotions he nearly always describes it in detail. But when the patient's expression is inhibited or when he wishes for some reason to hide part of the story, he may glide over essential details. In these circumstances the physician may need to ask questions until he has learned exactly who did or said what to whom.

The physician will often need to insert other remarks to draw the patient into a more detailed account of thoughts and fantasies. Some suggestions for appropriate remarks to aid this process are given later in this chapter.

### Reducing Irrelevant Material

In general, it is wiser to study the material produced during apparent irrelevancies than to cut it off. When a physician accuses a patient of being irrelevant, he may show that he has failed to understand the significance to the patient of what the patient is saying. Often much can be learned from apparent irrelevancies. Sometimes the patient is "filling in" time until he can bring himself to expose his inner anxieties. Sometimes he is feeling out the sensitivity and understanding of the physician on small issues before he presents him with major problems. Sometimes he is justifying his conduct against inner accusations projected externally. Sometimes the irrelevancies are the patient's unconscious or guarded manner of presenting his real problem. For example, a woman may talk at great length of her longing for a pregnancy when she really wants help with her relations with her husband. Often the physician can understand better when he asks himself: "To what unasked question could all of this talk be the answer?" Then he may find that a woman who talks at great length about her operations is, as it were, answering someone who said: "You have suffered a great deal in your life, haven't you? Tell me all about that suffering." The patient has a need to show how much she has suffered. Much of what patients talk about in apparently irrelevant remarks answers such unspoken questions.[9]

The advice to unravel the meaning of circumstantial talk by patients does not mean that this should be listened to interminably. When material is obviously repetitive or wastefully circumstantial, the physician, acting in the patient's interest as well as his own, should move to focus the conversation more sharply. He can say simply: "I think it would be helpful if we spent the remainder of our time talking about some of your other problems (symptoms). Tell me about such and such."

## *Breaking Unhelpful Silences*

Silences can help interviews or hinder them. A patient may simply stop talking in order to think better what he wants to say or remember more clearly some past event. The physician should learn to recognize and permit silences so used.

The physician should remember, however, that a thoughtful silence may merge with a censoring one in which the patient reviews and discards one thought after another while trying to find one which he dares expose to the physician. The physician may suspect that this is going on from signs, often slight, of tension within the patient. The patient may shift restlessly in his chair or his eyes may avoid the physician more than usual. Often the slight tension of the silence urges the patient to speak again. As the silence continues the tension usually increases until physician or patient speaks. The physician should learn to tolerate the silence and its accompanying tension so as to exploit its forcing quality to encourage the patient to talk. After he has been obliged to break the silence a few times, the patient will usually learn that he shares responsibility for the continuity of the interview and will respond accordingly.

Yet the physician must judge the tension in silences which the patient can tolerate. If he sees the patient becoming much distressed or continuing to become more tense without speaking, then he should speak himself to relieve the patient. He should not speak to relieve his own anxiety.

The physician should also speak to recall the patient from a reverie which has taken him too far away from the physician, the interview, or the topic under discussion. In such instances, the physician should interrupt the silence by saying, for example, "You seem to be having some more thoughts. What are they?" "I'm sure you didn't stop thinking when you stopped talking. Can you tell me where your thoughts went then?" Or he may say quite simply, "Go ahead," or "What are you thinking about now?"

Frequent long silences nearly always mean that the patient has excessive anxiety, either about the subjects of the interview, or about the imagined reaction of the physician to the terrible revelations which the patient is about to offer. Such silences usually require a discussion with the patient of the reasons for his anxiety, especially that focused on the physician.

## *Reducing the Patient's Anxiety*

As mentioned in Chapter 2, when the patient is anxious at the beginning of an interview, the physician can often help him to relax by asking more questions. An anxious patient should be relieved of the responsibility for starting and maintaining the conversation. This principle may apply also at any time during the first or subsequent interviews when the patient becomes markedly anxious. Anxiety felt with respect to other people drives the interview; that which is focused on the physician blocks it. The physician must therefore notice when the patient seems close to having a blocking anxiety and should change his activity accordingly. Instead of exhorting the patient to talk more, the physician should talk more himself. He can make much longer responses to the patient's remarks so that the ratio of, say, 9:1 between the respective volumes of talk of patient and physician becomes reversed to 1:9. He may draw the patient onto some topic known to be of interest to him and not disturbing. He may talk about himself and his own interests. In this situation, it is quite permissible for the physician to talk about himself with the goal of making the patient more comfortable. And usually any activity which lifts the burden of initiative from the patient does make him more comfortable. As the physician talks more, the anxiety of the patient often melts away and he may then begin to talk more freely again.

Certain rigid or isolated persons lack enough spontaneity to maintain an adequate flow of talk. Furthermore, they may believe that a physician who does not direct them is an unorganized, casual sort of person which for them means that he is weak and ineffective. They respond better if some tracks are provided along which they can travel narrowly. With these patients the physician needs to be more active not so much in talking himself as in directing and questioning the patient.

The physician therefore needs to maintain an optimal balance between intolerable silences and obstructive interruptions of the patient's flow of talk.

Often patients hesitate and glance across at the physician searching for signs of his continuing acceptance. This may be conveyed by the friendly expression on the physician's face. Or it may need more articulate communication by reassuring phrases. There should be no hesitation in offering these. The physician should communicate his interest and acceptance to the patient by interjecting comments from time to time such as: "Naturally, I can understand how you felt," "I see what you mean," or "That's not surprising." Or he may echo slightly the implied emotion of the patient by saying, for example, "It's easy to see that losing your job was quite depressing," or "I can see how that could easily make you angry." Sometimes he needs only to interject occasionally a simple world like "Surely" or "Naturally" to indicate an appreciation of the patient's feelings. The communication of appropriate reassurance and acceptance lubricates the interview as nothing else can.

The physician should not hesitate to encourage the patient to talk further and in doing so, to praise him for having talked well. It is often appropriate and important for him to make some remark such as, "Go ahead. You're doing well. Just keep on." Or the patient may say: "I don't know what to say or whether I'm telling you what you need to know." To this the physician could reply: "Why, really you've told me a lot so far. Tell me what other thoughts you've had about all this."

### Offering Reassurance

The physician offers reassurance to reduce the patient's anxiety. The only sound reassurance comes from understanding. It should therefore be connected with the salient facts of the patient's condition.

The physician conveys much of his reassurance in his explanations. However, the patient does not necessarily expect an explanation for everything, and provided he has been allowed to express his anxieties, he will usually accept the physician's reassurance. He becomes suspicious of reassurance when it precedes or precludes full expression of his fears.

The physician should focus his reassurance on the patient's anxiety as specifically as possible. Blanket reassurance which tries to smother everything such as that attempted in remarks like "Everything is going to be all right" have their place in the practice of medicine; but that place is when the physician decides the patient needs handling like a child in the arms of a loving parent. The physician's efforts to handle the patient as an adult include offering reassurance which specifically allays specific fears. It is unhelpful and sometimes dangerous to hose down the living room when a small fire breaks out in the kitchen stove. The preferability of specific over diffuse reassurance adds one more reason to many others for a thorough exploration of the patient's anxieties.

### Avoiding Premature Reassurance

Physicians more often offer too much rather than too little reassurance. Premature reassurance may make the patient think the physician minimizes his difficulties. The relatives of the patient have usually reassured him exhaustively and in so doing have usually also implied that he has exaggerated his difficulties. If the physician joins them in this, he cannot hope to encourage the ventilation and exploration of the patient's difficulties which the patient needs.

Moreover, premature reassurance may close a discussion before an anxiety has been adequately understood. For example, if the patient says: "I think I'm losing my mind and am going crazy," the physician may want to relieve the patient's anxiety. He may then say hastily: "I'm sure you're not going crazy. You don't have the symptoms." Such a comment, although it may be temporarily relieving, may also seal off the patient's anxiety so that it cannot be further expressed and understood. A more useful response would be: "What makes you think you are going crazy?" or "What do you mean by crazy?" The first question helps the patient to expose his fears more specifically. Usually some particular symptoms have given rise to the panicky fear of insanity and the physician needs to know what these symptoms are. The second question uncovers the patient's concept of insanity. Thus he may equate being insane with losing control of himself, with violence, with being sent away, or with loss of independence. Again, the question helps to uncover specific anxieties.

The above warnings against premature reassurance certainly do not mean that no reassurance should be given at all. After the patient's anxieties have been thoroughly exposed and discussed, they often dissolve. But some do not, and the physician should then offer whatever reassurance he can truthfully give for whatever anxieties remain. The physician should never allow a patient to leave an interview still loaded with burdensome questions asked but unanswered.

Physicians sometimes offer reassurance in order to reduce their own anxieties about topics or emotions which the patient presents. This is the least satisfactory of all motives for offering reassurance, and one which the physician must certainly combat in himself if he discovers it.

In summary of the foregoing, reassurance is probably premature or inappropriate in the following circumstances:

(a) If the physician offers reassurance before the patient has adequately ventilated his anxieties, so that the reassurance seals off the patient's fears from further expression.
(b) If the physician offers reassurance before the origins of the patient's symptoms or difficulties have been understood in adequate detail. Reassurance must be based on facts.
(c) If the reassurance has the effect of belittling or devaluing the importance of what the patient says.
(d) If the reassurance is offered chiefly to relieve the physician rather than the patient.

The patient often tells the physician of thoughts or acts he has experienced for which he feels guilty or ashamed. The guilt and shame bring to the patient a sense of isolation from other people. The physician may think to reduce the patient's isolation by reassuring him. He may say, for example: "What's so bad about that?" Such remarks may sometimes help, but if applied thoughtlessly, the patient may only think that the physician has failed to understand the enormity of his guilt or shame. Or again, suppose the patient says: "Doctor, there is something I have never been able to tell anyone." The physician may try to help the patient by replying: "What could be as bad as that?" But he would assist the patient more by saying simply: "Now would be a good time to tell it," or "I'd like to hear about it." That the physician listens to the revelations which follow without signs of shock, horror, or surprise nearly always provides abundant reassurance. In such moments the physician rarely needs to alloy golden silence with coppery comments, or at most a few words suffice to indicate understanding. The best relief for guilt and shame is the continuing acceptance of the patient by the physician, notwithstanding the origins of the guilt and shame. The patient may derive more reassurance in this area from the fact that the physician continues to listen interestedly than from any formula of verbal forgiveness which the physician may offer.

## Encouraging the Patient's Emotional Expression

Successful interviewing depends as much on the ability of the physician to encourage the patient's expression of emotion as upon his alertness in detecting whatever emotion is shown. For with regard to emotions the physician must know what to look for, must observe its slightest expression, and then must try to increase its expression, turning a trickle into a full stream.

The full expression of emotion is necessary for at least three reasons. First, it leaves no doubt about the particular emotions experienced. If a patient says he felt sad about a certain event, the physician knows only that the patient may have felt sad. If, however, the patient cries as he talks about the event, the physician knows positively that he felt sad. Secondly, the expression of emotions benefits the patient. He nearly always feels better for it. And thirdly, as the patient feels better, he wants to talk more. So emotional expression usually clears the way for improved communication between patient and physician.

However, the expression of emotions may be resisted within the patient by two factors. First, the emotions themselves are usually unpleasant, sometimes extremely so. Expression temporarily intensifies emotions even if it also reduces their strength. Secondly, the patient will often have found in previous experiences that expressing his emotions to other people evoked anger, coolness, derision or other discouraging responses in these persons. And such responses in turn brought further unpleasant emotions in the patient. The patient wishes to avoid a repetition of such experiences. His emotions must therefore often reach expression against the patient's natural wish to spare himself painful feelings. On the other side, the patient's anxiety about his condition and his hope for relief push him towards expression of his emotions. His situation therefore often resembles that of a man in whose house a fire has broken out between himself and the only exit. Already heated by the flames and choked by the smoke, he yet hesitates to run through the fire in order to reach safety.

Fortunately as the interviews proceed the patient's experiences with the physician encourage his further expression. He finds that the physician, far from condemning him, continues to listen with ever fresh interest and continuing acceptance. As the patient notices these things his confidence in the physician and his willingness to talk increase. Thus the expression of one fear facilitates the expression of another. The cumulative benefits of talking increase the patient's attachment to the physician.

Occasionally patients show an opposite reaction. They believe they have exposed too much of themselves and shown their weaknesses to the physician. They may then become less communicative rather than more so. But this can usually be resolved by discussing the matter with them.

The physician must therefore train himself to recognize the expression of emotions in the patient by the signs mentioned in Chapter 6. Without this detection he cannot channel the interview into the topics of importance and encourage the needed expression of emotion.

The following example illustrates unfortunate failure to recognize an upsurge of emotion and encourage the patient's expression of it:

PHYSICIAN: How have you been feeling recently?
PATIENT: Terrible. The other day I went to my priest and talked to him a bit. He tries to cheer me up. (*Suddenly becomes tearful.*) But that doesn't help much. I don't think he understands how I feel. (*Patient now on the verge of crying and looking down and away from the physician.*)
PHYSICIAN: Do you have enough of your medicine for the present?
PATIENT (*looking up and with eyes drying again*): Well, yes, I think I can get along with what I have. But I need to ask you about it. (*Tearfulness completely gone as patient continues talking about medicine.*)

The physician, in discussing this exchange later, said he had not noticed that the patient was tearful and about to cry. If he had noticed, he certainly would not have cut her off just as she began to expose her feelings. This illustrates the importance of constant alertness to the patient's changing emotions so that their expression may be enhanced rather than blocked.

The physician's failure to notice emotions and encourage their expression may arise from anxiety or other discomfort provoked by such displays in his patients. The patient's emotions naturally resonate to some extent in the physician. The latter may find himself becoming anxious or depressed when the patient becomes anxious or depressed. Or the physician may himself believe, as many patients do, that the expression of emotion is a sign of weakness and immaturity. Consequently, he will do nothing to aid their expression. Or he may be embarrassed by some emotional expressions such as tears, not knowing quite what to say to the patient.

Such a physician may, perhaps unconsciously, move to reduce the patient's expression. When he sees the patient starting to express some deep feelings, he may show increased aloofness, lose interest, or hurry the patient away from the subject under discussion by abruptly asking about something else. All these devices say to the patient, in effect, "Don't do that here, please."

### Premature Reassurance Inhibits Emotional Expression

Of all the devices for suppressing the expression of emotion, by far the commonest and most effective is premature reassurance. As the patient begins to show strong emotions, the anxious physician applies reassurance soothingly. Such reassurance is part of the human wish to reduce human suffering. But it may be inappropriate if the patient wishes and needs to talk more and if it has the effect of extinguishing his speech. The only permanent relief from suffering comes after understanding it. If the patient wishes to go on talking, he should be permitted to do so. Often he is actually suffering less than the physician imagines. The patient can endure a temporary discomfort of painful emotion to the end of a more enduring repair of health.

To succeed in interviewing, the physician must overcome any reluctance to witness strong emotions. Fortunately, experience nearly always brings increased ease in handling his own and others' emotions and thus makes him more skillful. To help the effects of experience, however, the physician should observe as much as possible his own emotions and responses as they are aroused by different patients. He should particularly notice tendencies to change the conversation abruptly, and to apply premature reassurance. He should ask himself whether the reassurance he gives is for the patient or for himself. Often when he becomes aware of his unfavorable responses to the patient's emotions he can make helpful corrections.

### Techniques for Facilitating the Expression of Emotions

Of techniques for encouraging the expression of emotions, the most important by far is simply listening with interest and keeping the patient on the same subject. The interest of the physician in the patient and the attention and acceptance he shows the patient, all encourage the patient to express himself freely. Thus encouraged, the patient tends to continue talking about the matters which mean most to him. The more he talks about any subject, the more freely he will express the emotions which rise to the surface with his thoughts. The physician can readily convince himself of this by observing the amount of emotion shown by the patient as he first approaches a particular subject and after he has talked about it for ten or fifteen minutes. These facts emphasize the need for allowing plenty of time for a history-taking interview. Much will emerge in an interview lasting forty-five minutes or an hour which could never be reached in a half dozen interviews each lasting ten minutes. In the short interviews, the patient can rarely become free enough to begin expressing himself thoroughly. Or if he does and is cut off just as he begins, he may not repeat the attempt.

Many of the emotions felt and shown during medical interviews repeat the emotions accompanying past experiences. As the patient retells the past he relives it and re-experiences the emotions he then felt. Different patients vary greatly in the extent of this re-experiencing. At one extreme one may listen to a detached and reportorial account of events which seem to have happened not to the patient but to someone else in whom he is only slightly interested. At the other extreme, the physician may witness a total engrossment of the patient in what seems to be a complete recapitulation of some past event. The patient may seem to lose all contact with his present surroundings and recreate some past scene and his part in it with extraordinary vividness. The extent of re-experiencing the original emotions depends, among other things, on the evocation of detail in the recall of the past events. Some persons can achieve such clarity much more readily than others. Simple unsophisticated persons rather easily slip into a present tense in their narration and will tell the physician what happened as if it is happening right now. Better educated persons are usually more inhibited in their recitals. But the physician can increase the emotion felt and shown by encouraging the patient to recall in greater detail. This he can do by asking the patient for examples of what happened and for details of the events related. The value of this technique for encouraging emotional expression adds another reason to those already mentioned for asking the patient for specific examples. Sometimes the physician will need to press a reluctant patient for these, as in the following example:

PATIENT: My father never seems to care about me.
PHYSICIAN: What do you mean?
PATIENT: Well, he just doesn't. I don't think he cares about me.
PHYSICIAN: Perhaps not, but how does he show it? What makes you think this?
PATIENT: Well, I've been here a week and he hasn't even bothered to ask my wife how I'm getting along. She told me he hadn't called. (*Beginning to show emotion.*)
PHYSICIAN: And is this typical of him? Has he done this before?

## HOW TO HELP PATIENTS TALK FREELY

PATIENT: He certainly has.
PHYSICIAN: When, for example?
PATIENT: I'll never forget the time I was in a play at school, had the lead part and it was a big thing for everyone. Once or twice he said he would come to see the play, but when the night came, he said he couldn't make it. Something came up at his office, he said. I was so disappointed I could have cried and had trouble going on with my part, but I did. (*Now showing strong emotion.*)

Sometimes the physician can catalyze the expression of the patient's emotion by appropriate comments indicating recognition and acceptance of the patient's feelings. The physician can encourage emotional expression by repeatedly emphasizing feelings in his remarks to the patient. For example, he can make such comments as, "I'm sure that must have made you sad," and "That could have made you feel quite angry."

As the patient moves towards the expression of an important emotion, the physician may name the emotion and this often has the effect of permitting or encouraging its full expression. For example:

PATIENT: This morning I left the house in a hurry after my daughter and I had a quarrel. I don't like to quarrel with her. It was my fault. (*Becoming tearful.*)
PHYSICIAN: And you get sad when you think about it?
PATIENT (*begins to cry*): Yes, I feel terrible for the things I do to her. I shouldn't have said what I did. (*Sobbing.*)

In this example, the physician's brief comment acted as if he had said to the patient: "Yes, you are sad, but it is all right to be sad and to cry about this. Go ahead." In this way the physician can sometimes aid the patient's expression of emotions by putting into words what he thinks the patient's anxiety (or other emotion) is about. He can say to the patient, for example:

"You look scared. I think you are worried about whether you are going to get over this illness."

"You seem depressed. Perhaps you condemn yourself for having to consult a doctor."

"This subject seems to make you anxious. Can you tell me what about it troubles you?"

The physician should only make such remarks after he has studied the previous remarks and behavior of the patient sufficiently to believe that he is aiming at the right target. If he is, the patient will frequently respond with a sigh of relief or maybe with tears, and then pour out a confirmation of the physician's guess. Sometimes the physician will score a near miss. The patient may then correct him and say: "No, you are wrong. I am really worried about such and such." Or the patient may deny altogether the relevance of what the physician has said. This does not mean that the physician has guessed incorrectly, although he may have. It does suggest leaving the topic until the physician knows more about the patient or until the patient has become more ready to expose the emotions linked to the topic.

Certain emotions, especially anger, are denied by many people. To be hurt is acceptable; to be angry implies destructiveness and lack of self-control which are much condemned in our society. Therefore, to help the patient recognize his anger or other emotions concealed by shame, the physician may have to press the patient gently by suggesting the emotion probably experienced but unverbalized, as in the following example:

PATIENT: So when Dad said Henry was no good and a loafer, I felt hurt.
PHYSICIAN: I can see you might have. Did you have any other feelings, too?
PATIENT: No, just hurt, that's all.
PHYSICIAN: Well, I could imagine that your father's remark might have made you a bit angry as well as hurt.
PATIENT: You know, for just a second I thought I was going to get really angry, but then I told myself it wasn't worth getting angry about. But maybe I was a bit angry.

The physician can often convey both acceptance and interest in an emotion with one sentence. For example, when a patient cries, the physician should let the patient do so without comment or interfering reassurance. Then when the patient's tears have diminished or stopped, he can say: "What were you thinking about while you were crying?" This assures the patient that the tears were not condemned by the physician or disturbing to him. At the same time it helps both patient and physician in the important task of seeing the connections between emotions and thoughts.

When the physician suspects an important emotion which the patient has not expressed or verbalized in response to the technique mentioned, he can still ask a direct question. This, as it were, confronts the patient with the fact of his having some strong emotion. His suppression or denial of the emotion may then collapse, especially if he finds the physician an interested listener. For example:

PHYSICIAN: How do you feel in general?
PATIENT (*with an appearance of bravery*): Oh, fine, really.
PHYSICIAN: Is that so? Well, I was wondering, how are your spirits?
PATIENT: What do you mean?
PHYSICIAN: I mean do you ever feel blue or sad?
PATIENT: Well, sometimes I do.
PHYSICIAN: Tell me about it.
PATIENT (*becoming more tense and slightly tearful*): I guess I'm that way a good deal of the time. I don't care to listen to music any more. It makes me sad.
PHYSICIAN: Can you tell me what that sadness is about?
PATIENT (*now beginning to cry*): It's been that way ever since last year. I think it started when....

Often the physician will have to help the patient overcome his reluctance to experience painful emotions which come up when he discusses his past or present stresses. For example:

PATIENT: Last year something terrible happened.
PHYSICIAN: Is that so? Tell me about it.
PATIENT: But it makes me nervous to talk about it, or even to think about it. Like right now I feel nervous.
PHYSICIAN: I can see you do, but that means that whatever happened is particularly important to you and should be talked about.

The capacity of the patient to express his emotions freely actually depends less on what the physician says than on the patient's attitude towards the physician and especially on his confidence that the physician will not hurt him if he exposes himself. Thus whatever heightens the attachment of patient and physician may facilitate emotional expression. Usually such growing attachments develop with the course of the interviews. Occasionally, the physician can increase the bond between himself and the patient at a particular moment when he wishes to encourage more emotional expression. Thus he may draw his chair a little closer, touch the patient with his hand, or perhaps call him by his given name if he has not already done so.

## References and Suggestions for Further Reading

1. BIRD, B.: *Talking with Patients*. Philadelphia, J. B. Lippincott Company, 1955.

2. Cobb, S.: Technic of interviewing a patient with psychosomatic disorder. *Med. Clin. North America 28:*1210, 1944.
3. Finesinger, J. E.: Psychiatric interviewing. 1. Some principles and procedures in insight therapy. *Am. J. Psychiat. 105:*187, 1948.
4. Greenhill, M. H.: The application of psychosomatic techniques to the general practice of medicine. *North Carolina M. J. 10:*1, 1949.
5. Meares, A.: *The Medical Interview.* Springfield, Ill., Charles C Thomas, 1958.
6. Menninger, K. A. (with Mayman, M., and Pruyser, P. W.): *A Manual for Psychiatric Case Study.* (2nd ed.) New York, Grune & Stratton, 1962.
7. Stevenson, I. and Matthews, R. A.: The art of interviewing. *GP 2:*59, 1950.
8. Sullivan, H. S.: *The Psychiatric Interview.* New York, W. W. Norton & Co., Inc., 1954.
9. Whitehorn, J. C.: Guide to interviewing and clinical personality study. *Arch. Neurol. & Psychiat. 52:*197, 1944.
10. Wolf, S.: Talking with the patient. *Current Med. Digest 19:*21, 1952.

# 9

# HOW TO GUIDE THE INTERVIEWS

The physician's activity in the interviews includes guiding the patient to talk about matters relevant to his illness. As the patient talks the physician tries to separate the more from the less significant topics and then channel the conversation into the more important topics while leaving the others behind.

The physician should guide the interview casually and inconspicuously. Forcible bending can cause a break, especially if, like an old twig, the interview is already dry. He should favor and use first covert methods of guidance, afterwards resorting to more direct methods if these become necessary.

## INDIRECT AND COVERT METHODS OF GUIDING INTERVIEWS

The physician's subtlest efforts to channel the interview simply involve his showing preferential interest for one topic rather than another. Thus if the patient touches upon an area which the physician wishes to open up, the physician may sit up in his chair and lean forward expectantly. Sometimes simply raising an eyebrow or nodding the head suffices. Sometimes "uh-huh" interjected from time to time adequately shows the physician's interest. The physician may supplement these gestures by the insertion in appropriate places of such remarks as: "Is that so?" "Naturally," "Surely," "I see," and "Of course."

Vocalizations such as "uh-huh" and other slight comments or gestures can powerfully influence the patient. This power a number of experiments have demonstrated. For example, some subjects were asked to speak words at random. As they did so, the experimenter muttered "uh-huh" behind them every time they spoke a plural word. This produced a marked increase in the number of plural words spoken by the experimental subjects.[1] Similar experiments have shown that "uh-huhs" can influence persons being interviewed to give more emotional responses[3] and to vary the types of memories recalled.[2] One can readily imagine that the slight utterances of a physician would be even more influential on a patient eager for his help. The physician should therefore avoid saying "uh-huh" or any other vocalization or showing any kind of behavior in an automatic way. And he should make himself aware of his use of such communications with patients. Different physicians (like their patients) find different topics interesting. Some have special interests in sex, others in religion, others in money, and so on. As different patients mention these topics the physician's interest may be aroused more by some topics than by others. This is to be expected. But if he then allows this interest to be strongly communicated to the patient, perhaps with a shower of eager "uh-huhs," the patient's pursuit of other topics may be delayed while he tries to satisfy the physician's special and unhelpful interest in one or two particular themes.

If the patient pauses in the middle of some significant topic, the physician can encourage him to continue by simple remarks. The physician may say questioningly, "And?" or "And then?" or he may repeat the last word or two of the patient's last sentence indicating his continuing interest in that topic. For example:

PATIENT: Things would be all right if my husband would help me out on Saturdays. (*Long pause.*)
PHYSICIAN: Saturdays?
PATIENT: Yes, that's when I try to do all the shopping and need him at home, but he says he has to work on Saturdays because customers want to talk to him in the store (he is the manager) and won't talk to a salesman.

The spontaneous association by the patient of one experience or event (e.g., a physical symptom) with another event or person (e.g., a close relative) usually provides a clue to important factors in the patient's illness or situation. The physician should, whenever feasible, pick up such associations with a further inquiry, as in the following example:

PATIENT: I seem to have these asthma attacks especially at night, and my husband doesn't understand that.
PHYSICIAN: What does he think about your attacks?
PATIENT: He says they interfere with our sleeping together.
PHYSICIAN: Does he? Tell me some more about how they seem to interfere.

# HOW TO GUIDE THE INTERVIEWS

As mentioned in Chapter 6 the physician should notice words and phrases used repeatedly by the patient. He may then repeat these to the patient in order to stimulate further associations and the fuller expression of the meanings for the patient of these themes. The physician should re-present such key words and phrases to the patient unobtrusively and in the natural course of the interview. He should not turn the interview into a word association test. The patient should not become aware of the reasons for the physician's re-presenting his own words to him. Often he will not even be aware that the physician is doing this. The following fragment of an interview illustrates the use of this technique:

PATIENT: Every time I get this pain I seem to be nervous.
PHYSICIAN: Nervous?
PATIENT: Yes, it makes me nervous all over. Sometimes I don't know which comes first, the pain or the nervousness.
PHYSICIAN: But you do feel nervous at these times?
PATIENT: Yes, I do. And sometimes I am irritable when the pain comes on, too.
PHYSICIAN: Being nervous and irritable go together?
PATIENT: They seem to, with me at least. I get so irritable I could scream or hit someone. Maybe that's my trouble.
PHYSICIAN: Are you saying you're angry when you're nervous?
PATIENT: Maybe I am saying that. I believe I do feel angry then.

Often one remark of the physician can serve two or more purposes simultaneously. It can communicate acceptance and interest and also slightly sharpen the focus of thought. The physician can do this when he restates what the patient has been saying or feeling. For example:

PATIENT: So if I can't get to feeling better, I may just have to stop working. I think anyone would get low if he knew he had something seriously the matter with his heart like maybe angina.
PHYSICIAN: So you're pretty sure you have heart disease and that's discouraging you?
PATIENT: That's right. At night I lie awake and think of all those bills and then I notice I'm breathing fast and then my heart starts racing and . . . .

Another example may illustrate this further:

PATIENT: My mother was always criticizing me, telling me that I could do better and should try harder. Even when I'd work as hard as I could, she'd find some fault.

PHYSICIAN: It seemed impossible to please her?
PATIENT: That's right. Whatever I did, I never seemed to satisfy her and she would always have one more thing she expected. I can't remember her ever saying she was really pleased with something I'd done.

Sometimes comments interjected by the physician in this way not only show his understanding of the patient's experience, but also clarify and perhaps openly announce what the patient had vaguely thought but never quite permitted himself to say out loud. For example:

PATIENT: My mother always seems to find something wrong in my sister's boy friends. She never likes them. She objected to my brother's marriage saying he was too young to marry. And she keeps telling me I should wait to get married myself, although I'm 28 now.
PHYSICIAN: It sounds as if she doesn't want to lose her children.
PATIENT: That's exactly it, I think. I never really saw it quite that way, but I'm sure she doesn't want to see us go.

## MORE DIRECT GUIDANCE OF INTERVIEWS

If the patient fails to respond to the physician's cues of interest mentioned above, the physician should encourage him further and more explicitly with such remarks as: "Go on," "I hope you can tell me more about this. It seems to be important to you," "What other thoughts do you have about that?" and "What else comes to mind in that connection?"

The patient may ignore even these signs of interest which the physician offers, and may instead move on to other topics. The physician should not necessarily force him back to the subject at the time, since this may interfere with the development of an equally important theme towards which the patient is pressing. However, he can later, at a suitable time, ask the patient to return and pick up the neglected topic. For example, he can say: "You mentioned a while back that your mother and father don't get along. Could you tell me some more about that?" The patient usually accepts readily such invitations to talk further, if the subject does not carry too much anxiety for him at the time.

The following example of evasion by the patient and direction by the physician illustrates some of the foregoing tactics:

PATIENT: When I first got this pain around my heart I didn't know what the matter was. I got really frightened. My father had a heart attack ten years ago and ever since then his heart has been bad.

PHYSICIAN (*trying to encourage patient to talk about his father's trouble*): Is that so?

PATIENT: Yes. You know when I get these pains I can't breathe right and I get weak all over. In fact, I can hardly stand up. It's going to be hard for me to go on working and I have a lot of bills. (*Pause.*)

PHYSICIAN: Bills?

PATIENT: Yes. You see I've had all my father's medical bills, and now I have a lot of my own. Another doctor told me I had nothing the matter with my heart. He said it was just my nerves. You don't believe that, do you? Besides he never took an electrocardiogram and I understand you have to have one of those or you can't tell whether a heart is good or bad. Will you take one? I hope so. This is really getting me down. (*Long pause.*)

PHYSICIAN: Can you tell me more about how it's getting you down?

PATIENT: It just is. I don't want to get like my old man and be a sort of invalid. (*Long pause.*)

PHYSICIAN: Do you think you have the same trouble your father had?

PATIENT: Well, it looks like it to me.

PHYSICIAN (*returning to topic of father's illness*): Can you tell me some more about his symptoms?

PATIENT: His doctor says it's called angina. His pain is really bad. I think I must have that angina too.

PHYSICIAN (*focusing more sharply*): A few minutes ago you said your father had a heart attack. Exactly what happened then as you remember it?

PATIENT: Well, it was in the middle of the night, too—in fact, just like mine. He just woke up and complained of terrible pain in his chest and weakness, and you could see he couldn't breathe right and . . . .

The physician's words should convey as much as possible. Nevertheless, striving always to say exactly the right thing every time may become tedious. The physician, no less than the patient, must feel comfortable in the interview. The task of choosing words carefully must not choke his own spontaneity. Fortunately, as mentioned earlier, the physician's attitude harvests more than the words he uses. With a constructive attitude he will find suitable words.

## GENERAL PRINCIPLES OF THE USE OF QUESTIONS

When the physician must fall back upon the more direct methods of guiding interviews he must usually ask questions which direct the patient to talk about a particular subject. The proper use of questions requires a knowledge of their advantages and limitations.

### *The Advantages of Questions*

Previous sections have already mentioned the value and the necessity of asking questions to obtain essential data about symptoms, people, and events which have to be located in time and place. But questions have other uses also.

First, they may help the physician focus the interview where he wishes. In this function the questions may either guide the patient towards an important topic or assist him away from a disturbing topic, helping him onto more comfortable ground. Questions often reduce the patient's anxiety by bringing his attention to some aspect of a problem which he had not thought of. A question of this kind may relieve the patient more than the physician's overt reassurance about the subject.

Secondly, appropriate questions may enhance the patient's flow rather than impede it. Questions nearly always help to communicate the physician's interest in the patient. The physician can best enter into the patient's world by asking questions about the details of his living. Such detailed questions about the circumstances of the patient's home, family, work, and hobbies communicate the wish of the physician to understand the patient. To this the patient responds by confiding more fully in the physician. Thus it often happens that silence on the part of the physician evokes silence in the patient, but a friendly questioning soon moves the patient to talk freely. The patient expresses his thoughts and emotions when he perceives the physician as interested in what he has to say. Silent listening, even when friendly, is not always the best way of showing this interest. The patient cannot always tell when a silence is friendly; but he can usually tell whether a friendly attitude lies behind questions.

### *The Limitations and Disadvantages of Questions*

Despite the value of appropriate questions, they do have important limitations and disadvantages. These the physician should also remember.

Often one hopes that the patient can answer questions about his marriage, his job, or his parents as he can answer questions about whether or not he has had bloody stools, jaundice, or swollen feet. Such hopes are best set aside. The patient cannot do this, and attempts to make him should be abandoned. But he will deliver the same information if he can be helped to talk and kept talking about his personal life in a free-flowing manner. Everything that is needed and more will emerge. Questions can guide his flow, they cannot produce it.

Moreover, the unskillful use of questions can interfere with the patient's spontaneity of speech. The questions can interrupt his train of thought, sometimes even pushing his thoughts completely away from a topic of greater importance than that pointed to by the interfering questions. Especially to be avoided are hasty questions about the time and place of events inserted by the physician out of a compulsive need to complete the record as an end in itself. Questions thoughtlessly inserted to allay the physician's curiosity or anxiety can also draw the patient away from his theme.

Questions invariably convey some suggestion to the patient. They may suggest a new symptom, disorder, or problem. The suggestion contained in the question may be picked up with resulting distortion of the information offered in response to the question. Or the suggestion may arouse anxiety in the patient.

Questions also communicate something of the answer expected, for one cannot ask a question without having a possible answer in mind. Patients know this as much as physicians and they usually try to guess the answer expected. Then a need to please the physician may lead them to furnish that answer. Or they may furnish any answer rather than admit to ignorance or forgetting.[4] The physician who asks many questions may hear routine sterile replies designed to satisfy social conventions. Both patient and physician may remain unaware of the various distortions resulting.

## *Reducing Suggestions in Questions*

To minimize the element of suggestion, the physician should at first phrase questions as generally as possible. For example, such questions as: "How are things today?" or "What's new?" do little more than invite the patient to talk. They convey no suggestion of what he should talk about. A question like "Tell me a little about your early life" focuses on a specific subject, but on a broad one; the question only conveys the physician's interest in the subject, and does not tell the patient what to say. "Tell me what you remember about your early sexual knowledge and experiences" is a more general, hence more useful question than such questions as "When did you learn about sex?" or "Who taught you about sex?"

At the end of the history of the present illness when the physician wishes to inquire about other symptoms, he may say: "Have you any other symptoms?" But symptoms for most patients are physical discomforts and if the patient has already spoken of his physical symptoms fully, he may have nothing further to say in reply to this question. The question phrased thus needlessly reduces the area of inquiry. However, the question "Does anything else trouble you?" omits the suggestion of symptoms and the patient may then talk of other important topics such as some financial anxiety or a difficulty in personal relationships.

In addition to minimizing suggestions, general questions stimulate the patient to think about himself and to accept some responsibility for exploring his difficulties. The physician, therefore, should open a subject with general questions and as these fail or the responses dry up, he can fall back upon more and more specific questions.

Even in asking specific questions, however, the physician should always seek to reactivate the patient's spontaneous flow. He should prefer open questions which the patient must answer with a sentence or more and avoid questions which offer alternatives or which the patient can answer with "yes" or "no." This suggestion derives from the fact that the more the patient talks, the more he will reveal his significant attitudes and emotions. A little experience in watching the effects of both kinds of questions will soon teach the physician the value of open questions. To illustrate:

| Examples of Closed Questions | More Appropriate Open Questions |
| --- | --- |
| "Do you like your work?" | "What things do you like and dislike about your work?" |
| "Do you like sports?" | "What things do you enjoy when you're not working?" |
| "Do you and your wife quarrel much?" | "How has your marriage been?" |
| "Was the pain sharp?" | "What was your pain like?" |
| "Did you have a lot of pain with your heart attack?" | "What was your heart attack like?" or "How was it?" |
| "Do you have a bad temper?" | "How is your temper?" |
| "Are you happily married?" | "How are things at home?" |

When the physician must resort to narrower questions which can be answered in one word, he should put questions which minimize the element of suggestion by offering alternatives from which the patient must choose. Finally, and only when the physician has exhausted all these other resources, he may use leading questions. He can thus arrange

questions in a kind of hierarchy of desirability as follows:
1. General questions with no focus or topic
2. General questions with choice of one topic, but no suggestion to the patient of what to say
3. Special questions about a smaller topic which cannot be answered with one word (open questions)
4. Special questions which offer a choice (minimizing suggestion), but which can be answered with one word
5. Questions which offer direct suggestions and which can be answered with one word (leading questions)

The following fragment of an interview illustrates in compressed form the serial retreat of the physician to these different types of questions. In many interviews these questions would not proceed to such a sharp focus so quickly as in this example.

PHYSICIAN: Have you had any other difficulty than the one you mentioned?
PATIENT: No, I don't think so.
PHYSICIAN: Any other symptoms of any kind?
PATIENT: No, I don't believe so, doctor.
PHYSICIAN: Have you ever had any trouble with your digestion or bowel function or appetite?
PATIENT: No, really, all that's been pretty good.
PHYSICIAN: Have you had any diarrhea or constipation?
PATIENT: Not that I can recall, doctor.
PHYSICIAN: How many bowel movements do you have?
PATIENT: About one every two days.
PHYSICIAN: Have you always had that many?
PATIENT: No, doctor. I used to have one every day.
PHYSICIAN: Then there's been a change in that?
PATIENT: Yes, I guess there has been a change now that you mention it. I hadn't thought much of it.

The foregoing remarks about the greater value of general and open over specific and leading questions should not restrict the use of leading questions in many places where they are quite appropriate, as for example, in inquiring about dates, places, ages, and many other essential details which the physician must learn. But the frequent need for specific direct questions should not form a thoughtless habit in the physician so that he continues their use in other places where they can powerfully and harmfully influence the responses of the patient.

### Avoiding the Suggestion of Conventional Attitudes and Emotions

The physician especially needs to avoid suggesting attitudes and emotional reactions to his patients. Direct questions about emotions and attitudes can hardly be asked without the patient's wondering whether the physician will approve his answer or not.

If the physician asks the patient: "Are you interested in your job?", the patient may be unwilling to expose himself to possible criticism for lack of interest. Hence he may answer guardedly that he is interested in his job. On the other hand, if the physician asks: "Is your job interesting?", the patient feels free to talk about his job instead of himself. But in talking about his job he will naturally reveal to the physician his interest in that job. So a slight change in wording may greatly increase the amount of information obtained by the physician. As further examples, the following three questions are given in order of merit:

"How did you feel when you had to sell your house?"
"Did you feel bad when you had to sell your house?"
"You must have felt bad when you had to sell your house, didn't you?"

The last two questions assume an attitude on the part of the patient which, although common, is not universal and hence may be one which he does not have. He may have been secretly or openly glad he had to sell his house. Perhaps he really wanted to move to another neighborhood, or perhaps he found some other advantage in selling. But sensing the physician's expectation of the conventional reaction, he might reply to the last two questions: "Yes, I really felt bad. Anyone would, too." On the other hand, to the more open first question he might reply: "Well, I did feel bad, but it wasn't all bad. There were some good sides to it, too. . . ."

The physician needs no more time to say: "How do you feel about what happened?" than to say: "You must have been angry when that happened, weren't you?" He can as readily say: "How do you feel now that your daughter is away?" as he can say: "Do you miss your daughter?" Yet the first question of each example is open: the second weighted with expectations which are bound to influence the patient's response, if not to that question, then to others and to the physician himself.

Sometimes when the physician notes a discrepancy between what the patient says and other signs of emotion, or when the patient denies having a reaction to some common stress to which most people react in a rather uniform way, the physician may draw out the patient's expression by suggesting an emotion in a question. In the foregoing example, if the physician believed that the patient's first reply concealed other attitudes he might suggest: "Perhaps you weren't altogether sorry to see your house go?"

## FACILITATING THE FULL EXPRESSION OF THE PATIENT'S THOUGHTS AND FEELINGS

Careful observation of himself and his patients will show the physician how readily he can facilitate the expression of their thoughts, and just as readily inhibit this expression. Listed below are a number of remarks by a patient beneath each of which is placed an interfering and a facilitating response on the part of the physician.

PATIENT: I'm always afraid people are talking about me and criticizing me.
PHYSICIAN (*interfering*): How do you know they are?
PHYSICIAN (*facilitating*): What would they find to criticize about you?

PATIENT: When I saw that girl at the party, I thought sadly about my own marriage.
PHYSICIAN (*interfering*): How could a thing like that upset you?
PHYSICIAN (*facilitating*): What about the girl made you think of your own marriage?
PHYSICIAN (*alternative facilitating response*): What thoughts did you have about your marriage?

PATIENT: I feel I need affection and can't get it.
PHYSICIAN (*interfering*): Well, we all need affection.
PHYSICIAN (*facilitating*): What interferes with your getting it?

PATIENT: Last night my wife and I had a big quarrel.
PHYSICIAN (*interfering*): Again?
PHYSICIAN (*facilitating*): What happened?

PATIENT: I'm afraid I may lose control of myself.
PHYSICIAN (*interfering*): Would that be bad?
PHYSICIAN (*facilitating*): What do you think would happen if you did?

PATIENT: I was afraid of my parents as a child.
PHYSICIAN (*interfering*): Yes, a lot of children are.
PHYSICIAN (*facilitating*): What do you think you were afraid of?

PATIENT: My mind keeps wandering to all sorts of things.
PHYSICIAN (*interfering*): Does it? I imagine that bothers you a lot.
PHYSICIAN (*facilitating*): What thoughts does it wander to?

| | |
|---|---|
| PATIENT: | I have enormous debts and bills. |
| PHYSICIAN | (*interfering*): How did you spend so much money? |
| PHYSICIAN | (*facilitating*): What brought about those bills? |
| PATIENT: | I think I get too much rest. |
| PHYSICIAN | (*interfering*): I don't see how that could be. |
| PHYSICIAN | (*facilitating*): What makes you think so? |

In the foregoing examples, the interfering remarks offer gratuitous suggestions, premature reassurance, and reproaches to the patient. They trip him. After each such remark the patient may stop and think: "What did he mean by that?" If the physician smoothly facilitates the expression of the patient, the patient will never have time or need for such a thought about him.

Despite warnings running throughout this chapter against giving the patient suggestions of what to say, sometimes the physician may prompt the patient a little by saying for him something which the patient is struggling to say and cannot quite articulate without help. This technique has already been mentioned in Chapter 8 as a useful means of facilitating the patient's expression of emotions.

The physician should do this only when he has good reason to believe he is not suggesting some thought not already in the patient's mind. When given in these circumstances, such assistance is not a form of suggestion, but rather a kind of lubricant to the patient's own expression. The patient usually responds to the physician's assistance. It shows him that the physician does understand him. Moreover, the patient can usually then go on to speak what was in his mind but blocked in utterance. It is as if he has received permission from the physician and so can proceed. The following example illustrates a typical exchange of this kind.

| | |
|---|---|
| PATIENT: | I've just no interest in going out socially at all. I don't feel comfortable with other people. |
| PHYSICIAN: | Do you have any idea what that is about? |
| PATIENT: | No, I don't know. I feel nervous, that's all. (*Becoming tense and hesitating.*) |
| PHYSICIAN: | It sounds as if you were afraid of the other people. |
| PATIENT: | I think maybe I am. |
| PHYSICIAN: | Why should you be afraid of them? |
| PATIENT: | I don't know. There's no reason. But I am. |
| PHYSICIAN: | Perhaps you are afraid they will criticize you. |
| PATIENT: | That's it. I am afraid of that. I always think they'll see how bad I am. |

## HOW TO GUIDE THE INTERVIEWS

*Helping the Patient to Reveal Specific Thoughts and Fantasies*

Often the patient will hint at some thought or fantasy without fully revealing it. Simple interjections by the physician can then facilitate the patient's exposing his thoughts in full detail, when he otherwise might not do so. The following examples illustrate such remarks. In them the physician inquires about the patient's thoughts gently but rather firmly, partly drawing, partly squeezing more words from the patient.

PATIENT: My husband can hurt me.
PHYSICIAN: Can he? In what way?
PATIENT: The things he says.
PHYSICIAN: What sort of things does he say?

PATIENT: I get these depressed feelings.
PHYSICIAN: What thoughts do you have when you're depressed?
PATIENT: Sexual thoughts.
PHYSICIAN: Can you tell me about them?
PATIENT: Well, when I'm with women, I think of doing these things.
PHYSICIAN: Such as what?

PATIENT: I think part of the trouble with my marriage is my fault.
PHYSICIAN: Which part?

PATIENT: My parents say doctors are greedy.
PHYSICIAN: Do they? What do they say about that?

PATIENT: I like to be alone.
PHYSICIAN: What kinds of things do you think about when alone?
PATIENT: I think about things that happened in the past.
PHYSICIAN: What things?

PATIENT: I'm scared of marriage.
PHYSICIAN: What about it scares you?
PATIENT: I think it may not work out.
PHYSICIAN: What could prevent it from working out?
PATIENT: Well, there's a lot of responsibility involved.
PHYSICIAN: What about that bothers you?

PATIENT: I've been thinking a lot about my father.
PHYSICIAN: Have you? What sort of thoughts have you had?
PATIENT: Oh, a lot of stuff.
PHYSICIAN: What stuff?

PATIENT: I seem to get too emotional about things.
PHYSICIAN: Such as what?
PATIENT: Oh, weddings and funerals and things like that.
PHYSICIAN: Whose funeral, for example?
PATIENT: Oh, the other day a cousin died, and he never did mean much to me, but I cried like a baby.
PHYSICIAN: And did you think there was something wrong with that?
PATIENT: Yes, I never used to do that. I thought I was going to pieces.

### Excluding the Physician's Thoughts from the Questions

The physician should avoid not only the suggestion of conventional attitudes to the patient; he should not suggest any attitude whatever. Yet often physicians interject little suggestions or comments with their questions and these can influence the patient's replies. The physician should want to hear the patient's associations to any question. If he offers his own first, he will probably influence the patient's replies. The following example illustrates clumsy intrusion of the physician's own associations into his questions:

PATIENT: Last night I got so mad at my husband. I was afraid I might do something I'd regret.
PHYSICIAN: What did you have in mind? Hitting him?
PATIENT: No, not that. I thought of going away.
PHYSICIAN: Why would you want to go away? To hurt him?
PATIENT: No. I just thought if I could get away for a while things might be better. I mean, I'd calm down.
PHYSICIAN: Where would you have gone? To your mother's home?
PATIENT: No. I told you mother is poor and couldn't afford to have me. I'd go to my aunt's house.

In this example, the physician's associations have simply cluttered up the path of the patient's movement. Moreover, the physician's suggestions have shown that he considers the patient a much more violent, revengeful, and thoughtless person than she believed herself to be. In future answers she may avoid exposing herself to such implied accusations again. In each of the physician's comments he would have obtained better results by simply omitting the second question with its unnecessary and unfounded suggestion.

### Avoiding Premature and Irrelevant Interpretations

Initial interviews with patients have often been marred by rash interpretations of the patient's symptoms or behavior by the physician.

Most patients, unless they happen to have stuffed their minds with psychological theories, come to the physician quite unprepared to understand the influence of their thoughts within their bodies and in forming their behavior. Often they have not even seen the all-important relationships between symptoms and life stresses. If the physician then offers such a patient a symbolic interpretation of a symptom or piece of behavior the patient will probably respond unfavorably. The patient may conclude that the physician is either cruel or incompetent, or possibly both. And perhaps he is right. Interpretations of motivation and intent of behavior will rarely evoke any more enthusiasm than interpretations of symbolic meaning. The physician should similarly avoid abrupt confrontation of the patient with his own emotions which he may be quite unready to acknowledge. For example, the physician should think carefully before telling a patient in an initial interview: "Your impotence comes from your being angry at your wife."

The foregoing is not intended to exclude all such interpretations and confrontations from initial interviews. They certainly have their place both as part of the examination of the patient to test his understanding, and as part of the explanations to the patient. But the physician must carefully suit remarks in this category to the present needs and comprehension of the patient. Above all he should avoid damming the patient's flow by gratuitously increasing anxiety.

## TECHNIQUES FOR REDUCING THE PATIENT'S ANXIETY

The material discussed in medical interviewing arouses anxiety in most patients. Successful interviewing requires the reduction and maintenance of this anxiety to levels which do not interfere with the patient's ability to talk usefully. Accordingly, the physician must bring into play a variety of techniques for asking his questions in such a way that they arouse little or no anxiety.

### *Phrasing Questions To Disguise the Physician's Reasons for Asking Them*

Since patients tend to furnish the physician with answers that they think he expects or would approve, the physician must often disguise the purpose of his questions. In this way he leads the patient to reply to a question other than the one actually asked. The following example illustrates obstruction of the patient's expression by a poorly worded question.

PHYSICIAN: How do you get along with your father?
PATIENT: Why, we get along just great. No trouble at all.

The patient interpreted this question as part of a scrutiny of his behavior towards other people. Accordingly, he defensively denied any trouble between himself and his father. Another question might evoke completely different information about the same topic. For example:

PHYSICIAN: Can you tell me something about your father?
PATIENT: Well, he's all right, really a good guy. He just always wants his own way in everything and I'm not going to give in to him all the time. Why, the other night....

The second question invites the patient to paint an ostensibly objective portrait of his father. In his reply to this question the patient gave the desired information about his own relations with his father. This kind of question exploits the fact that when $A$ tells $B$ about $C$, he tells $B$ more about himself ($A$) than about $C$.

Other useful questions for eliciting the same information would be: "How do they treat you at home?" or "How does your father treat you?" As the patient talks about his family's behavior towards him he will inevitably tell much about his behavior towards them.

As mentioned in Chapter 7, patients sometimes have difficulty in describing their own parents or other close relatives. The suggestion was made there of having the patient tell what some other person or persons think of the relative in question. Thus the patient who cannot talk comfortably about his mother may be asked to say what her brothers and sisters think about her. In reporting what others think of someone else the patient invariably exposes something of his own thoughts and feelings. His voice and manner will indicate whether or not he agrees with the opinions of the other people he quotes.

The physician cannot often get direct information about a patient's motives in any action. In the first place, the patient is often not aware of his motives or is aware of only a portion of them. Secondly, he wishes to show the physician only laudable motives. For example:

PHYSICIAN: Do you remember why you got married?
PATIENT: I just loved my wife, that's all. Why does anyone get married?
PHYSICIAN: You had no other reason?
PATIENT: No, why should I?
PHYSICIAN: Well, I was wondering what attracted you in your wife.
PATIENT: Well, she was good-looking and physically attractive. Then I remember she was awfully kind to me when I was feeling low after losing my job. She was working herself at the time

and that made it possible for us to get married right after I got my next job.

In this example, the first question proved useless. The second question, which uses the patient like a camera, helps him to reveal some of the motives for marrying which a few seconds earlier he had denied having.

The physician should therefore use oblique questions for any information which might possibly show the patient in an unfavorable light. Such information is obtained best by asking him to describe situations or people as he witnesses them.

Asking the patient to describe himself as others see him often provides useful information because the patient may again reveal something of himself which he would not express in answer to a direct question. For example:

PHYSICIAN: Well, you've told me pretty well what you think about your illness. I gather you feel it's all due to the bad weather we've had this month and your getting your feet cold and sitting in that draught. I was wondering what your wife thinks of your illness.
PATIENT: Oh, her. She's got it all worked out differently. She says I've been nervous over nothing for the past four months. In fact she says I get nervous every time she's pregnant and that's my trouble.
PHYSICIAN: What do you think about that idea?
PATIENT: Well, it could be, I suppose, but . . . .

## *The Importance of Tact in Questioning*

Questions, by their very nature, open up new, unexplored territory. The physician does not know what sensitivities of the patient he may stumble upon. In exploring new areas he needs more gentleness than zeal. The questions asked should always give the patient maximal credit for maturity and "being in the right."

It is helpful to remember that part of tact is the ability to describe a person as he sees himself. The physician should phrase questions with respect for the patient's concept of himself. For example, when a patient ventilates much hostility to a boss, the physician may be tempted to say: "Do you always have trouble with bosses?" The patient, however, will respond more freely if asked: "Have you found other bosses as troublesome as this one has been for you?" When a patient mentions receiving assistance from the Department of Public Welfare, the physician may want to say: "Have you been on relief often?" He can encourage the patient to talk more by asking instead: "Have you had much trouble finding work?" A question such as "Why don't you take your wife out more often?" can immediately make the patient anxious and perhaps angry. The physician can avoid this by asking instead: "What prevents you from taking your wife out more?" This has much less of an accusatory quality while still including the possibility that the difficulty is within the patient himself.

Questions of the form, "Why did you do so and so?" nearly always arouse the patient's expectation that his reasons will be questioned and perhaps found faulty. Such questions can often be put to patients when the physician knows them well. But in the early interviews physician and patient show each other cautious scrutinies and tentative acceptances so that the physician should phrase questions about motivations in a form such as: "What led up to your doing so and so?" or "How did it happen that . . . ?" or "What influenced you to decide such and such?"

When the interviewer suspects but does not positively know that a patient has experienced some severe mental illness, he will not wish to frighten the patient or offer a harmful suggestion, and may rightly hesitate to ask a direct question about it. He can, however, give the patient an opportunity to discuss such an illness by saying something like: "When you tell me all you have been through, I'm surprised it didn't get you down and even interfere with your health."

With some patients the physician can be much more direct than with others. Moreover, timidity is no part of tact. A question firmly put may bring a better answer than one offered tentatively. The physician should have no diffidence about asking any question which his professional work requires.

### The Use of Indirection in Questioning

Closely related to the foregoing emphasis on tact in questioning is the use of indirection in helping the patient to see relationships between symptoms and other events, such as emotions or the actions of other persons which produce emotions. For example, when the physician asks a patient abruptly if he thinks his headaches are related to emotional disturbances, the directness of the inquiry may arouse anxiety in the patient. He does not know what terrible question might come next. He thinks if he encourages the physician in this line of inquiry the physician may start asking questions which throw doubt on his sanity. And so he is prompted to deny the relationship and spare himself further anxiety. However, if the physician makes the patient a kind of colleague or ally in a scientific quest, the patient can often be led to see and admit the correlation of symptoms and emotions himself. With this approach the patient knows the direction of the physician's movements, and he can see where he is being led. This reduces his anxiety, and encourages him to participate more actively. For example:

PHYSICIAN: Now getting back to your headaches. You don't have them every day, do you?
PATIENT: No, not really every day, but almost every day.
PHYSICIAN: Still, they do seem to fluctuate some. Can you say what makes them worse or better?
PATIENT: No, I can't really. I have no idea.
PHYSICIAN: Perhaps you have noticed that they are connected with something else that's going on. I was thinking of such things as exercise, fatigue, a heavy meal, nervousness, or bright lights.
PATIENT: Well, they do come on when I'm tired, and also when I'm nervous.
PHYSICIAN: They do? Tell me about that.

In the above example, the physician embeds "nervousness" in a group of other common factors related to headaches. This makes "nervousness" seem much more ordinary and acceptable to the patient than he might think if it were offered to him alone.

Indirect approaches of this kind take more time than blunt inquiries, but they almost invariably reward the physician for the additional effort.

As mentioned already, many topics arouse anxiety and must be approached gently. Often the subject of sex arouses anxiety in patients. Many educated, sophisticated patients talk readily of sexual matters in the first interview. But for many other patients the subject is quite unapproachable during the first period of the patient's acquaintance with the physician. Women especially may find it difficult to discuss sexual matters with men. But patients of either sex may defend themselves against direct inquiries or become irritated by them. If the physician plunges into the subject of sexual intimacies during the first interview, he may only alarm and silence the patient.

The patient himself may wish to bring the subject up and should not be dissuaded if he does so. But he will not bring it up unless the anxiety associated with the problem exceeds his fears of talking about it with the physician. If the patient does not himself broach the subject, the physician cannot know how much anxiety the patient feels in connection with it. He will proceed best if he assumes that the patient has some anxiety. He will have to judge individually in each case when the patient is ready to discuss the topic. Often he should wait until some later interview when the patient has become accustomed to talking about himself in connection with a wide range of subjects. The sexual experiences then become just another topic about which the physician inquires as he does about other matters.

If, however, time is limited and the physician thinks he should at least touch this topic in the first interview or two with a patient who shows marked anxiety, he can do so through questions which are routine for the physical history. Thus he may approach sexual experiences as part of the review of functions. For example, physicians customarily ask, and female patients usually expect to be asked, about pregnancies, menstruation and pelvic operations. After a patient has mentioned the number of her pregnancies, she may be asked: "How did it happen that you didn't have more (any) children?" If the reply to this question fails to furnish full information, the physician can next ask: "Did you want any more?" If the patient did not want more (or any) children, the physician may ask if the patient did anything to prevent pregnancies. If she practiced contraception, the physician can inquire naturally about whether this interfered with her sexual experiences. If the patient states that she did want more children, the physician can naturally ask how it happened that she did not have more pregnancies. Possibly the sexual relationship was not adequate. An inquiry about sexual relationship would again be natural in this context. And so, whatever the answer to the first question about the number of pregnancies, the physician can usually lead the patient to talk about sexual experiences with a freedom not attained so readily when he approaches the subject directly.

Similarly when the physician interviews an unmarried girl he should not plunge into the subject of sex with a question about sexual intercourse. If he wishes to ask the girl about this topic, he should usually approach it gradually across less guarded territory. The following series of questions illustrate one means of reaching the topic without frightening the patient.

"How about your social life now? I mean what do you do with friends?"
↓
"Do you have any special friends, girl friends or boy friends?"
↓
"Do boys attract you physically?" or "Does your boy friend attract you physically?"
↓
"Do you get each other sexually aroused?"
↓
"How far have you gone in sexual play?"

## HOW TO GUIDE THE INTERVIEWS

Many other question besides those concerning sex are charged with anxiety either for themselves or for their implications. Patients are especially sensitive to questions which imply to them a suggestion that they may be "crazy" or "insane." And they may resent questions which seem to suggest weakness or lack of self-control. Questions touching on such subjects lose much or all of their charge when embedded in a matrix of other questions which the patient expects or does not object to.

To give another example, if the physician asks a patient directly about awareness of loss of memory, the patient may sense and resent an implication that he is "crazy." However, if the patient is asked a series of questions such as the following, he will probably answer easily and without anxiety:

PHYSICIAN: Do you have any headaches?
PATIENT: Well, a few, but not bad ones.
PHYSICIAN: Do you notice anything else in connection with the headaches?
PATIENT: No, not particularly.
PHYSICIAN: Have you had any buzzing in your ears?
PATIENT: No.
PHYSICIAN: Have you had any trouble concentrating on what you are doing or reading?
PATIENT: Why, yes, it seems hard for me to read a newspaper all through now and I used to read every word every night.
PHYSICIAN: I see. And have you noticed any trouble in remembering what you read?
PATIENT: Yes, I think so. As a matter of fact, my wife says I don't have any memory at all like the one I used to have. Why the other day she sent me to the grocery for some groceries and I forgot half of them.

Direct questions about subjective feelings or changes in emotions and mood often stimulate anxiety and lead to meaningless denials. Questions about these subjects also can be embedded in a context of other questions. For example:

PHYSICIAN: Has anything else been bothering you?
PATIENT: No, absolutely nothing.
PHYSICIAN: Well, have you been any more tired or fatigued lately than you were?
PATIENT: Yes, I guess I have been.
PHYSICIAN: Could there be a difference in your energy or "pep?"
PATIENT: I guess that's it. I just don't have the old pep I had.

PHYSICIAN: Well, how about your spirits, or your mood? Has that changed?
PATIENT: What do you mean?
PHYSICIAN: Well, when people lose pep it's often because they are really a bit low in spirits or feeling blue.
PATIENT: Oh, I see. Yes, I guess that's me, too. I have been sort of blue recently. Maybe that has something to do with . . . .

Direct questions about factors underlying anxiety also often arouse defensiveness. When asked directly whether anything is worrying them, many obviously anxious patients deny any fears or worries. However, the physician can sometimes approach fears and worries in some of these patients through inquiries about the vital functions such as sleep and appetite, and the things which interfere with these. For example:

PHYSICIAN: Then you've had no trouble with your appetite or your bowels?
PATIENT: That's right, doctor.
PHYSICIAN: How about sleeping?
PATIENT: Not so good. Matter of fact, I don't sleep at all well.
PHYSICIAN: Is that so? What seems to be keeping you awake at night?
PATIENT: Can't think of anything in the world.
PHYSICIAN: When did you first have trouble sleeping?
PATIENT: It was around last December, I guess.
PHYSICIAN: What was happening then?
PATIENT: Nothing much that I think of now. Well, Alice and I did have a big quarrel then. But it's all over now.
PHYSICIAN: What do you think about when you lie awake trying to get to sleep?
PATIENT: Mostly I think about not getting to sleep and how tired I'm going to be in the morning because I haven't slept.
PHYSICIAN: Anything else?
PATIENT: Sometimes I think about Alice and how I'd hate to have her leave me, but I just can't go on letting her have her way in everything.
PHYSICIAN: Then the quarrel you had in December was pretty important to you?
PATIENT: Yes, I guess it was. It was a sort of a showdown. You see . . .

### *The Use of Direct Questions To Flank Anxiety*

Although in general the physician should prefer an indirect and gentle approach to the topics charged with anxiety for the patient, at times he will find a direct approach more helpful. Sometimes he can phrase questions which take the patient by surprise by boldly implying an event or attitude so that the patient cannot or will not deny it. For example, in inquiring about childhood punishments the physician can say: "Did your parents punish you often?" Many patients would detect in this question a hint of criticism of the parents. They do not wish to criticize their parents because they think this is disapproved by other persons, including the physician. So to this question such patients are likely to say (when the truth may be quite different), "Why, no, they hardly ever punished me." The subject has then reached a dead end. If the physician asks instead: "For what offenses were you punished as a child?" or "How did your parents punish you when you were a child?", the patient may reply differently. The fact of punishment, which is indeed universal, is assumed. The patient cannot answer with a simple "yes" or "no," and therefore he must inevitably tell something about his early relations with his parents and their attitude towards discipline. In this case a direct question gives the patient's anxiety less opportunity to interfere than an indirect approach might have done.

The physician can use this technique in exploring other matters about which patients are usually defensive. For example, if the physician asks: "When did you first masturbate?", he will probably open up the subject of masturbation more effectively than if he suggests, more tentatively, "Have you ever masturbated?"

However, abuse of this technique may make the patient more defensive rather than less. Suppose, for example, the physician wishes to inquire about relations between the patient and his wife. He may say: "How often do you and your wife quarrel?" This can offend since the patient knows quarrels are made by two, and he does not wish the physician to think he is a quarreler. "Do you and your wife quarrel often?" is a little gentler, but gives the patient an easy chance to say: "No, we never quarrel." "What sort of things do you and your wife quarrel about?" assumes, like the first question, that quarreling takes place. Although it may open the subject further, it may also irritate the patient or evoke a defensive denial from him. A better question than any of these would be: "What things have you and your wife found you disagree on?" Disagreement, even if only in matters of taste, is universal and does not imply exchange of hostilities. The patient can talk first about whatever areas of disagreement he wishes to mention. When he has revealed these, the physician can then inquire further to discover the intensity of disagreement, that is, whether the couple respect in each other simple differences of opinion, or have more serious disagreements of various degrees up to physical brawling.

### Offering Questions Rapidly To Reduce Evasiveness in the Patient

While the physician should always cultivate the spontaneous flow of the patient's remarks, he should also remember that when the patient chooses the topic of discussion he can also select what he will say. So although the patient may seem to talk freely, he may actually be concealing a great deal. If the physician believes that such evasiveness seriously interferes with the value of the interview, he may vary his technique and start throwing questions rather rapidly at the patient. This can be done in a kindly, yet firm manner. When the physician asks questions rapidly, the patient thinks that the physician expects a rapid answer. So he gives one. He has no time for selection of thoughts or their concealment. He is likely to give the first answer which comes to his mind, which is what the physician wants in preference to the patient's third or fourth thought put in place of the censored first thought. Before the patient has time to become anxious about having spoken so freely, the physician asks him another question and so it continues. After the patient leaves the interview, he may be surprised to realize how freely he has talked in responding to the questions of the physician.

Each of the physician's questions in this technique should rapidly follow the end of the patient's answer to the previous question. They should not precede that end, thus cutting into what the patient is trying to say.

The physician must judge whether the patient can respond to this technique of questioning. Some patients will become more anxious or irritated and perhaps blocked completely. They require other tactics.

## ALLOWING THE PATIENT TO ANSWER QUESTIONS FULLY

When the physician has asked the patient a question, he should, as it were, step aside again until the patient has had a chance to answer the question fully. He must not get in the patient's way by inserting premature reassurance, asking another question, or losing interest half way through the patient's reply. Often the physician may think that the patient's first few words or sentences have answered the question satisfactorily. He may then be tempted to cut the patient off if he tries to continue and elaborate. The physician should resist this impulse, because the most useful part of the patient's response to the question often comes in his associations and after-thoughts which are stimulated by the questions and the first part of the answer. As mentioned earlier, the physician should rarely interrupt the patient when he is talking. The physician gains nothing if he uses one question to start the patient talking and with another cuts him off.

## ASKING THE PATIENT TO CLARIFY HIS MEANING

If the physician censors his own questions before asking them he will often notice that what he was about to ask for, the patient tells him a moment later. If he waits a little longer, an obscure point may clarify. But often it will not. Then it is unhelpful for the physician to allow the patient to continue while he himself lingers in a fog of confusion. Instead he should stop the patient and say, "I didn't understand what you were telling me there. Can you say that another way?" or "I'm afraid I don't understand the connection of this with that. Will you go over that again, please?"

## SUMMARIZING WHAT THE PATIENT HAS SAID FROM TIME TO TIME

The physician can facilitate the interview if, from time to time, he summarizes briefly what the patient has been telling him. When he does so, he may be astonished to have the patient point out that the physician's summary is quite incorrect and inadequate. This response, however, merely emphasizes the need for some such summarizing if the physician and patient are to communicate effectively. The summaries of the physician should be brief and do not need to cover everything the patient has said. They could not do this even if it were wise to try. But they can throw back to the patient for consideration what the physician has thought most important in what the patient has said. A typical summary at the end of some questioning about the present illness might be the following:

PHYSICIAN: Well, as I understand what you have told me, you believe that what you eat, and changes in the weather, affect your asthma, and that it sometimes comes on when you are tense, but you don't connect this tenseness with anything or anyone in particular. Is that right?

PATIENT: That's about it, but you left out that the asthma gets worse if I take a lot of exercise; and I can't understand why it should be worse on weekends.

PHYSICIAN: Well, let's look into that a bit. What do you make of it?

### References and Suggestions for Further Reading

1. GREENSPOON, J.: The reinforcing effect of two spoken sounds on the frequency of two responses. *Am. J. Psychol. 68:*409, 1955.
2. QUAY, H.: The effect of verbal reinforcement on the recall of early memories. *J. Abnorm. Soc. Psychol. 59:*254, 1959.
3. SALZINGER, K., and PISONI, S.: Reinforcement of verbal affect responses of normal subjects during the interview. *J. Abnorm. Soc. Psychol. 60:*127, 1960.
4. STERN, W.: *General Psychology from the Personalistic Standpoint.* Trans. H.D. Spoerl. New York, The Macmillan Company, 1938.

# 10

# VARIATIONS IN INTERVIEWS

As already mentioned, the physician must adapt interviews to suit the particular needs of each patient. Such adaptations will be required by differences in the personalities of patients and also by differences in the main symptoms or problems which patients bring to physicians. Previous chapters have already included some examples of necessary adaptations in the interviews. As further illustrations, this chapter will describe some commonly encountered types of patients and the special handling they require in interviewing.

## DEPRESSED PATIENTS

In interviewing and examining depressed patients, the physician's first task is to recognize that the patient is depressed. This may seem obvious, but yet the physician can be misled by the fact that many depressed patients do not describe their complaints in language which suggests a disturbance of mood. The physician may hear only physical complaints, or at the most, complaints of loss of energy, vitality, or "pep." Some such depressed patients are sometimes actually unaware of the change in mood and may only become aware of it after they have improved or recovered. This is especially likely to be the case in mild, chronic depressions which come on gradually and which extend over many years. Other patients who deny mood changes are aware of these, but unable to confess such symptoms because to do so would be to label themselves "weak," or "lacking in self-control." Still other patients with both anxiety and depression may focus their attention exclusively on the anxiety which then may conceal the underlying depression until specific inquiries uncover it.

The physician should consider the likelihood of a depression in any patient who speaks or moves slowly. Depressed persons have little to say and that little they speak slowly. Such signs do not prove depression, but only suggest it. This is because slowness of speech and movement may be long-standing habits, sometimes even part of a cultural pattern. As always the physician should especially note a change from what is usual for the patient.

When the physician identifies or suspects depression, he should carefully explore the quality of the patient's experience by relating the patient's feeling state to his thought contents. It is important to distinguish several rather different experiences which may be labeled as "depression" and accompanied by approximately similar feeling states.[12] These are as follows:

- (a) Conditions of guilty fear. This is the commonest experience included under the heading of depression. The patient believes that he has committed acts which are morally wrong and for which he is being, or will be, punished.
- (b) Shame. In this experience the patient's unpleasant feelings are associated with ideas of inadequacy and failure in achievements of which he supposedly ought to have been capable. The patient is ashamed for what he is or is not, in contrast to the guilty patient who is remorseful for what he has done.
- (c) Discouragement. In this experience the patient's feelings are associated with ideas of despair and hopelessness about his future. Such states frequently accompany severe illness and calamities such as the burning down of one's house or its loss in a flood, or the loss through death of an important supportive relative.
- (d) Loneliness. Affective stimulation seems necessary for affective expression. Persons deprived of companionship through deaths, moving, quarrels, imprisonments, or other events, may come to feel and exhibit an impoverished affective state, perhaps more accurately called apathy, but frequently labeled depression.
- (e) Immaturity reactions. Certain immature persons unused to ordinary frustrations may respond to disappointments and deprivations with marked emotional disturbances in which tears and crying form the principal modes of expression. While this kind of reaction has elements of discouragement in it, there is also a mixture of (usually concealed) anger. The significance of this pattern here is that such patients also may be considered depressed.
- (f) States of inhibited anger. A patient may enter a state of anger which he is reluctant to express or admit to others. He may indi-

## VARIATIONS IN INTERVIEWS

cate some of his emotion to other persons by speaking less to them, by avoiding them, or in other ways which fall short of overtly expressing the anger felt. To such a state the patient or his family may apply the word "depression" either through ignorance of its real quality, or because there are admixtures of guilt (which produce the inhibition of the anger), or because anger is too dreadful a state to bear admission and must be concealed under some more acceptable label such as depression.

The foregoing complexes may exist together in various combinations. For example, grief and mourning usually include elements of guilt, loneliness and discouragement.

That any of the experiences mentioned above may be reasonably labeled "depression" by either patient or physician demonstrates the importance of understanding emotional states and thought contents together. If the patient does not reveal his thoughts spontaneously, the physician should ask, "What do you think about when you are feeling low?" Failure to elicit the thoughts accompanying apparently similar affective states will lead to serious confusion of different experiences.

The distinctions the physician can make about the depressed patient's experiences may guide him in his further interviewing of the patient. For example, with morbidly guilty patients, the physician should especially avoid premature reassurance or efforts to assuage the guilt by minimizing the crimes which the patient attributes to himself. Such behavior on the part of the physician may actually make matters worse. The patient may think that he deserves no kindness and the demonstration of it may simply increase his guilt; or the patient may think that the physician has gravely underestimated the enormity of the patient's sins. In this last respect, the patient may be right in one sense. His guilt, however, comes from his thoughts, not from any overt acts. In any case, irrational guilt such as that of moderately and severely depressed patients can only be relieved over a period of time and the physician should avoid attempting to do so in one interview. Shame likewise must be handled over a period of time since its origins usually extend backwards many years. One does not help a patient who thinks he is ugly or stupid by telling him that he is beautiful or clever. Rather the physician should try to find out how the patient came to have such ideas about himself. Discouragement is best handled by appropriate study of the situation evoking it, whatever that may be, and of those attitudes which give rise to discouragement when this comes on easily. Usually irrational discouragement is a product of excessive dependency which leads the patient to expect other people to do for him what he needs to do for himself. Discouragement about illness requires not only the appropriate treatment for the illness, but also appropriate reassurance.

## *Estimating the Degree of Depression and Suicidal Risk*[4, 13, 15, 17, 19]

When the patient is found to be depressed, the physician should try to find out the degree of depression, whether or not the patient has suicidal ideas, and the strength of these. He should start his inquiry with questions about the degree of the depression. He should not plunge directly into the subject of suicide, since the patient may have had no such ideas and may be frightened or irritated by the question. On the other hand, if the earlier questions indicate the possibility of suicidal thoughts, the physician must not shrink from direct questions about these.

In ascertaining the degree of depression, some of the following questions may prove useful. The physician should find out, for example, the extent of interference with the patient's ordinarily pleasurable appetites. He may ask, "What do you enjoy doing still?" or "Is there anything you enjoy doing now?" In the more severe depressions all enjoyment vanishes. The physician may also ask the patient about the origins of his illness with such questions as "What do you think caused your illness?" "Did you bring this illness on yourself?" or "Do you deserve to be ill?" Again in the more severe depressions with irrational guilt, the patient will readily attribute his condition to his own miserable and unforgivable sins. The physician may also ask the patient about how it will all end. He may say, "Do you think you are going to get well?" or "What is going to become of you?" Less depressed patients will concede they have some hope of recovery; more depressed patients have abandoned such hope and think they are surely doomed and deserve to be. In addition, the physician should ask the patient directly about the degree of his depression. There is no better authority, although he may not tell all he knows.

The following example illustrates a possible sequence of questions and answers in an interview with a depressed patient.

PHYSICIAN: From what you've told me, it seems this depressed feeling is the main thing that bothers you. Just how low do you get?
PATIENT: Sometimes I get so low I don't want to go on.
PHYSICIAN: You mean then that life doesn't seem worth living?
PATIENT: That's right, doctor. I'd just as soon die and be done with it all.
PHYSICIAN: And have you ever thought of killing yourself when you were in one of these moods?
PATIENT: Yes, I have, many times.

PHYSICIAN: What did you think you would do?
PATIENT: Once I walked along the harbor bridge with the idea of jumping in, but I decided to try to hold on for a while longer and get some help.

Suicidal thoughts usually derive from mixtures of hostility directed toward the patient and toward other persons. These ingredients vary with different persons. The physician should find out what he can about the motivations behind suicidal thoughts. When the patient's hostility is directed mainly toward other persons, the suicidal fantasies or attempts are intended chiefly to manipulate these other persons. In a suicidal gesture, the patient usually adopts less dangerous means (e.g., a light slashing of wrists or a swallow of iodine) and arranges things so that he is likely to be saved. Conversely, the use of dangerous means in suicidal attempts (e.g., jumping off high buildings, firing a revolver at the heart) indicates serious intentions. The physician may obtain clues to the patient's motivations by inquiries concerning any previous suicidal attempts, the methods which the patient has contemplated using, and his fantasies about the reactions of other persons to his suicide. The question: "What would happen after you were dead?" may help to uncover the patient's fantasies about other people.

When a patient asserts that he had suicidal thoughts or intentions but has them no longer, the physician can learn much by asking: "Why did you give up the idea of suicide?" Among other data, the answer to this question will usually tell the physician whether the patient has really abandoned thoughts of suicide or merely pretends to have done so as a means of concealing his intentions. The patient who wants to live can usually give reasons for his change; the patient who wants to die may fumble or fail in presenting reasons for living.

The physician should not become excessively involved with the suicidal ruminations or attempts and their immediate motivations. These must not distract attention from the important task of discovering first the origins of the depressing thoughts and feelings, and secondly, why the patient was unable to consider and adopt a more constructive solution for his difficulties than suicide.

## CHILDREN[6, 9, 14, 20]

In general, the principles of interviewing adults apply to children. Most children who can use words (usually those over the age of three) can participate in an interview, even in one dealing with their personal difficulties. Since young children are often less inhibited than adults, they can frequently talk more easily about personal difficulties than can adults. On the other hand, children have limited conceptual ability, and the physician should not use words beyond their grasp. This does not mean he should use childish language. The child should be met on his own ground, but the physician should not pretend that he is himself a child.

Because the child's concept of himself is often rudimentary, he may have difficulty in expressing his feelings and conflicts verbally. Often he can do this more easily with drawings, or while playing with toy people, or with clay. Often children will tell their dreams, daydreams and wishes rather easily, and these will also provide clues to significant difficulties.

Nearly always the child should be seen alone without anyone else present. The child's mother may wish to accompany the child into the interviewing room, but her presence may inhibit the child. On the other hand, sometimes a child cooperates more if his mother comes into the room with him, and then she should certainly be permitted to do so. In any case, the physician should observe carefully the behavior of the mother and child together in the waiting room.

Interviews can often be combined with the physical examination of a younger child. The physical contact is often wanted by the young child and helps him to relate to the physician. When he is sitting on the physician's lap, for example, he may be examined physically to some extent, and also engaged in conversation.

The physician should never deceive a child, although the amount of information given to him must naturally vary. If the physician intends to inquire about the child's personal difficulties, he should tell the child briefly the purpose of the interview. When the child's difficulties include distrust of other people, and especially fear of the parents, the physician should tell the child that what he (the child) tells the physician will remain confidential between them. This may help the child to talk more freely. In other circumstances, however, such a statement might suggest distrust to the child when none exists, thus perhaps making the child more anxious. All explanations to the child should be brief, and he should not be flooded with unassimilable information.

## PATIENTS WITH ANXIETY STATES

Previous chapters of this book, especially in a section of Chapter 3 on anxiety, have offered suggestions for interviewing patients with anxiety states. In this place, therefore, only two points will receive further emphasis.

First, the physician must take time to hear the patient through a thorough ventilation of everything connected with the patient's anxiety. This precludes his offering premature reassurance against which the reader has been warned in Chapter 8.

Secondly, the physician must remember that what the patient first attributes his anxiety to is rarely the only or the most important source of his anxiety. Acute anxiety states nearly always occur in persons who have experienced chronically lesser degrees of anxiety which they have managed to control in one way or another. The study of the acute anxiety states must include a careful survey of the origins of the chronic anxiety.

The symptoms of chronic anxiety are often minor or capable of being ignored or kept out of awareness. Those of acute anxiety are frequently alarming and compel attention. They include marked and sometimes startling physical and mental dysfunctions, e.g., palpitations, dyspnea, impaired attention and poor memory. These symptoms are commonly interpreted by patients as signs of heart disease or mental disease or perhaps some other equally serious affliction. Such interpretations naturally augment the patient's anxiety further and intensify his symptoms. By the time the patient reaches a physician he may have become totally preoccupied with his fears of some serious disease. The circumstances of the original anxiety may be forgotten entirely by the patient, and unless the physician remembers this possibility they may be forgotten by him also. From this derives the importance of careful reviews with the patient of the circumstances in which the patient's first anxiety attack or attacks occurred. In his concern about what he supposes to be the gravity of his condition, the patient may resist such detailed inquiries as quite irrelevant to the present emergency. At this point the physician's adherence to the first point emphasized may find one of its rewards. For if he has carefully listened to what the patient wants to say he may then succeed in persuading the patient to talk about earlier and to the physician equally important events.

## PATIENTS WITH PSYCHOPHYSIOLOGICAL REACTIONS

Previous sections of this book have included much that pertains to the interviewing of patients with psychophysiological reactions. In one sense, every patient falls into this group, and the physician must constantly study the interplay of the physical and psychological factors in his patients. Psychophysiological reactions can occur in anyone and do occur in everyone at some time or another. The task of the physician in this area then is that of estimating the extent to which psychophysiological reactions contribute to the total disability of each patient. In some patients this element will be slight, in others it may be the only mechanism of disease. Moreover, the physician must pursue this task unimpeded by prejudices with regard to the presence of structural disease. Structural diseases provide no immunity against the powerful influence of life stresses and the occurrence during them of psychophysiological reactions. On the contrary, they may render the organism even more susceptible to the physiological disturbances which can accompany stresses. The person with advanced structural disease often hangs precariously balanced between comfort and invalidism or death. One might say without exaggerating that his physician needs to understand psychophysiological reactions not less, but more than a physician attending a patient without structural disease. John Hunter said: "My life is in the hands of any fool who cares to annoy me," and afterwards proved this by dying in an attack of angina pectoris which occurred when he became angry at some colleagues.

Psychophysiological reactions have two main mechanisms. First, in some of these reactions, the physical symptoms are concomitants of emotions or sequelae of the sustained emotions. Secondly, such reactions can be the physical expression of ideas within the mind of the patient. The interviews must deal with somewhat different matters in order to study both these mechanisms. Both mechanisms may occur in one patient at the same time.

## *Temporal Correlations of Stresses, Emotions, and Symptoms*

With regard to the first mechanism, the physician should study temporal correlations between emotions and symptoms. The patient will frequently be unaware initially of any emotion, or if he is, he may deny it and reject a suggestion that it was present at the time of the symptom. He is chiefly or only aware of his physical symptom or symptoms. Nevertheless, any initial unawareness or defensiveness on the part of the patient can be flanked by correlating the symptoms with stresses and temporarily omitting consideration of the associated emotion.

### Demonstrating Fluctuations in the Symptoms

The first step is to establish the fact that the symptom or symptoms fluctuate. This will usually have come out in the preliminary history of the present illness. Most symptoms fluctuate, some more than others. Even if the symptom never entirely goes away, the physician may learn that its intensity varies; this provides at least some leverage for the next move.

Patients sometimes deny any fluctuations in the symptoms when there is reason to suspect these. Sometimes also the illness is of short duration and insufficient time has elapsed for the occurrence of any significant changes in the symptoms. In these instances, the physician must patiently observe the patient over a period of time, talking to him at intervals of a week or so and noting the occurrence or absence of such fluctuations.

Sometimes fluctuations in symptoms may occur in the presence of the physician during an interview. The patient may be disturbed by some topic broached in the interview, or he may be relieved by the expression of his emotions. These emotional changes may be accompanied by changes in the symptoms.

Sometimes a more direct effort may be made to change the patient's psychological state with psychotherapy or sedatives. These measures may also be accompanied by relief symptoms.

The physician therefore has several opportunities for establishing the fact that the symptoms fluctuate, viz.,

(a) in the taking of the past history of the illness,
(b) in a day to day, or week to week, observation of the patient,
(c) during any one interview, and
(d) with the application of psychotherapy or drugs which alter the psychological state.

Examples of correlations of life situations and symptoms by means of these different methods are illustrated in Figures 6 to 12.

### Relating Changes in Symptoms to Life Stresses

When the physician has demonstrated the occurrence of fluctuations in symptoms, he must next show that these fluctuations are significantly related to stresses in the life of the patient. To the patient, it must be remembered, such fluctuations usually "just happen." They do not always make any meaningful pattern to him, although some exceptional patients do show much ability to correlate their symptoms and stresses. The physician should try to enlist the patient as a scientific collaborator. The two should look together at everything that happens or has happened in the patient's life and note whether a consistent relationship between symptoms and stresses emerges.

Mention has already been made in Chapter 9 of some useful methods of indirection for helping the patient study such correlations. For example, the physician can pursue references which the patient makes to his life situation during the description of his symptoms. If the patient says, "The pain is getting so bad, I may not be able to work," the physician may say, "Is your work hard?" and the patient will almost certainly

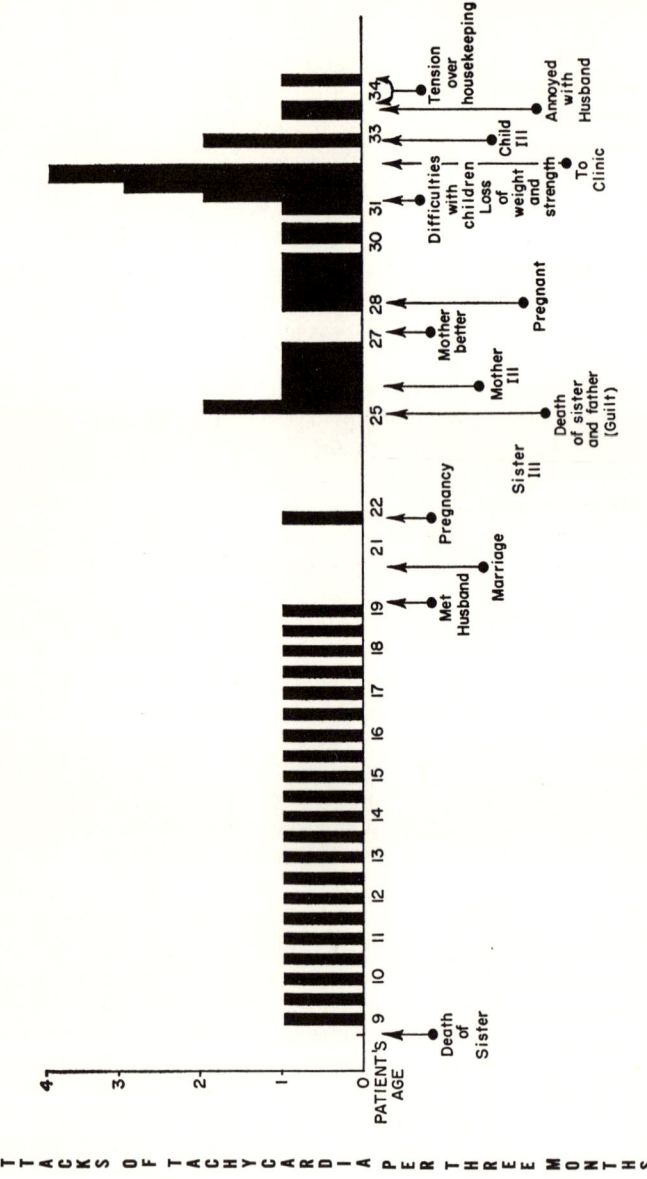

Fig. 6. Correlation of symptoms and stresses in the history of the present illness. The patient suffered from paroxysmal auricular tachycardia. Throughout the history of her illness the frequency and severity of tachycardias correlated closely with the circumstances of her life.

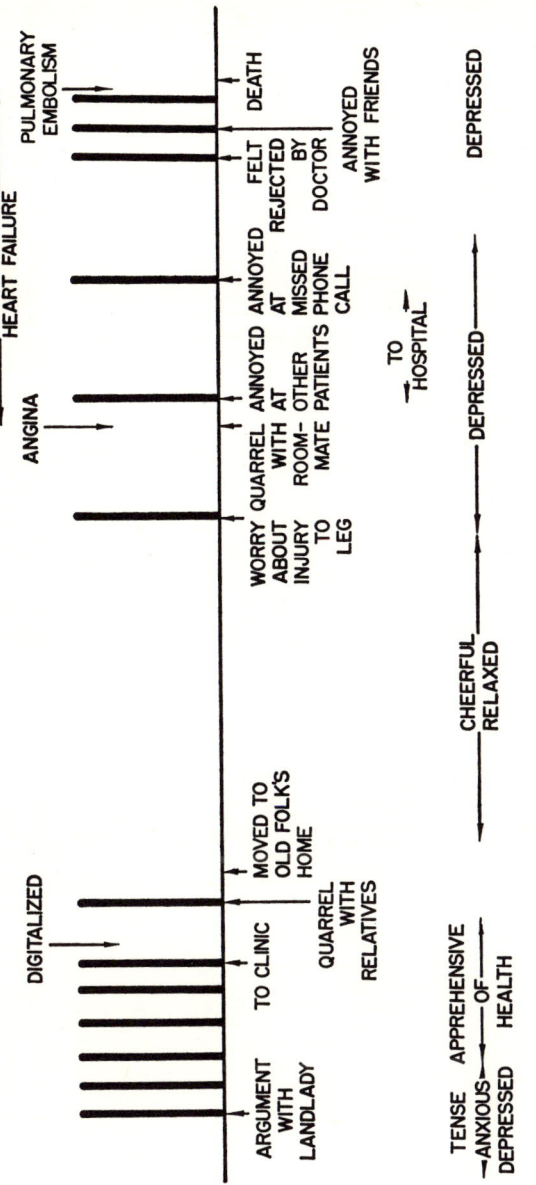

Fig. 7. Correlation of symptoms and stresses during observations of a patient at weekly intervals. At each visit symptoms, emotions, and life events were reviewed and correlated. The patient was a 74-year-old woman with arteriosclerotic heart disease. The black bars represent attacks of paroxysmal auricular fibrillation which correlated closely with stressful events in the patient's life. The patient died with symptoms suggesting a major pulmonary embolism.

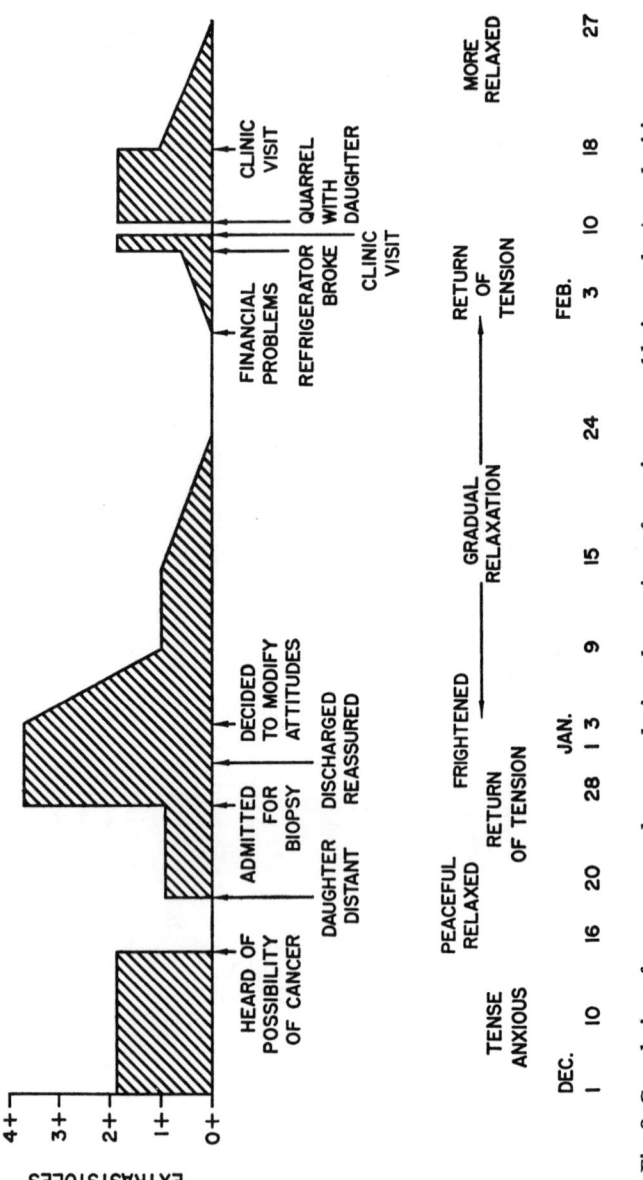

Fig. 8. Correlation of symptoms and stresses during observations of a patient at weekly intervals. At each visit symptoms, emotions, and life events were reviewed and correlated. The patient was a 45-year-old woman with advanced rheumatic heart disease, including cardiac hypertrophy and mitral stenosis. She complained of palpitations and was found to have many auricular extrasystoles. The diagram above shows the correlation between the frequency of extrasystoles and the events of the patient's life.

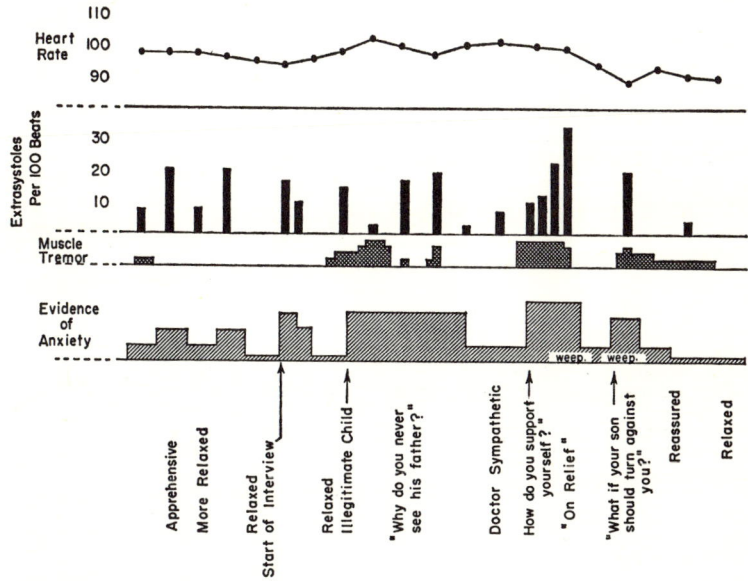

Fig. 9. Correlations of symptoms and stresses during an interview with a 55-year-old woman with arteriosclerotic heart disease. She complained of palpitations and "nervousness." She was found to have numerous ventricular extrasystoles. The top columns correlate the topics of the interview with the data of the electrocardiogram. The bottom column estimates the degree of anxiety shown by the patient in speech, facial expression, and other behavior. At two points (weep), the patient became tearful in discussing the fact that she was on relief and the possibility that her only child might leave her. The second column from the bottom estimates the patient's muscle tension during the interview as indicated on the electrocardiographic tracing. Figure 10 reproduces a section of the electrocardiogram before, during, and after discussion of the fact that the patient was on relief.

begin to talk about his work and how he feels about it. Then there may emerge correlations between what happens at work and the patient's symptom of pain. Or again the patient may say, "My wife doesn't seem to understand how much I suffer with these headaches," to which the physician may reply, "What does she think about them?" The patient will then probably begin talking about his wife's attitude to his illness. The correlation between his relations with his wife and his headaches may then become apparent.

Sometimes references to life situations in the initial history of the illness do not occur, or lead the inquiry no further. Then the physician should

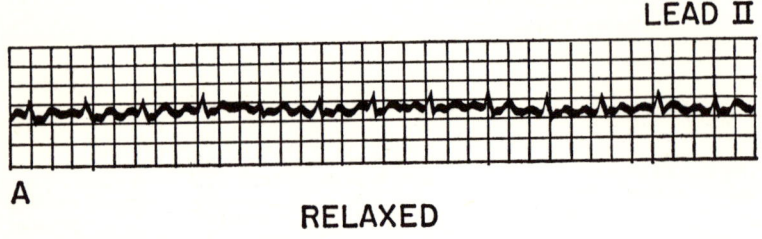

**A**

**RELAXED**

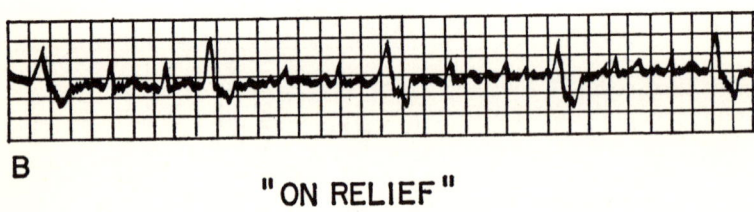

**B**

**"ON RELIEF"**

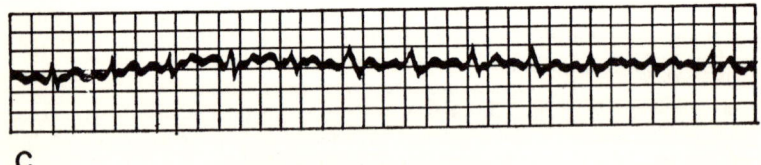

**C**

**RELAXING AGAIN**

Fig. 10. Correlations of symptoms and stresses during an interview with a 55-year-old woman with arteriosclerotic heart disease. Ventricular extrasystoles occurred during anxiety. The tracing was taken during the interview illustrated in Figure 9. The three strips shown are taken from periods before, during, and after the maximal emotional disturbance when the patient was discussing her financial difficulties. In the middle strip the evidence of muscle tension associated with the anxiety can be seen.

make more direct inquiries concerning correlations. Among suitable opening remarks for this are the following:

"Your symptoms vary a lot, don't they? What do you make of that?"
"You said your symptoms come on when you're nervous. What kinds of things make you nervous?"
"Have you noticed what's going on at the time your symptoms come on?

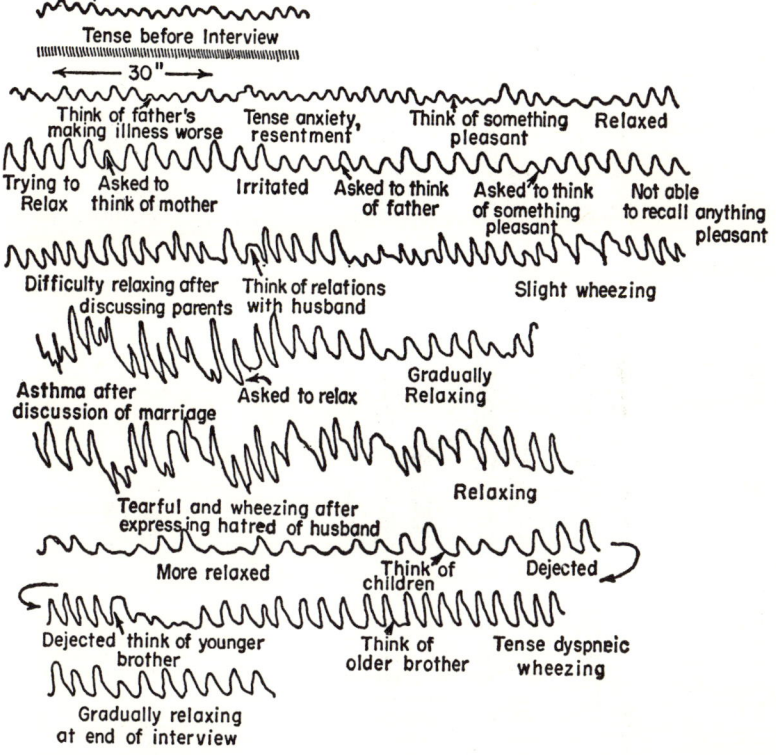

Fig. 11. Correlations of symptoms and stresses during an interview with a 35-year-old housewife with bronchial asthma. The diagram reproduces pneumographic tracings of respiration during an interview touching on some of the patient's current life stresses. Note the initial shallow, rapid breathing compared to the deeper, slower respirations at the end of the interview when the patient was relaxed. Periods of resentment and dejection were associated with changes in the rate, depth, and rhythm of breathing. On three occasions during the interview the patient showed dyspnea and wheezing during emotional disturbances.

I mean they don't just come from nowhere. Something must be happening to bring them on. What can you think of?"
"Have you noticed anything connected with the ups and downs in your condition? I mean why should your symptoms change so much?"
"Something must make your symptoms come and go. What do you think it could be?"

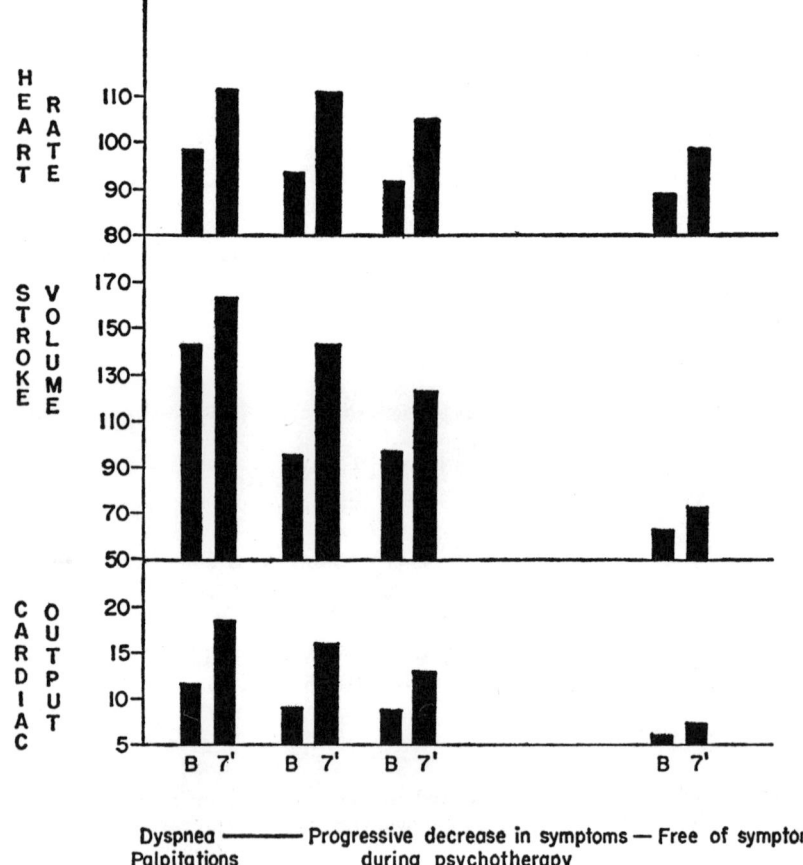

Fig. 12. Correlations of symptoms and stresses before and during psychotherapy. The patient had a patent ductus arteriosus. In addition, she experienced marked anxiety and psychophysiological cardiovascular disturbances when she was first examined. The bars give measurements of her cardiac functions before (B) and seven minutes after (7′) a standard exercise. During the course of psychotherapy her symptoms ceased and her performance during exercise improved markedly. Residual dysfunction due to structural disease persisted and is demonstrated by the delay in return to resting levels of function after the last exercise.

Many patients pick up such statements and work with the physician to find correlations. Others do not respond helpfully. They insist that changes in the symptoms do not occur or occur "spontaneously." The failure of the patient to see relationships between symptoms and stresses, even his vehement denial of such connections, should not deter the physician from further search for these. However, nothing is gained by insisting to such patients that they are overlooking or denying the stresses which must be there. After all, the physician's initial impression can be wrong and the patient may be right. The matter is better handled by a more tentative approach. The physician may say, for example, "Well, let's take a look at the different times when your symptoms have been worse and better and see if we can make any sense of it together." The physician and patient can then go into greater detail about the events reported in the history of the illness, in the past personal history, and in the review of the patient's current life situation. The material for this study should already be at hand. An adequate history of the present illness will have included whatever fluctuations have occurred in the symptoms. An adequate personal history will have included whatever has been stressful to the patient. The two histories may then be apposed, if they have not already been entered on a life history form such as that of Figures 4 and 5. When the two records are placed together, they will often be found to match as well as the two parts of a piece of paper torn down the middle. Figures 6 to 12 illustrate some other useful ways of correlating the data of symptoms and stresses in graphical forms.

Or the physician may ask the patient to give a detailed description of everything he has done in the past week. Out of this account important relationships may become apparent.

A 30-year-old housewife with severe headaches first reported that these had been constant all week. Later she modified this statement to say that there had been some changes, but she could not connect them with anything. Still later she was asked to describe the activities of the week, and the following pattern was revealed:

| *Day of Week* | *Events* | *Feelings and Symptoms* |
| --- | --- | --- |
| Saturday | Clinic visit | No headache |
| Sunday | Rested | No headache and felt fine |
| Monday | Heavy laundry and children were "bad " | Moderate headache |
| Tuesday | Nothing unusual | No headache |
| Wednesday | Husband announced he was going to races with pay check | Moderate headache |

| Day of Week | Events | Feelings and Symptoms |
|---|---|---|
| Thursday | | Worry over husband. Moderate headache. |
| Friday | Early in A.M. husband returned drunk after being away all day and night gambling. | Severe headache which started as patient opened door to let husband in. |

As the patient remembered and described the start of her most severe headache (Friday) and the circumstances surrounding its onset, she began to recognize for the first time the emotional tensions behind these headaches.

The physician should remember that the patient's failure to perceive correlations between symptoms and stresses may derive from either ignorance of what to look for or defensiveness against acknowledging the influence of stresses. These two types of patients require different management in the interviews.

The patients who do not know what to look for have simply to be taught this by the physician and instructed again at each interview until the physician becomes confident they are reporting all the data relating to possible correlations.

Patients defensive against the acknowledgement that social stresses could play a part in their illnesses usually fear the (imagined) implication that they will be considered "weak," "neurotic," or "crazy." The fear such labels arouse in them may prevent them from even making the attempt to correlate symptoms with the events in their relations with other people. The physician can often desensitize such patients by providing abundant explanations and reassurances of the significance of correlations supposing they are found. He may then gradually persuade them to join him in a study of possible connections.

The physician should collect as many instances of temporal correlations as he can. The more correlations between apparent stresses and symptoms occur, the more likely are the stresses to be significantly related to the symptoms.

### Relating Symptoms and Emotions

When correlations between apparent stresses and symptoms have emerged, a third step remains. The stresses and symptoms must be shown connected through an associated emotional state. By demonstrating the meaningfulness of the stress for the patient, such a connection confirms the relevance of the stress to the symptom. Otherwise the physician may attempt to correlate the symptoms with events in the patient's life which had little significance for the patient. The physician should try to estab-

# VARIATIONS IN INTERVIEWS 233

lish the meaningfulness of the supposed stresses to the patient by finding out whether the patient experienced some emotion at the time of the stresses and the symptoms or does experience some emotion as he talks of them in the interviews. Chapter 6 has already reviewed the various clues to the significance of different topics which the patient gives the physician in his remarks and behavior as he talks.

As already mentioned, patients may deny the occurrence of any associated emotion at the time of the symptoms. Sometimes they may not be aware of such emotions at first. The patient may not notice his emotions because his main symptoms such as headache or palpitations absorbs all his attention. Yet careful inquiries may demonstrate significant emotions at the time of the symptoms. Close questioning of the patient concerning the details of symptoms additional to the main one often reveals the symptoms of tension states, depressions, or anxiety. For example, the physician may find that a patient complaining of palpitations also suffers from insomnia, nightmares, impotence and anorexia which he has not initially mentioned. Such symptoms certainly suggest an emotional disturbance. When the physician uncovers these or other symptoms, he can try to relate their occurrence to the life stresses and the main symptom.

A patient came to a clinic with the sole complaint of severe parietal headaches. He at first insisted that these were constant and resulted from an old head injury. However, during an interview it soon became clear that he had periods free of headaches. The patient was then led to talk about his current life situation and quickly revealed difficulties with his employer and great anxiety about losing his job. Inquiries about other symptoms showed that he had been having severe nightmares which started at the time his current exacerbation began. The physician was then able to say to the patient, "It looks to me as if your headaches and your nightmares are both coming from your being upset about your job. What do you think?" The patient agreed.

In establishing temporal correlations between life stresses, emotions, and symptoms, the physician must remember some of the difficulties in making such correlations which were mentioned in Chapter 3. One additional aspect of the problem deserves notice in this place. The patient may condition himself to his own fear so that symptoms may occur in situations which would not ordinarily be stressful.

A patient had severe anxiety attacks with symptomatic emphasis on the cardiovascular system. Both his parents had died of heart disease, and he became much afraid he would follow them in the same manner. He became afraid of damaging his heart by any exertion. This fear became so strongly enforced that for some years afterwards the mild exertion of gardening would be followed by the symptoms of anxiety and exhaustion quite out of proportion to his actual physical exertion. In this case the fear of exertion had become conditioned to an activity which he consciously enjoyed, but which unconsciously reminded him of his fear of heart disease and death.

Such conditioning often interferes with a convalescent patient's return to work. The patient perhaps returns to work before he has entirely recovered from his illness and encounters some unexpected weakness or fatigue. He may then become frightened about these symptoms and conclude that the work is damaging him. The next time he tries working he may therefore have not only the symptoms of weakness and fatigue, but also the conditioned symptoms of anxiety. This simply reinforces his conviction of a disability. Such a patient can with perfect sincerity tell the physician: "I want to work, but can't because I get this weakness every time I do." Moreover, the patient may equally sincerely deny awareness of any distressing emotion at the time he tries working. He may be quite unaware of the mixture of anxiety in his symptoms or that he has conditioned himself in the manner described.

This mechanism may occur in a wide variety of other symptoms. For a further example, dietary loathings and fads can arise from a conditioned fear of certain foods starting at a time when these foods were actually distressing to the patient. During a period of gastrointestinal dysfunction the patient may find fatty or greasy foods unappetizing and even nauseous. The experience may later be reported as, "I can't eat fats." It is not to be inferred from this that all dietary avoidances have such origins, but many do.

Sometimes the physician cannot successfully demonstrate the significant emotion connecting a life stress and a symptom. This may occur when the patient cannot permit himself to admit an emotion such as fear or anger which he thinks might be discreditable to him. And it can also occur when the emotion itself is so mild or attenuated as to be little noticed. Weak emotions over a prolonged period of time may have as greatly damaging effects as strong ones sustained more briefly. An emotion may be largely neutralized in conscious experience by an opposite attitude so that the patient can genuinely deny awareness of its presence. In such instances the physician may nevertheless correlate the symptom and the stresses by noting their repeated temporal coincidence in remissions and exacerbations.

A middle-aged housewife cared devotedly for an invalid and irascible husband over many years. During this time the patient worked to support her husband and children and to educate the children. At home she also filled the role of cook and nurse. She constantly deprived herself in the interests of her family. Throughout this period of her husband's illness, she suffered from severe headaches of the muscle tension variety. It was impossible to discover in her any signs of anger at her husband or disappointment in the part which she had been called upon to play in life. However, her headaches had first occurred at the time her husband became ill. It seemed probable that they were a somatic expression of the stress she experienced, although this stress was accompanied by a diluted emotion of which she was unaware.

### Stimulating the Resistant Patient's Interest in His Emotions

As already mentioned, patients show varying resistances to talking about personal problems and revealing their feelings, emotions, and attitudes. Many patients glide readily into fuller discussion of their personal lives if the physician shows interest in these and gives the proper cues. They do not notice the transition to talking of personal difficulties, or if they do notice, they do not object or even are eager to go into such matters. However, other patients cling tenaciously to some particular topic, usually their physical symptoms, and will not talk spontaneously or willingly of anything else. In such a situation the physician should ask himself whether he has been encouraging the emphasis on this topic by his own interest in it. If, for example, the physician himself has restricted his interest in the patient to the physical symptoms, the patient can hardly be expected to talk about his psychological symptoms or life stresses.

But even when the physician is interested in hearing about personal problems and has demonstrated that interest to the patient, the patient may resist his efforts to channel the conversation appropriately towards life situations or psychological difficulties. When the physician drags the patient to these subjects, as it were, he is unable or unwilling to study them. Such a patient, for example, may reply with bland denials to direct inquiries about disturbances of feeling or mood. When asked about his goals in life, he insists that all are more than satisfied and smilingly assures the physician: "Why should I worry? I have nothing to worry about." But the physician, noting signs of emotional disturbance in the patient, may still believe there is an important connection between this disturbance and the patient's symptoms. The physician should recognize, however, that the patient cannot easily expose his psychological difficulties because they make him too anxious. Then the physician must judge to what extent the patient can be urged to acknowledge and discuss his difficulties. If he thinks the patient is ready, he may gently confront the patient with the evidence of emotional disturbance which he has observed already in the patient. For example:

PATIENT: I'm sorry, Doctor. I'm sure you're on the wrong track. I've got a good job, a fine wife, and three grand kids. I'm well fixed financially; own my own home and car. What else could a man ask for? I just don't have anything to worry about or anything I want that I don't have.

PHYSICIAN: Well, I could be wrong, of course. But you impress me as being pretty nervous about something. I mean, right now as I watch you, you seem to be rather nervous.

PATIENT: Why, what do you mean?

PHYSICIAN: Well, your face looks serious and glum, although you say you're not worried about your physical condition. And I notice you move around in bed restlessly, and your eyes keep looking around. Now, really relaxed people don't do those things. What do you think?

PATIENT: Maybe you're right at that. I know I haven't been able to sleep well at night. It's been hard to say what's bothering me. I don't think I really know. It might be . . . .

Many such patients are not so grossly anxious as the one in the above example. But many others do show some evidence of emotion as they talk, and the physician can then point this out to them to arouse their own awareness of their emotions. To give another example, if a patient blocks or hesitates the physician can say, "This subject seems to be upsetting you. I wonder why. Perhaps it's more important to you than you thought it was." More open displays of emotion, such as weeping or overt anger, make it even easier for the physician to help the patient link his symptoms to his emotions and begin talking about his feelings and attitudes. The patient may try to deny the importance of the emotion he showed by saying, "It was nothing." To this the physician should reply firmly by some such remark as, "I think it was something. People don't cry (get angry, become frightened) over nothing. and I'd be interested in hearing more about it."

Once the physician has shown the patient the possibility of connecting his symptoms and his emotions, he should encourage the patient to study himself more closely at the time of the occurrence of the symptoms. The physician should not say anything like, "I'll bet you're really angry every time you have a headache." This kind of remark seems to chide the patient, and he may have to deny that he is angry in order to preserve his own respect. But the patient cannot object to reporting either the thoughts or the feelings he notices just before or during the occurrence of the symptoms. So the physician can say to him, for example, "Well, the next time you feel like overeating, see if you can notice the thoughts that go through your mind," or "Try to watch yourself and see if you notice if you have any other feelings besides your headache the next time one comes on."

When the physician and patient have identified the relevant stresses and emotions, there remains the further task of finding out why the patient reacted to the stresses in the way he did. But in this part of the inquiry, the technique of interviewing does not differ from that needed for other patients.

## *Correlations of Thoughts and Psychophysiological Reactions*

Many physical symptoms express thoughts held by the patient. Morbid thoughts find expression more readily through the central nervous system (as in hysteria), but may also affect the organs served by the autonomic nervous system. The inquiry should explore the various ways in which ideas may have entered the mind of the patient and thereafter found physical expression. Two such ways will be mentioned.

First, the patient may have been offered direct suggestions or may have elaborated into a suggestion a remark made by someone. Examples of this kind are the remarks made by parents to children which, while inquiring about the children's activities, also suggest these to the children. For example, a parent who repeatedly tells a child, "Don't lie to me," or "Don't let men take advantage of you," may actually promote the ostensibly prohibited behavior in the child. Many patients pick up suggestions about illness from members of their families and from physicians.

Secondly, patients may acquire ideas about disease not only from what is said to them, but from what they observe in other people. A wide variety of physical symptoms ranging from constipation to convulsions and almost any behavioral trait may be imitated by a patient who has seen it once. The conditions necessary for such imitation are by no means well understood. The patients are usually more suggestible than average. They are sensitive to what other people say and do, and readily model themselves on other people. A second factor in such imitation, not a necessary condition, but a facilitating one, is a strong attachment between the patient and the person imitated. The attachment may carry devotion or resentment and guilt.

The widespread occurrence of symptoms which are suggested to the patient, or expressed by him in imitation of others, adds further importance to the family history. The physician should inquire whether other members of the patient's family (or friends) have ever had the disorder of which the patient complains. Relevant disorders need not be exactly similar to that of the patient, and the patient need not always have actually seen the sick person he imitates. Sometimes the patient's imagination may amplify or modify an illness, the original idea of which he derived from another person. The family history and the study of the patient's current life situation will also need scrutiny for the presence in the patient's arena of persons who have been offering him morbid suggestions which he has adopted.

## HYPOCHONDRIACAL PATIENTS

Hypochondriasis consists of a focusing of irrational anxiety on the body. The patient either imagines he has an illness which he does not have, or he misinterprets and exaggerates the severity of an illness he does have. The first of these conditions is rather rare: few patients complain of physical symptoms without any physical disorder whatever. The physician will rarely encounter actual delusions about the body, and if he does, he will almost certainly recognize a schizophrenic reaction or paranoid state. But the second condition, a hypochondriacal attitude toward physical (or psychological) disorders is exceedingly common. Anxiety about a physical symptom can be more disabling than the physical disorder itself.

Interviewing and examining these patients must include a thorough study of the physical symptoms. This is partly to permit the physician to dissect the layer of hypochondriacal attitudes from the layer of physical dysfunction and partly to provide the physician with sound knowledge to support his later explanations to the patient of his illness.

The first principle in interviewing such patients is to avoid giving the impression of thinking the symptoms are delusional. For the patient, everything he says about his symptoms is true. For the physician, only part of what he says is true. But if the physician's approach implies to the patient that the physician thinks the symptoms are "imaginary" or "delusional," only a useless collision of words will result.

Instead of confronting the patient with contradictions, or with what may be construed as contradictions by the patient, the physician should simply ask the patient for more details in a benevolently skeptical manner. Especially, detail should be drawn out around the question of how the patient's symptoms account for his disability. For it is this, the discrepancy between the real and the imagined disability, which is the point at issue in many cases of hypochondriasis, especially those in which problems of employment and compensation are concerned. The following example may illustrate this maneuver:

PATIENT        (*concluding his account of his symptoms*): And so I gave up working because I kept getting this fluttering in my heart.
PHYSICIAN:     What is your work?
PATIENT:       I am a bank clerk.
PHYSICIAN:     Then I don't understand how the fluttering keeps you from working.
PATIENT:       Well, I just can't work when I don't feel well. There's no telling what might happen to me.
PHYSICIAN:     What do you think might happen?
PATIENT:       I just don't know, but I know I can't work.
PHYSICIAN:     I'm afraid I haven't understood that yet. I can see you're uncomfortable when you work and these symptoms come on, but as you know, a lot of people don't feel perfectly well when they work, and I don't understand in what way your symptoms keep you from working.

In interviewing hypochondriacal patients, the physician should attempt to show fluctuations in the symptoms and correlations between the symptoms, emotions, and life stresses just as he does with patients having psychophysiological reactions. It is also helpful to explore in detail the patient's vital functioning and his functioning in areas outside the principal occasions of his complaints. For example, if a patient claims inability to work because of severe backache, a doubt is aroused about his claim if he also reports no limitation on a vigorous sexual life. Or if a patient says he is too weak to work as a store salesman, but reports engaging in comparable strenuous activity such as repairing his own automobile, further inquiries naturally follow.

Hypochondriacal attitudes are often betrayed not so much by the symptoms themselves as by the language in which they are described, the interpretations given to them, and the explanations of their origin. For example, a patient may describe discomfort in his heart as: "My heart seems to be exploding with every beat. I can't go on like this much longer. It all started because I ate those dried figs." The diagnostic information furnished by such wild explanations provides another reason for eliciting the patient's explanation of his illness which was recommended in Chapter 3.

Interviews with hypochondriacal patients should not become arrested at the level of the physical symptoms and their description. The physician should try to understand how the patient came to adopt a hypochondriacal attitude and what purpose it seems to serve for him. Several ingredients can enter into the formation of hypochondriacal attitudes, usually in varying mixtures. Some of these are the following:

1. The patient is usually preoccupied with himself and has a lessened interest in other people and events. This may be a long-standing trait or occasioned by some other illness or other stress.

2. The patient has developed an excessive fear about his physical condition, frequently based on some psychophysiological disorder. For example, hyponchondriacal states often begin with an anxiety attack or tension state accompanied by such physical symptoms as palpitations and dyspnea. The patient imagines that he has heart disease. He may then rapidly develop a fixed idea that his symptoms arise from a serious physical illness.

3. The organs which are the site of symptoms have a special meaning for the patient. Such meanings may arise from imitation of other persons, e.g., a parent who died of heart disease, or because past experiences have given them a particular significance, e.g., the nose as a source of ugliness. The sexual organs are frequently involved in hypochondriacal attitudes perhaps because the patient's preoccupation with himself inhibits normal sexual expression and results in an excessive, unrelieved frustration of sexual impulses. In other instances, the explanation may lie in previous experiences (e.g., excessive proscription of sexual curiosity and activity by parents) which have focused attention on the sexual organs. The patient then becomes abnormally sensitive to slight functional changes in these organs to which changes he adds imginatively.

4. The patient finds that illness provides him with a new status which is socially acceptable. It permits him approved dependency and he receives special attentions which would not ordinarily come to him. Many hypochondriacal patients can use their illnesses as media of communication with other people from whom they might otherwise be cut off by their self-centeredness. Thus they frequently haunt the offices of physicians and the clinics of hospitals, not expecting any relief from their symptoms, but because the symptoms bring them into contact with other people.

5. The illness removes the patient from some responsibility or other burden he would like to avoid. It is generally a mistake to believe that patients take refuge from the strife of the world in illness. But when illness comes they may find themselves unexpectedly relieved of unpleasant cares. A mother may graciously abdicate her responsibilities to her children when she becomes ill; a father may plausibly explain that he cannot work much because his condition requires him to rest a great deal. Once accustomed to the role of invalid, patients may doubt their ability in any other role; and this fear, rather than a special pleasure in being an invalid, may delay recovery. To discover the task from which an illness

may separate the patient, the physician can ask: "What would you do if you were well?" To this a hypochondriacal girl may reply: "I'd get married." This answer would suggest, although it certainly would not prove, that the girl was clinging to the illness to avoid her fears of sex and marriage.

A further complication comes when the patient believes he is completely disabled for work and eligible for compensation of one kind or another. Chapter 3 contains a further discussion of this topic under the heading of Apparent Gains Arising from the Illness.

6. The illness and its suffering assuages the patient's sense of guilt. After a severe illness patients frequently feel purged of guilt as if the illness had punished them for their crimes. In some patients the purification never finishes. It seems as if these patients cannot believe in their right to be healthy and whole. They repeatedly search for some evidence that just punishment has come to them. Often this process occurs covertly and is only uncovered with effort. It is seen in its most extreme form in patients with psychotic depressions whose guilt induces delusions about all kinds of destruction and rot in their bodies.

Hypochondriacal symptoms may totally absorb the morbid thoughts of a depressed patient so that he appears in good spirits while he has his physical symptoms and can talk about them. He may sincerely deny any abnormality of mood. When the interviewer succeeds in diverting the patient away from his recital of physical symptoms to talk of, say, a distressing situation at home, he may then be astonished to see the patient suddenly cry as depressive thoughts come to the surface.

The guilt of many hypochondriacal patients may be expressed not only in depression, but also in angry, paranoid projections. Thus the patient may insist that his illness has been inadequately treated or even maliciously caused by other people, sometimes physicians. Such charges strengthen the patient's conviction about having a physical illness and at the same time help to suppress further the guilt which the symptoms may partially express. Many paranoid reactions begin with hypochondriacal symptoms; the physician should always ask the patient for his opinion as to the causes of his condition. He should carefully ascertain the patient's attitude toward previous physicians and their treatments. The next section discusses further the interviewing of paranoid patients.

Mixtures of the foregoing motives and other factors occur much more commonly than single isolated ones. Furthermore, the patient usually knows little or nothing of the psychological origins of his symptoms. The physician cannot expect him to reveal these origins in response to direct questions. The foregoing discussion of underlying motives therefore simply provides some guidance about the topics over which the interviews with these patients should range.

The physician should remember these powerful motives underlying hypochondriacal symptoms in order to preserve his calmness when interviewing such patients. Otherwise he can become exasperated by the smile or grin on the face of the patient during the recital of apparently horrendous symptoms. He can become irritated also when he repeatedly blunts the tools of persuasion against the patient's unyielding insistence upon the explanation of the symptoms which he favors. The irrational derives its support from strongly entrenched, although often hidden motives which are inaccessible to reason. The physician may use this fact diagnostically, because when a patient fails to accept his explanations he should suspect hypochondriacal attitudes in the patient, although other factors may lead to such a rejection also.

Despite the need for a clear understanding of the patient's symptoms and of their mechanisms, the physician must not follow the patient in becoming solely occupied with the symptoms. Part of the patient would like nothing better than that they should spend all their time talking about his symptoms; nothing would be more futile. Instead the physician must try to deflect the conversation towards other aspects of the patient's living. It may at first appear that these have shrunken to an insignificant size and that the patient has no life outside his interest in his body. But this is less true than appears. References to other people and events will break through from time to time, and the physician can use them to widen the area of discussion. If the patient never refers spontaneously to other people and events, thus providing useful tangents, the physician can always ask the patient, "What does your wife (husband or whoever) think of your illness?" This at least gets someone else into the discussion. The physician can then gradually enlarge this opening and guide the patient to talk further of his current life situation and relations with other people. The gentle but persistent interest of the physician may eventually train the patient to talk of the events of his life and to express his emotions in doing so. The rewards of the physician may finally include the patient's forgetting all about his physical symptoms and talking only of his personal relationships. But this may require many interviews.

## INTERVIEWING SUSPICIOUS, DELUSIONAL, OR PARANOID PATIENTS[5, 17, 18]

When the physician interviews patients who are suspicious or paranoid, he should avoid becoming defensive or apologetic. He should not

# VARIATIONS IN INTERVIEWS 243

try to ingratiate himself with the patient or appease him. The physician should be kindly, but firm. Statements by the patient about the physician which are obviously delusional or grossly distorted should be countered with definite statements of the facts. If the physician fails to do this, the patient may incorporate the physician in his paranoid system.

When the patient presents delusions which do not include the physician, they should be handled less bluntly. The proper attitude for the physician is one of tacit skepticism. It is tacit because the physician should avoid, if he can, contradicting the patient openly; this can antagonize the patient, and may disrupt his relationship with the physician. And it is skeptical because the physician should not endorse the delusions or in any way encourage the patient in his belief in them.

Experience will bring skill to the physician in his efforts to help the patient talk about delusions without either offending the patient or appearing to endorse the delusions. The usual rules of tact apply doubly here since a careless remark can block the patient and deprive the physician of necessary information and the patient of necessary help. For example, a patient may declare that people are talking about him. The physician may be tempted to say immediately, "What makes you think they are talking about you?" But this seems to challenge the patient's assertion, and he may become annoyed. Better responses would be "Who do you think talks about you?" or "What do you think they are saying about you?" None of these responses agrees with the patient's statement. None contradict it. All simply encourage him to tell more.

Sometimes the patient may press the physician for an open statement of agreement or disagreement with him. The physician should then not avoid stating his disagreement with the patient. But he can often present this to the patient while at the same time acknowledging some element of truth in what the patient says. And he can always convey to the patient his understanding that the patient is thoroughly convinced of the truth of what he is saying. Often the patient is not so concerned with converting the physician to his exact point of view as with establishing some other crucial point such as that he is not altogether wrong, that he is not as bad as others seem to think him, or that he is not completely unreasonable and hence "crazy." Such hidden aspects of the patient's questions and remarks illustrate again the importance of attending to the anxieties lying beneath the patient's verbal remarks and questions.

The physician must reconcile himself to the irrational quality of delusions. This means that he should not expect to correct them immediately with rational explanations although, as mentioned above, he should sometimes offer these. Still less should he try to knock down the patient's delusions with contradictions, or get drawn into a wrangling argument about them. Delusions are the patient's irrational explanations for his experiences, including often his illness. They can only be removed by changing his experiences and by gradually helping him to accept alternative explanations for his experiences. This is the work of psychotherapy and not of initial interviews.

The patient may have delusions about some subjects and not about others. Or he may be correct about what has happened and delusional about why it happened or about the motives of other people involved in the event. The physician should respond appropriately to the rational aspects of the patient and avoid handling him in a manner which might be necessary for a dissociated or delirial patient.

The physician should find out as much as he can about the details of the delusions. For example, does the patient believe himself persecuted by an indefinite "they," or has he identified his enemies clearly, thus focusing his own animosity on one or more persons? The physician should also try to explore the origin of the delusions in the patient's mind. In what situation did they first occur? Are they simple imaginative elaborations of the motives of other people who have frustrated him? Or are they explanations with which he has provided himself in order to account for unusual experiences (e.g., physical sensations and symptoms) which he has had? What purpose do they seem to serve in his total psychological functioning?

In talking to a patient with paranoid attitudes, the physician should not become so absorbed in the study of the patient's anger as to forget the underlying fear which fires the anger. The physician needs to find out how the patient has come to believe himself threatened. Three psychopathological processes promote paranoid distortions. First, anxiety brings loss of perceptive discrimination so that friend and foe are confused. Secondly, the discomfort of fears associated with a sense of failure can be reduced by attributing the failure to other people. It is less painful to blame others than to accuse oneself. Thirdly, paranoid distortions are closely related to passivity. To the patient other people always have the initiative; he himself is powerless, a mere bystander. This sense of detached innocence is also motivated by the wish to avoid blame. So long as the patient does nothing, he cannot be accused of anything. And if things go wrong, which they will do, someone else is at fault. It nearly always happens, therefore, that interviews with paranoid patients eventually, (although this may take a long time), move away from the surface angers and fears of the patient and enter the topics of praise, blame and responsibility. In talking to such patients we need constantly to remind ourselves that they want to be loved like everyone else, but that they cannot love others because they cannot love themselves. We need to learn what they feel guilty about and why. And we need to learn how they have come to believe that their supplies of affection and approval are threatened, or more threatened than they really are.

## PATIENTS WHO ARE MARKEDLY SHY, WITHDRAWN, OR TENSE

Patients of this type are unable to participate spontaneously in an interview. Often they have difficulty enough in talking about their complaints, and much more in speaking about their personal lives. The physician must take the initiative in the interviews and usually keep it for a long time. He must guide the patient by questions.

Some topics are much more suitable for discussion with these patients during initial interviews than others. For example, the patient can usually be questioned about his complaints and the reason for coming to the physician. Often he can talk readily enough about his current life situation, his interests such as hobbies, and about his physical functioning. At the same time he may resist exploration of his emotions, fantasies, and thoughts about other people. The physician should not press these patients on such matters if they do not volunteer any information. Also, they are frequently stirred up too much by reviews of their past lives. These comments may seem to restrict the conversation greatly. Nevertheless, it seems best to keep such patients talking at first chiefly about their current life situations and day-to-day living. In this way they gradually come to trust the physician and eventually can offer him more of their thoughts and feelings.

Shy and withdrawn patients are usually extremely sensitive to control by other persons. At the same time their withdrawal and detachment from practical matters frequently stimulates other people, usually their parents, to supervise them and care for them to an unusual extent. The patients resent this supervision. The physician needs to avoid falling into the same pattern. He should especially avoid an appearance of aligning himself with the patient's relatives or of taking secret counsel with them about the patient. The contacts of the physician with the patient's relatives will naturally be influenced by special circumstances and some of the general principles outlined in Chapter 12. What needs emphasis here is the avoidance by the physician of anything which will interfere with the already slow development of the patient's trust in him.

The physician needs special flexibility in dealing with such patients.

To shyness many of these patients add rebellion and defiance of social customs. They may come late or break appointments. They may be surly and overtly uncooperative. With all this the physician must go along, at least for a time, until the patient has formed an attachment for the physician which will permit the scrutiny of some of these patterns of behavior. This belongs to psychotherapy, but the matter is mentioned here because the physician will never reach the point of doing psychotherapy with these patients unless he adapts himself flexibly at first to their idiosyncrasies. Chapter 11 contains some further discussion of interviewing involuntary patients.

## PATIENTS WITH SEVERE PHYSICAL ILLNESSES

It may be thought that persons with severe physical illness should not be interviewed at all beyond the requirements of obtaining a clear history of the present illness so that necessary and sometimes urgent treatment can be applied. In general, this is true; certainly patients who are seriously ill should not be exhausted by the discussion of the no longer relevant past or of fantasies or emotions which can have no possible bearing on their conditions. Nevertheless, these patients also, for several reasons, need often to have the opportunity to talk freely with a physician.

First, the physician needs especially to understand how the patient feels about his illness. Any severe illness can puzzle and confuse a patient and make him anxious or discouraged. Frequently the symptoms of the main illness mask the signs of such anxiety or despair. Several of the symptoms of anxiety and of congestive heart failure (e.g., dyspnea, tachycardia, fatigue) are similar. If he relies on visceral signs alone, the physician may have as much difficulty in telling when a patient in heart failure has anxiety as in saying when a Negro has a tan. Accordingly, the physician must watch for other signs of anxiety such as occur in the patient's words or gestures. In any case, he can assume the patient has some anxiety which needs expression and appropriate reassurance.[7]

Secondly, the seriously ill patient frequently has burdens upon his mind which he may wish to confide in someone else. He may want to talk about the past and of acts of which he feels guilty. Or he may want to discuss the future which for him may be death. There may be no one else to whom he can talk about these things except the physician. Or he may choose the physician deliberately because the physician shows a kindly interest in the patient as a person, and thereby makes himself a worthy confidant.

Thirdly, patients of this group frequently have left behind them when they enter the hospital various items of unfinished business. These may be financial or they may be more personal. But in any case the thought of such matters may weigh heavily upon the patient. Again he may have no one better than the physician to help him by talking about these problems and counseling appropriate action.

In talking to the patient about the three topics mentioned above, the physician should not think he is offering incidental services only to the patient. The emotions associated with each of these problems may add a large component to the patient's disability. And the relief provided by talking about them may be enough to turn the patient's course towards health and ultimate recovery.

## References and Suggestions for Further Reading

1. ATKIN, L.: Difficult delusions. *Lancet 1*:213, Jan. 31, 1953.
2. BACHRACH, A. J.: Notes on the psychopathology of delusions. *Psychiatry 16:* 375, 1953.
3. BALINT, M.: *The Doctor, The Patient, and the Illness.* New York, International Universities Press, 1957.
4. BIRD, B.: *Talking With Patients.* Philadelphia, J. B. Lippincott Company, 1955.
5. BOVERMAN, M.: Some notes on the psychotherapy of delusional patients. *Psychiatry 16:*139, 1953.
6. CAPLAN, H.: Some interview techniques in child psychiatry. *J. Pediat. 38:* 128, 1951.
7. CARTER, A. B.: Reassurance. *Brit. Med. J. 2:*671, Sept. 10, 1955.
8. COBB, S.: Technique of interviewing a patient with psychosomatic disorder. *Med. Clin. North America 28:*1210, 1944.
9. COLEMAN, J. V., SHORT, G. B., and HIRSCHBERG, J. C.: The intake interview as the beginning of psychiatric treatment in children's cases. *Am. J. Psychiat. 105:*183, 1948.
10. DUNBAR, F. E.: Psychosomatic history and technique of examination. *Am. J. Psychiat. 95:*1277, 1939.
11. GREENHILL, M. H.: The application of psychosomatic techniques to the general practice of medicine. *North Carolina M. J. 10:*1, 1949.
12. MENDELSON, M.: Depression: The use and meaning of the term. *Brit. J. Med. Psychol. 32:*183, 1959.
13. OLIVEN, J. F.: The suicidal risk. *New England J. Med. 245:*488, 1951.
14. POTTS, W. J.: The heart of a child. *J.A.M.A. 161:*487, 1956.
15. STENGEL, E.: *Suicide and Attempted Suicide.* Baltimore, Penguin Books, 1964.
16. STEVENSON, I., and MATTHEWS, R. A.: Detection of the dangerous paranoid patient. *Postgrad. Med. 11:*12, 1952.
17. STEVENSON, I.: *The Psychiatric Examination.* Boston, Little, Brown and Co., 1969.
18. SULLIVAN, H. S.:*The Psychiatric Interview.* New York, W. W. Norton & Co. 1954.
19. WALL, J. H.: The psychiatric problem of suicide. *Am. J. Psychiat. 101:*404, 1944.
20. WITMER, H. L. (Ed.): *Psychiatric Interviews With Children.* New York, Commonwealth Fund, 1946.

# 11

# DIFFICULTIES AND FAILURES IN INTERVIEWING

Although most medical interviews run smoothly enough, difficulties and failures can occur and may be fewer through considering their origins and appropriate management.

### THE MARKEDLY ANXIOUS PATIENT

A fear of disturbing or even harming patients has inhibited many physicians from the investigation of personal matters in their patients. Such physicians have heard that patients have become more ill, more disturbed, or even agitated and violent after talking of personal difficulties. Consequently, they hesitate to open up areas of sensitivity for fear of saying the wrong thing, or making the patient worse. The following remarks should dispel such fears.

The discussion of personal problems rarely harms patients. Patients may indeed become somewhat disturbed as they talk over events of their lives which have been fraught with emotion. But this process helps rather than injures them, even though it may distress them at the time. Moreover, the disturbance passes off quickly in most cases. Some patients do become disturbed for longer periods, but prolonged disturbances will not occur if the physician observes a few simple precautions.

Whenever trouble does ensue, it usually stems from the wrong attitude on the part of the physician rather than from the wrong words. As mentioned earlier, if the physician's feeling for the patient's suffering is right, the right words will come out. The physician who shows a kindly, considerate attitude toward the patient will rarely irritate, even when he asks for the most intimate information. He will automatically phrase his questions tactfully so as to preserve or increase the patient's self-esteem.

of this group do have psychoses and can be given other reassurances but not this particular one.

The patient's resistance may also arise in ignorance of how talking will help him. He may defensively deny that he needs any help at all. To such a patient the physician can say, "You seem to have troubles even though you may not know exactly what they are. You would not be here if everything were going well. People often get a lot of help from talking about their difficulties. Often they see better exactly what is bothering them after they have talked to someone else. I'm here to help you do that."

Sometimes the patient is markedly confused about his illness and especially perplexed and anxious over what may be done to him. Such anxiety can sometimes be reduced by the physician's stating frankly that the patient has a mental illness which requires study and treatment. The kind of study and possible treatment recommended may then be described and discussed. Such a discussion may helpfully reassure the patient, especially if his relatives have previously told him that nothing important was wrong and that he "just needed a check-up and a tonic." To have some competent person recognize the gravity of his illness and take steps to treat it may relieve the patient greatly and at the same time open gates for his emotional expression.

In confronting a psychotic patient with the fact of his mental illness, the physician should use tact with his firmness. The patient may be jolted and hurt by being told abruptly, "You are crazy and must go to a hospital." This could immediately arouse in the mind of the patient all kinds of fears of confinement in the more horrible mental hospitals. The physician can do better by saying: "You have a severe mental illness for the treatment of which you must go to Blank Hospital. We will be able to get you better much more quickly there than at your home."

If a psychotic patient says: "Am I insane?" then the physician can say something like: "Yes, in some respects you are. At least you have some insane thoughts. But that doesn't mean you are all insane, or that you can't get well. Lots of people get temporarily insane when they get drunk. They get over it and so can you. But you need to talk about the things which bother you."

A patient's belief that the physician will ally himself with the patient's family may increase the patient's reluctance to talk. Since in many such cases the family has taken the initiative in consulting the physician, he is believed *a priori* to have sided with them. Chapter 12 offers some suggestions for talking to relatives without damaging the patient's confidence in the physician, which will not be repeated here. However, with an involuntary patient, the physician must, more than ordinarily, avoid ency only becomes excessive when it interferes with treatment. Such interference more often occurs during convalescence or in minor illnesses. The physician may then need to check the patient's excessive dependency. He should usually discuss the situation with the patient. A suitable opening to such a discussion would be: "It seems to me you are expecting rather more than I can give you. This may be keeping you from doing all you can for yourself. Let's talk about it a little."

## THE INVOLUNTARY PATIENT

Sometimes physicians must interview patients who come involuntarily. Some of these patients are reluctant to participate in any part of the examinations. Others may agree to a physical examination, but are unwilling to participate in a review of their personal histories. Many such persons are children. However, some adults also meet the physician's endeavors in this area with important resistance. Some patients come to the physician only to please their families, or because their families bring them with various amounts of pressure. Such a patient may bring his body, but not a spirit of cooperation. Reluctance occurs frequently when relatives try to get an unprepared patient to see a psychiatrist, but any physician trying to explore psychological problems may encounter reluctance and lack of cooperation from patients. Yet these patients need help as much as those who come voluntarily or eagerly.

In this situation the physician should first seek to convert the patient's reluctance into interest and cooperation. He should not attempt this with zealous urging or preachments. Rather he should make a few remarks designed to counteract the usual causes of poor cooperation.

The commonest cause of poor cooperation is ignorance of the need for study of the personal history and emotions of the patient. The physician should therefore explain briefly to the patient that certain aspects of his illness are inexplicable otherwise than by reference to his thoughts and feelings, and therefore some study of these is necessary. At this point, the patient may erroneously think that the physician believes his symptoms are imaginary. He may interrupt the physician to protest that his illness is a real one. This response at least tells the physician where the patient's anxiety on this subject lies. He can then try to correct the patient's misunderstanding, perhaps giving simple explanations of psychophysiological relationships to show that the symptoms can have a psychological component of origin and still be genuinely physical in experience. Some of these patients need reassurances that an exploration of emotional disturbances does not mean they are psychotic, "insane," or "crazy." Others

If a patient starts out exceedingly tense, but as he talks gradually loosens up and even smiles or jokes a bit, he is being helped and the interview should continue. On the other hand, if the talking is accompanied by increasing restlessness, if the patient's mouth gets steadily drier and he blocks more or appears abstracted, it is wiser to direct the conversation to some neutral topic, such as the routine details of his daily living. The patient has reached his dosage limit for the day and can be seen another day for further history-taking when he is more relaxed. If such a patient is allowed to continue, he may become frightened by the anxiety or other emotions which are evoked. This may lead him to deny all the psychological aspects of his problems and to suppress and repress his feelings, rather than face such discomforts again. And this in turn will deprive him of further assistance with his psychological difficulties.

The foregoing precautions apply also to the management of another group of patients, those with psychotic reactions. Patients who are known to be psychotic, or suspected of being close to an overt psychosis, should not undergo extensive reviews of their past lives in the early interviews. At these times the physician should focus on the current situation of the patient, or on his principal complaints. The past history may later come out gradually as the patient wishes and can tolerate this. This recommendation derives from the fact that occasionally an overt psychosis has occurred in a patient already close to psychosis, after extensive personal history-taking. The emotions thus aroused exceeded the threshold of endurable tension. If the physician suspects his patient of having a latent psychosis, he should follow the suggestion made above of watching the tension of the patient during the interview. If the patient becomes more tense rather than less, the physician should divert the interview to other topics or terminate it.

When the patient is already fully psychotic but dissociated, interviewing can hardly make his condition worse. But in these cases the physician may have great difficulty in obtaining any history at all. Nevertheless, he can learn much from interviews with psychotic patients. This subject has received further discussion in a later section of this chapter.

## THE EXCESSIVELY DEPENDENT PATIENT

The physician must judge in each case whether and when he should discuss with a patient an excessive dependency upon the physician. In acute and severe illnesses patients naturally become markedly dependent on the physician. In these situations the patient's dependency on the physician often usefully increases his hopes and his cooperation. Depend-

## DIFFICULTIES AND FAILURES IN INTERVIEWING

Although nothing else outweighs the importance of the physician's attitude, some further points need remembering. A patient should never be forced to talk if he does not wish to do so. The physician's attitude in this matter may be helpfully modified if he abandons entirely the surgical concept of "probing" with respect to history-taking, and substitutes the idea of a collaborative exploration between patient and physician of everything which might bear on the patient's illness.

If the physician believes the patient unready to discuss a certain topic, he can present it to the patient tentatively. He can say, for example, "You may think this a personal question, but I was wondering if you could tell me something about so and so." An inquiry phrased in this way encourages the patient to pick up the subject, but also tells him he can decline to talk about it, if he prefers, without offending the physician.

If a patient blocks or says he finds talking too painful, the physician may encourage him gently. He may say, for example, "Of course, I know it is hard for you to talk, but that's because you're upset now, and when a person is upset he really needs to talk more than ever. For one thing, it will help me to help you if I know what's troubling you. And also, when people can talk about what's upsetting them, they feel a lot better afterwards. The fact that it upsets you to talk about these matters is a sign that you need to talk about them so as to become less upset by them and think more clearly about them."

If a patient is overtly uncooperative, or resentful rather than anxious, the physician may firmly but kindly pass the responsibility back to him by some such remark as, "We have to work together on this, you know. It's a sort of collaboration between us, and I can't help you unless you can talk to me a bit more about your difficulties (symptoms)." If after such statements the patient still refuses to talk, or seems unable to do so, the physician should withdraw gracefully, saying perhaps, "Well, I can see it's hard for you to talk, so let's leave it there. Perhaps some other time you'll feel more like it, and then we can try again."

As indicated in Chapter 10, patients who are exceedingly tense and anxious should not be engaged in much discussion about the past during the first or early interviews. With them it is better to confine one's interest at the initial interviews to the symptoms and the current life situation. If areas of past conflict are opened up, the patient's anxiety may increase beyond his endurance. On the other hand, if an anxious patient wishes to talk about a problem, he should be allowed to do so. Rarely does any harm come from a patient's talking when he wants to talk. The physician should watch the patient and try to detect whether he is becoming more relaxed or more anxious as the interview proceeds.

acting or appearing to act in the interests of someone else to the exclusion of the interests of the patient. Sometimes other people must be protected from the patient, just as he must sometimes be protected from them. But always the physician should remember and demonstrate his prime responsibility to care for the patient.

At some time during the interview with the patient, the physician should point out to the patient that although he came involuntarily, the physician considers the patient the chief recipient of his interest and his endeavors. Patient and physician should discuss together any interviews which the physician believes he should have with the patient's relatives. The reasons for these should be explained to the patient. They should be held to the minimum necessary for obtaining essential historical data and for providing the responsible relatives with explanations of the patient's disorder and recommendations for treatment. After these discussions with the relatives, the physician should avoid further interviews with the family whenever possible. Sometimes the members of the family may wish for many further unnecessary interviews. But it is unwise for the physician to undertake such interviews. He can spend his time much more profitably in working with the patient to arouse his interest in necessary treatments. Repeated interviews with members of the family in such cases may merely confirm the patient in his original mistrust of the physician.

The patient who believes that the physician will side with the family also often fears that the physician will pass on to the family whatever the patient may say. The physician should therefore assure the patient that whatever he says will be held in strict confidence. This should be a true statement and not merely verbal appeasement of the moment.

Many involuntary patients gradually become less resistant to discussing psychological symptoms and personal relationships after the above matters have been clarified. Others do not. The physician should make every effort to help the patient discuss the reasons for his reluctance. If he can get the reluctance into the open, he may be able through discussion to overcome many of the patient's doubts. Often the mere willingness of the physician to discuss the matter in a friendly way can establish his good faith with the patient.

## THE INACCESSIBLE PATIENT

Some patients are not only reluctant, but completely uncommunicative, at least in words. Some of these patients are negativistic children; others have schizophrenic reactions; and still others are severely depressed persons. Usually they receive communications much better than they send them. The physician should talk to them as if they understood what is said to them. After recovery they are often found to have understood perfectly what was said to them when they were mute. Often they will carry out simple requests or orders, but give no verbal responses. In approaching such a patient, the physician can simply say, for example, "I am Dr. A. B. Your wife has asked me to see you. You seem to be sick. It seems hard for you to talk now, but I want you to know that I am trying to help you. It certainly would help me if you could tell me a bit about yourself." If the patient shows some response to this, but also continued hesitancy, the physician can mention some of the reasons for reluctance to cooperate mentioned in the preceding section. He can then ask the patient if any of these reasons apply to him. Sometimes such patients will talk after such suggestions.

The physician should carefully note signs of response in the patient as he talks. Thus the patient may look more penetratingly, frown slightly, or relax his facial muscles at some comment of the physician. Using such cues, the physician in his own remarks may then develop further topics which seem to evoke such responses and gradually increase the patient's communication with him, passing eventually from the nonverbal to the verbal levels. All this requires great patience and kindness. The physician must expect to spend much time with such patients, often in complete silence or with the patient remaining silent. The patient's mutism indicates his severe distrust of other people and despair about the value of communicating with them. To overcome these the physician must offer a devotion even stronger than the patient's silent and fearful antagonism.

Although every patient deserves information about his next meeting with the physician, this becomes particularly important with mute patients. They may appear outwardly indifferent, but when they begin to form an attachment they will exhibit greater dependency and a greater need for the physician, and for his being reliable, than less frightened patients.

Some patients who are inaccessible for history-taking are confused from some physical (e.g., structural or toxic) interference with cerebral function. The physician should introduce and identify himself first and find out if the patient is oriented. If he is not, then the physician should orient the patient. He can say, for example, "I am Dr. A. B. You are in X. Y. hospital. This is your bed here. This is Miss Q., who will be looking after you, etc." Such orientation is often reassuring to these patients and may, by reducing their anxiety, also reduce their confusion and enable them to communicate more effectively.

Physicians and other persons should never discuss a mute, delirious, or confused patient in his presence. Such patients often give a false appearance of inattention. When they seem to be quite out of touch with their surroundings, and actually are in one sense, they can nevertheless record mentally everything that is said to them. It is not for this reason alone, however, that physicians should always treat them with courtesy and respect, which are the natural due of every person.

## HELPING THE PATIENT TO TALK ABOUT THE PHYSICIAN

Many difficulties in interviewing arise because physician and patient do not understand each other. Patients frequently misperceive the physician and irrationally assign him powers and responsibilities which he does not have. The physician should know about such distortions, and the best means of keeping himself informed lies in helping the patient to say what he thinks of the physician. Many patients will make comments about the physician spontaneously; others need encouragement or to be asked direct questions on the subject.

Patients sometimes ask questions about the physician's professional qualifications. The physician should answer these simply and briefly. Such questions are by no means always irrational. The patient has a right to know about the physician's competence to treat him, and although he may ask questions which are obscure and inept, his inquiry may be reasonable in itself.

Sometimes these inquiries are the patient's means of discovering the general type of physician he is talking to; that is, whether the physician is an internist, general practitioner, psychiatrist, or other specialist. As already mentioned, one patient may confide personal matters to a psychiatrist, but hide them from an internist on the grounds that the latter would not be interested or would not understand. Another patient may be exceedingly guarded wih a psychiatrist, fearing that this physician can pronounce him "crazy." Such a patient may speak more freely to an internist about his personal difficulties.

When the patient asks many question about the physician's qualifications, the physician should become curious about the reasons for this. As with all the patient's questions, the physician should study their intent as well as their content. Sometimes he should ask the patient about the questioning, taking care not to rebuff the patient. He can say, for example, "I notice you ask a good deal about my training and experience.

I'm sure it's important to you, but I wonder in what way?" The answers to this question vary widely. They may reveal the patient's desperate concern about whether anyone can help him, as a part of which concern he thinks that only the best physician could possibly do him any good. Or the patient may be preparing to make critical comparisons of the present physician with his former ones.

Sometimes questions about professional qualifications serve as an opening for questions of a more personal nature about the physician. Some physicians have no objection to answering a few questions about their personal lives. Often this helps the patient to think that the physician is more approachable and hence they can confide more readily in him. On the other hand, the physician may reasonably prefer not to talk about his personal life, and this is his privilege. In that case he should try to deflect the questions without irritating the patient. When a patient persists in asking many questions of a personal nature, the physician should inquire about this. He can say, for example, "I don't think it will help you to know about my personal life. Otherwise I would certainly tell you. But tell me why it interests you."

The answers to this question may in turn reveal more about the patient's attitude towards the physician. Especially likely to emerge are some of the patient's less rational expectations of the physician, such as that he should be a model citizen, a perfect husband, and a doting father. Given these attainments, the physician must then also be the magical healer whom such a patient seeks.

In addition to direct questions about the physician, the patient may make comments about the physician. Such comments are among the most valuable data the physician can obtain, and the physician should encourage them as naturally as possible. If the interviews are progressing satisfactorily, it is rarely necessary and often unwise for the physician to invite comments about himself. He does not need to undress himself psychologically, so to speak, in order to receive the blows of the patient. These will fall often enough without asking for them. Moreover, direct requests for comments may deter the patient from making any by suggesting to him that the physician is looking for praise or reassurance. What is needed in this connection is simply that the physician keep open the channels of communication with the patient, so that if the patient wishes to comment about the physician, he may do so easily. When the patient becomes seriously blocked, the physician may helpfully invite the patient to tell what thoughts about him inhibit the patient's expression.

In helping the patient to tell his thoughts about the physician, the

## DIFFICULTIES AND FAILURES IN INTERVIEWING

latter should particularly avoid any devaluing belittlement of what the patient says. For example, suppose the patient says, "Doctor, you remind me so much of my father." The physician may be tempted to reply to this with something like, "Is that so? Yes, a lot of my patients say that to me." Such a reply will surely end the discussion. A more helpful reply would be, "Really? In what way do I remind you of him?" This will assist the patient to bring out the details of his fantasy. The physician will learn whether the patient notices a resemblance in appearance, in behavior, or in some other aspect. He may then be able to judge the amount of perceptive distortion which entered into the patient's awareness of a resemblance between himself and the patient's father.

The physician should also avoid becoming defensive about anything the patient may say about him. For example, the patient may tell the physician: "I don't like your moustache." To such a comment the physician may reply testily, "Well, it suits me and I intend to wear it the way it is," or he may become apologetic and say, "Why, it's just a small moustache." Much better responses than either of these replies would be, "What don't you like about my moustache?" or "Why does it bother you?"

If the physician succeeds in permitting patients to talk about him freely, he may need to fortify himself against the candor of many patients. He can do this best by first remembering that the patient's remarks may contain elements of truth, although these elements will vary in importance and in associated distortions. But every physician can learn from his patients, and the physician's first task is to identify, and if possible correct, whatever may be reasonable in the patient's complaints. The searing heat of a psychotic patient's abuse often hurts less than the stings of almost invisible barbs thrown by less disturbed patients. This happens because one can readily shrug off a torrent of invective on the grounds that it cannot all be true. Yet the physician should strive conscientiously to profit from the remarks made about him by any patient. At such times he might remember the comment of Goëthe: "We should love our enemies, because they tell us our faults." And no patient will ever become our enemy if we can practice this maxim.

Secondly, the physician should remember the extent to which the patient's perceptions of the physician are influenced by his illness, by his previous experiences with other people, and by his previous experiences with other physicians. The reader will find a fuller discussion of these factors in Chapter 1. Here it is important to repeat that the patient may displace onto the physician some anger originally provoked by someone else, perhaps a person of the distant past of whom the physician reminds the patient.

Thirdly, the physician should attend to the anxiety which underlies angry or derogatory remarks the patient may make about him. Angry people are nearly always frightened people. Anger means that the patient believes that he is threatened. It is the physician's business to discover and often to help the patient see the real or imagined dangers which provoke the patient's anger, or other negative responses to the physician. The physician should apply the same effort to expose underlying motivations when patients heap on him unrealistic praise and adulation. Such patients may fear the physician as much as those patients who become openly angry at him. But they try to forestall his imagined wrath or derision by propitiating him in advance.

## FAILURES IN INTERVIEWING

### *The Importance of Discussing Impasses and Failures with the Patient*

Whenever an interview halts or fails altogether, or whenever the patient indicates reluctance to continue, or an intention to return no more, the physician should investigate the difficulty with the patient. When things go wrong, nothing can be done until the difficulties are understood. And to bring this understanding, nothing can substitute for a thorough discussion of these difficulties. Some useful ways of starting such a discussion are the following:

"It seems hard for you to talk to me about yourself. Can you tell me why?"

"Something seems to be holding you back. Could it have anything to do with your thoughts about me?"

"I've been wondering if the difficulty you're having in talking comes from your wondering how I'll react to what you tell me?"

"We don't seem to have made much progress. Can you tell me what we're doing wrong?"

"We're not getting along very well. What do you think is the reason?"

Patients may at first be taken aback by the frankness of these remarks. Then almost immediately they may respond with renewed interest, recognizing that the physician is sincere and that he genuinely wishes to help. When obstacles are brought into the open and discussed, they frequently melt away. After the patient has stated his objections or his anxieties, he can usually go on once again, often with more spontaneity than before.

The physician should avoid, in so far as this is possible, becoming involved in arguments or disputes with the patient. Some suggestions have already been offered for studying the patient's anger towards the physician. If the physician should happen to become angry with the patient, this too needs study. But management requires more than study. The sources of the patient's (or physician's) anger should nearly always be discussed between them. Worse things can happen than an angry exchange between physician and patient; and one of these would be a failure to discuss what the anger is about. In such a discussion the physician should certainly avoid a "calmer-than-thou" attitude which might intensify any guilt the patient may have about his behavior.

The question may arise whether physician and patient should continue to work together after getting angry with each other. Sometimes it may be wise for them to separate, especially if residual irritations which interfere with cooperation persist. However, it usually turns out that separations come only when the two cannot talk about their difficulties. When they can do so, the episode may actually enhance their attachment to each other and their ability to work together.

## *The Patient's Contributions to Failures*

The contributions of patients to failures in interviewing may arise in several sources. The involuntary and inaccessible patients superficially seem to want the interview to fail, although beneath this attitude usually lies a strong wish for help. Other patients bring a desire to cooperate, but are unable to do so. Many have serious anxieties about the purpose of the interview, or about particular questions asked or topics discussed. The anxiety aroused by the interview itself, or by parts of it, may overwhelm an otherwise strong desire to talk.

### The Patient's Fear of the Physician as a Common Cause of Failure in Interviewing

When interviews do arouse much anxiety, the patient usually fears the physician. The patient does not fear the topic discussed so much as he dreads the physician's reaction to what he will say. He thinks the physician will condemn him, or belittle him, or laugh at him. As mentioned earlier, these fears rarely arise in the attitude of the physician himself. Usually they started much earlier in experiences which the patient had with earlier significant persons in his life. At crucial times these persons did show, or seemed to show, the rejecting or destructive responses which the patient now fears. The patient has carried into later life a fear that others will treat him similarly. He looks at the present through the eyes of the past. And, as also mentioned earlier, the physician may unwittingly promote such distorted reactions in patients. Thus anything in the physician's personal appearance or behavior which suggests the persons of unhappy experiences in the patient's earlier life can reinforce the patient's negative reaction to the physician. Even the physician's social role of a somewhat authoritative person may stimulate responses provoked earlier by tyrannical, authoritarian parents. The physician should notice these irrational attitudes of patients towards him. When an interview becomes sluggish or fails, the physician should ask himself whether the patient has confused him with some other person. And if he will think to himself, "What are my patient's thoughts about me?" he may then be able to modify his own attitude somewhat so as to reduce the patient's fear and encourage his expression.

### The Patient's Fear of His Own Emotions

Sometimes interviews fail because the patient becomes alarmed at the emotions evoked by discussing personal problems. For example, in discussing some important relative, the patient may experience a welling up of resentment of which he had been previously unaware. Its sudden appearance when the patient imagined himself to have sheltered only the most loving thoughts about that person can frighten the patient. Patients are sometimes afraid of experiencing other strong emotions also. Patients who fear the strength of their emotions often equate emotional expression with loss of control. And loss of control for them may imply "insanity." They may prefer to avoid all discussion of emotionally charged topics rather than face revelations of strong, unpleasant, and seemingly uncontrollable feelings in themselves.

### The Patient's Fear of Examining Himself

Somewhat similarly, some patients may dislike all investigation of their personal histories because of implications that they will be revealed as weak, inadequate, lacking in self-control, or having other undesirable traits. Such patients are not afraid of their emotions as such. They simply have little self-esteem and what they do have is supported by defenses against examination of themselves. Although such an examination should also bring out their assets, they expect that it would expose only their weaknesses.

### The Patient's Fear That the Information He Gives May Reach Others

As mentioned earlier, the physician should not allow anything the patient confides in him to reach other unauthorized people. Yet, even if the physician is as conscientious in this respect as he should be, the patient may still have doubts about the physician's ability to keep information confidential. Such doubts may inhibit the patient from speaking freely. This situation arises sometimes in small towns where many physicians know most of their patients through business or social occasions. Such relationships can help the physician by adding to his knowledge of the patient. In such a setting the physician can acquire almost without effort many of the detailed data needed for the practice of comprehensive medicine. The physician must use this information discreetly, however, and must scrupulously keep to himself whatever his patients impart to him in private. When a physician cannot fulfill this requirement, his patients will naturally prefer to take their illnesses and confidences to another physician in another town.

## The Physician's Contributions to Failures in Interviewing

As mentioned earlier, the contributions of physicians to failures in interviewing arise more often from defects in attitude than from technical blunders. Patients forgive most mistakes made by physicians, except lack of interest and lack of kindness. They do not even object if the physician does not understand them; they value more highly his effort to understand them. Any physician who makes this effort wholeheartedly will not contribute much to the failure of an interview. Nevertheless, it may be helpful to remind the reader of four common errors of physicians. All are committed unintentionally, but all can be interpreted adversely by the patient and interfere with the interviews or ruin them.

### Failure To Communicate Interest and Warmth Adequately to the Patient

Physicians frequently have much more interest in their patients than the latter know about. Failure to communicate interest is a special, if paradoxical, hazard of interviews focused on psychological difficulties. In the interests of staying out of the patient's way so that the patient can say what he wants to say, the physician may say so little as to give the impression to the patient that he is mute. Young psychiatrists especially may misapply to initial interviews what they have learned as one technique of psychotherapy. Whatever the merits for certain kinds of psychotherapy of saying little or nothing to the patient, this behavior makes no sense to patients who have become used to the sharp questions and freely flowing comments of other physicians. Certainly when the patient has been maneuvered onto the ground of his psychological difficulties, the physician should say only enough to encourage and covertly guide him. But the average general medical patient only reaches that position after some time and effort on the part of both physician and patient. Such a patient, in the initial interview with the physician, needs more than the grunts and grimaces of the physician to sustain his conviction that the physician is someone worth talking to. The physician must move out towards the patient, actively seeking to enter and understand the world of the patient. How and when he should show his interest are matters to be learned by experience and influenced by the needs of the patient before him. But he will be less likely to hinder the interviews by showing his interest too much than by hiding it too much.

### Failure To Inform the Patient about What the Physician is Doing

The physician needs to remember that the patient is usually confused and anxious about his condition. He is also intensely interested in it and in what the physician is doing for him. But if the physician fails to explain what he is doing and to carry the patient along with him, then the patient's confusion and anxiety may mount to the point where he will prefer and seek another physician. This does not mean that the physician should tell the patient what he has in mind for every question he asks. Patients will go along if they understand the general direction in which the physician is moving. But they must not be asked to submit to procedures or treatments for which they have had no reasonable explanations. The physician must watch for signs of confusion, hesitancy or doubt in the words, face, or manner of the patient. These should then be inquired about and the necessary explanations offered.

### Failure To Uncover the Patient's Hidden Anxieties

Patients frequently break off interviews because they have not been able to tell the physician something they wanted to tell him. It may seem harsh to attribute this failure to the physician and certainly he is not entirely responsible. Nevertheless, the physician should remember that what the patient talks about most easily is not necessarily his greatest burden. The physician must often help the patient to go through one layer of anxiety after another until he can confide everything which troubles him. If the physician fails to facilitate the patient's revelations, the patient may become impatient or decide (quite erroneously) that the physician lacks interest in him.

### Too Rapid Exposure of the Patient's Psychological Difficulties and Emotions

The physician should remember that he can interfere with his interviews through an error the exact opposite of the one just discussed.

He can plunge the patient too rapidly into the discussion of personal difficulties. This can occur when such personal difficulties are irrelevant to the main disorder and also when the patient cannot tolerate the accompanying exposure of emotions and inadequacies.

That first things should come first has been a frequent theme of this book and the advice of all experienced physicians. A patient's gastric hemorrhage may have started the day after a competitor was promoted ahead of him at work. But the patient naturally wishes his hemorrhage stopped before he discusses such matters. Premature entrance into such topics may simply alienate the patient from their serious study later. Yet many patients with severe physical illnesses do wish to talk about personal matters and many are more accessible to the physician's inquiries at such times. Later when the emergency has passed they may again deny what they clearly saw for a day or two and become reluctant to discuss these things. Thus the physician must put out verbal skirmishers, as it were, and carefully estimate the most propitious time, neither too soon nor too late, for broaching the patient's psychological difficulties.

What we can confide to someone else depends greatly upon our assurance of trust in that other person, including the conviction that he will not use what we say to hurt us. A patient will usually only show anger or describe events about which he feels guilty when he thinks these revelations will not influence the physician's opinion of him. In the early interviews he often cannot know this. The physician can lead the conversation too hastily into areas where the patient will be forced to show feelings which he would rather have concealed. At the time all may seem to go well. But following the interview the patient may have a reaction to his confession. He may decide he has told the physician too much, that he has shown the physician his weaknesses and that the physician cannot possibly continue to like him. Or he may resent the fact that the physician has squeezed out of him, so he thinks, precious secrets he never told anyone before. For the patient the only solution may seem to lie in not seeing the physician any more. Experience will teach the physician to estimate how much to let the patient reveal of himself at each interview. Thus he will often be able to avoid these reactions. And when one does occur, he should discuss it with the patient.

# 12

# INTERVIEWING MEMBERS OF THE PATIENT'S FAMILY

## TALKING TO RELATIVES ABOUT THE HISTORY

### Reasons for Interviewing Relatives

Whenever possible, the physician should interview one or more members of the patient's family. Such interviews furnish valuable historical material, and they can also enlist the aid of the family in the treatment of the patient. Most physicians today interview members of the families of children and patients who are psychotic. Such patients can rarely furnish a coherent account of their difficulties or recount accurately the history of their earlier lives. For this information the physician must depend almost entirely upon relatives. Because adult patients who are not psychotic can give a history which is superficially consistent and plausible, the physician often goes no further in his search for historical data. Yet in a different and more subtle way, the histories given by patients with other illnesses may contain as much distortion as those given by psychotic patients. One can easily prove this by interviewing systematically the spouses of a group of patients, obtaining from each couple two accounts of the experiences which they have shared. Sometimes the stories differ so much that the interviewer cannot believe the two informants have actually described the same events. And the considerable distortion concerning events of the relatively recent past is often far exceeded in the reports of more remote occurrences. A few experiences of this kind will convince the physician of the value of interviewing relatives.

Probably relatives help the physician most with the psychological side of the history. They can also often furnish valuable data about the physical aspects of an illness. Thus a spouse may have a much clearer memory than the patient of the time of the first occurrence of the symptoms, or of the circumstances surrounding their occurrence. A relative often observes a connection between a patient's symptoms and some external event, e.g., eating, exercise, or a social event, which the patient himself may overlook. Moreover, relatives can often furnish a more accurate account of the disability arising from a symptom than can the patient himself. A patient may minimize or exaggerate his disability to a physician, but he can hardly continue such distortions for long in the presence of those who know him intimately. Consequently, if the physician suspects that the disability exceeds or falls short of what the patient states it to be, he can often obtain further helpful information on this point from the patient's family.

The information furnished by relatives can help especially in identifying previous illnesses of the patient. The patient himself may remember little about such illnesses for a number of reasons. He may have been a child at the time. He may have had a psychotic reaction for which memories are usually extremely poor. Or he may have experienced some shame concerning the illness, and for that reason have repressed or concealed its memory. What the patient may pass off casually as a "slight nervous breakdown," the family may reveal to have been an illness lasting six months, in which the patient was mute and had to be fed by hand. Or "a couple of bouts of fever as a child" may be shown to have been a series of episodes of acute rheumatic fever.

In addition to the historical details of the patient's past life, about which his memory may be vague or lacking, relatives can furnish a descriptive portrait of the pre-morbid functioning of the patient. In the first states of illness abnormality is suggested not so much by a deviation from an average for all people as by a deviation from what is usual for the patient under study. The family, therefore, draws for the physician a base-line, as it were, of the patient's functioning. From this the physician can measure deviations of pathological significance.

## *Preparing the Patient for the Physician's Interviews with Relatives*

When the physician talks to relatives of patients, several precautions will help him to avoid interfering with the objective of helping the patient.

The physician should always consult the patient before he interviews a relative. This applies whether the physician initiates the interview with the relative or whether the relative requests an appointment. In the latter circumstance especially, an interview should rarely be held without the patient's consent.

In proposing an interview with a relative, the physician will find it helpful to emphasize the use of this interview for obtaining more information about the patient. This may prevent the patient from thinking that the physician is going to blast his family on his behalf. And it will also prevent the invited relative from concluding that he is going to be chided by the physician for his behavior towards the patient. The subject can be introduced by some such statement as, "I think it would be helpful for me to talk to your wife (father, or whomever). It may be that she has noticed some things about your illness that you have missed, and I think what she can tell me will help me to help you more. Is it all right with you if I see her?" If the patient demurs, he may need some additional reassurance about the confidential nature of what he has told the physician. The latter can say, for example, "Of course, I don't need to tell her any of the things you have told me, unless you wish me to. I merely want to find out whether she can add anything to the information we already have."

Frequently relatives who request appointments with the physician are more bent on seeking information than on giving it. If the patient does not wish the physician to interview members of his family, he should not do so in most cases. Exceptions occur when the patient cannot communicate at all, for example, when he is comatose or delirious. Exceptions also often occur in the cases of young children or psychotic patients. In such cases, the physician needs one or two interviews with members of the family in order to obtain a preliminary history. If he failed to obtain such information, he might miss crucial data. But with this accomplished, the physician should usually respect the wishes of even children and psychotic patients in this matter. The patient must believe that his remarks do not reach beyond the physician and they should not. Otherwise he cannot speak freely. The physician should not rely on his simply reassuring the patient that he holds what the patient has said confidential. He should not talk further to the relatives unless the arrangements for treatment or the treatment itself requires this. If the patient watches repeated interviews between the physician and his relatives, he will probably doubt the physician's ability to withstand the urgings of his relatives who may press the physician for confidential information about the patient. A real or imagined violation of the patient's confidence may irreversibly damage the trust of the patient in the physician and make treatment by the physician impossible. This is a risk not worth taking.

The foregoing remarks should not deter the physician from discussing with relatives the general nature of the illness, the strategy of treatment, and the necessary practical, including financial, details of the patient's treatment. Clearly the persons responsible for the patient are entitled to a full discussion of these matters. But they can have this without revelations of the contents of the physician's interviews with the patient. A later section of this chapter will consider how much to tell relatives about the patient's illness.

*How To Interview Relatives*

When the physician has requested the interview, he should understand that the request may puzzle the relative. The latter may not understand how his information can help the physician. Or he may think erroneously that the physician will blame him for the patient's illness. Therefore, early in the interview the physician should put the relative at ease by explaining to him the purpose of the interview. This will bring much greater cooperation from the informant. A suitable introductory statement would be: "I asked you to come in because I thought you could help me understand your husband's illness better. Will you tell me all you know about it and what you think about it?"

When the relative has requested the interview, the physician should discover, if he can, the motives behind the request. Many times close relatives like husbands and wives request an interview to give or receive necessary information. But less rational and constructive motives may also underlie a request for an interview. Requests for interviews may also come from relatives who have little to do with the patient. The physician need not feel obliged to see these people. On the other hand, he should do so if he can spare the time, because he can thereby learn more about the patient's relations with other people and their attitudes towards him.

If the physician requests an interview or agrees to one, he should hear the relative to the finish if possible. The relative, like the patient himself, will only talk freely if he experiences the physician's unhurried attention. Often relatives, again like patients, speak under pressure and ventilate matters of great feeling and importance to them. The physician should not cut them off abruptly. His loyalty to the patient need not prevent him from helping a relative to unburden himself of a few anxieties. Moreover, if a relative assumes the role of informant, often a painful one, he should receive whatever information and reassurances about the illness the physician can transmit without sacrificing the confidence of the patient. Often the physician can offer sufficient of both to make the relative an important ally in future treatment.

Nevertheless, the physician should try to confine interviews with relatives to matters which will help the patient. This rule prevents any relative from taking over the interviews for discussion of his own problems to the complete exclusion of those of the principal patient. It precludes a long series of interviews of any kind as a result of which the patient may come to believe, perhaps quite incorrectly, that he is no longer the center of the physician's interest. (Such a series of interviews is natural if the relative himself becomes a patient of the physician, but this change should then be explained to the first patient). And finally, it precludes the use of the interview by the relative for efforts to have the physician influence the patient along lines laid down by the relative.

In interviewing a relative, the physician should evaluate the reliability of his informant. In this connection, he should notice the informant's memory. Does the informant show difficulty in recalling names, places and dates? Is he aware of his liability to error, or completely assured about his statements of the past? A humble recognition of the imperfections of memory often indicates greater reliability than the appearance or assertion of a perfect memory.

The physician should also note the attitude shown by the relative towards the patient. The attitudes shown by relatives towards patients vary as much as the attitudes shown by patients themselves. A few of the commoner attitudes of relatives deserve brief mention.

Relatives frequently become defensive when asked to discuss the personal affairs of the patient's family. They may consider mental illness a stigma on the family and hence fear a revelation of mental illness in the patient or the family. So if the illness is primarily psychological, or if the relatives suspect the physician tends to view it as primarily psychological, they may protectively conceal facts which would lead to such a conclusion.

Relatives also frequently feel guilty towards the patient. If they accept the fact of psychological factors in the illness they will usually know that environmental stresses contribute to psychological disorders. Consequently, their guilt can lead them to see and depict the patient as a faultless paragon. The physician may have to listen quietly while the relatives canonize the patient. They do this more often in the early phases of the examination when medical help is first being sought. A little later in the course of the illness, much more rarely at the start, solicitude often yields to indignation at the patient. The patient is then often seen as "not trying to get well," needing to pull himself together," or "just lacking in will power."

Of no less importance than the attitude which the relatives take up towards the patient's illness is the patient's response to that attitude. The physician needs to know what the patient thinks about what his family thinks about his illness.

The physician should also notice whether the family of the patient promotes or endorses his behavior or his symptoms. It frequently happens that parents will covertly (more rarely openly), encourage antisocial behavior or psychophysiological reactions in their children. In these instances the children are, in effect, expressing the impulses of the involved parents. Sometimes wives or husbands may similarly encourage the symptoms of their spouses because these symptoms vicariously express their own wishes and needs. People rarely mature more than they must. When immaturity persists in the patient, one can nearly always find one or more relatives who find the patient's behavior suitable to their own needs.

In subsequent interviews with the patient, following an interview with a relative, the physician may be tempted to expose what he has learned about the patient from the other informant. This temptation he should usually resist. To yield may give the patient the impression that the physician does not trust him as an informant, and one does not trust those who show distrust. The physician may, however, use the data furnished by the other informant to lead the conversation with the patient towards important topics about which he would like to hear the patient talk further. Exceptions to the foregoing rule may occur when the physician's recommendations for the patient, e.g., hospitalization, hinge upon data furnished by the relatives but withheld by the patient. The patient may conceal some serious symptom such as an act of violence. The physician may then find it necessary to tell the patient what he has learned from the relatives. The patient would otherwise find it difficult to understand why the physician makes a particular recommendation (e.g., for hospitalization) rather than another one. Sometimes also the physician can mention important stresses in the patient's life about which he has heard from others but which the patient himself has not mentioned. He might say, for example, "In asking your wife about things which might have troubled you, she mentioned severe financial difficulties. You haven't told me about these yourself and I wonder why not? Perhaps you can tell me about these now."

## TALKING TO RELATIVES ABOUT THE EXAMINATIONS AND TREATMENT

Most adult patients can readily understand the explanations of the physician and carry out his recommendations. In some instances, however, the nature of the patient's illness, the patient's attitude towards the illness, or an obstructive attitude on the part of his relatives prompts the physician to offer explanations to the relatives also. When to do this requires judgment of individual circumstances. The physician should not demote a responsible adult patient to the status of a child. To do so will certainly alienate the patient. On the other hand, he cannot allow an irresponsible patient to destroy his treatment when enlisting the aid of relatives might save it. Similarly, if interference comes not from the patient, but from his relatives, the physician needs to reach them.

Temptations may arise, especially if the physician is busy, to exclude significant relatives from information about the patient's illness. The physician may try to justify this on the grounds that the relatives take up a great deal of time, that they meddle, or that he does not need their assistance. The first two objections may often be valid, but the third is not. Relatives can influence treatment markedly. Their alliance may sustain the treatment when the patient himself shows reluctance or lack of cooperation. And their resistance may sabotage an otherwise effective program of treatment. Altogether apart from considerations of courtesy, since any illness concerns those around the sick person, the physician contributes greatly to the treatment of the patient when he enlists the cooperation of relatives. And this requires offering them some explanations of the illness.

It is no contradiction of the above for the physician to choose which relatives he will talk to. In general, he should select those who are closest to the patient by ties of affection, blood, and responsibility. He should not feel obliged to enter into a discussion of the patient's illness with any relative whose curiosity moves him to make inquiries.

As in interviewing relatives for history-taking, the physician should ask the patient's permission before talking to relatives about the diagnosis and formulation of the illness. Exceptions to this rule may occur when the patient is a child, or is delirious, comatose, or pyschotic, but rarely otherwise. Physicians may think that patients do not mind having their physical illnesses discussed with relatives even if they recognize objections to the discussion of mental symptoms. But patients can be as sensitive about physical ills as they are about emotional disturbances. Asking the patient's permission is an act of courtesy which the physician himself would greatly appreciate if he were a patient.

The patient should know with whom the physician discusses his illness. Sometimes relatives call the physician on the telephone to make secret inquiries about the patient's illness. In this situation, the physician should first decide whether a discussion of the patient's illness with this particular person would help. If he thinks so, then he should next tell the

## INTERVIEWING MEMBERS OF THE PATIENT'S FAMILY 271

relative that he will gladly talk to him provided he first obtains the consent of the patient. When the relative is genuinely interested in helping the patient, he will usually agree to this. When he is merely serving his own interests, he usually protests angrily at the physician's lack of confidence in him. To this the physician can best reply by asking the relative in a kindly manner how he would like the matter handled if he were the patient.

The physician must consider the reliability of the relative to whom he talks. Some relatives cannot keep any information to themselves and soon find means of passing everything they are told along to the patient. The physician cannot always distinguish these persons in advance from other, more discreet ones. Consequently he should rarely tell relatives anything which he does not tell the patient himself. Exceptions to this may occur with illnesses having grave prognoses such as carcinoma.

Relatives can readily distort the information they receive from the physician. Consequently the physician should not rely upon the relatives to communicate explanations or instructions for treatment to the patient. Their efforts may sometimes supplement, but should never replace the physician's explanations directly to the patient. Sometimes such supplementation may help to reduce a suspicious patient's belief that the physician has withheld sinister information from him. Thus if a doubting patient hears from a relative, who has talked with the physician, an account of his illness which differs in no important feature from what the physician told the patient directly, he may finally believe the physician was telling the truth.

Sometimes the physician can reduce apparent contradictions between what he tells the patient and what he tells the relatives by giving his explanations to all at the same time. There will be times, although these should be few, when the physician will want to say some things to the relatives which he cannot say to the patient; and the reverse may occur much more often. But in some other instances, he can save himself time and trouble by talking to all concerned at once.

The chief value of talking to relatives almost certainly lies not in their acquiring deep understanding of the patient's illness, but in their coming to have confidence in the physician. The relatives of the patient, like the patient himself, usually have a fantasy of the physician before they meet him. Into this fantasy enter a mixture of past experiences with other people and other physicians, and also an assortment of rational and irrational wishes and fears. Such mixtures solidify often into a stereotype of physicians bearing little resemblance to any one physician. The various myths depict physicians as inhumane scientists experimenting on human "guinea pigs," as omnipotent philanthropists, as meddlesome trouble-makers, and as countless other types. Such fantasies thrive in the absence of corrective perceptions. But when the person carrying some such fantasy actually meets a physician in person, the fantasy becomes weakened, if not abolished entirely. So even five or ten minutes with significant relatives may suffice to correct major distortions about the physician. Even when the physician has said little to the relative in words, the relative may go away thinking or saying, "Why, he's really an agreeable person. I expected someone quite different." The physician should certainly make no special effort to impress relatives with his skill, benignity or other desirable attributes. An impression of these should arise naturally from his having them, not from his pretending to have them.

If the physician remembers the foregoing, he may be less disappointed over his frequent failures to educate relatives about a patient's illness or persuade them to adopt a more rational approach to it. Physicians who have reconciled themselves to dealing with the irrational in their patients often become exasperated when they meet irrational behavior in the patient's relatives. This inconsistency often suggests that the physician identifies himself with his patients against the families. At any rate, the physician can reduce his impatience with relatives by reducing his expectations of them. Often he must be content if they merely endorse him and do not actively interfere with the treatment. And he can attain these essentials by spending some of his time with them.

The physician should resist efforts on the part of relatives to make him a special communicator or influencer for them. Thus he should not undertake to tell the patient what to do upon the instructions of the relatives. On the other hand, he may helpfully interpret the patient's interests and attitudes to the relatives, if the patient is unable to do so. At the same time he should encourage the patient to explain himself to his family.

The physician should always avoid a conspiratorial atmosphere in which he seems to align himself combatively with the patient against the relatives, or with the relatives against the patient. To be "on the patient's side," which has been a frequent recommendation of this book, means to be against the patient's illness, not against his family.

Some of the foregoing suggestions are illustrated in the following portion of an interview with a patient:

PHYSICIAN  *(at the end of his explanations to the patients)*: Now I think it would be helpful for me to talk also with your wife.

| | |
|---|---|
| PATIENT: | Why do you need to see her? |
| PHYSICIAN: | I think I can explain to her the things I have told you, and this will help her understand better what we are trying to do. |
| PATIENT: | But I don't want her to know all the things I've told you. |
| PHYSICIAN: | She won't. I don't intend to tell her anything of what you have told me. All I want to do is try to explain to her how I understand your illness and how I think she can help you get well. |
| PATIENT: | Oh, I see. Well, in that case, it sounds like a good idea. |
| PHYSICIAN: | Is there anything you would like me to tell her? |
| PATIENT: | You'd better tell her how long this will take and how much it's all going to cost. |
| PHYSICIAN: | I don't understand. I'll be glad to discuss that with her, but can you tell me why you can't tell her yourself? |
| PATIENT | (*becoming anxious*): Oh, I don't know. It's just that we never have been able to talk about money. She pays all the bills. It works better that way. |
| PHYSICIAN: | Well, I'll go into it with her, but it sounds like something important which we ought to talk about more ourselves. |

In this exchange the physician has prepared the way for an interview with the patient's wife, reassured the patient about the confidential nature of what he has said, and uncovered another important source of the patient's anxiety.

Sometimes the relatives of patients present obstacles to the treatment of the patient which the physician has not time to handle himself. He may need to refer the relatives to other persons for the help they need. However, he himself should always interview the responsible relatives of each patient first, to survey their attitudes and determine what further needs to be done. After this, he may refer the relatives of some patients to social workers or other physicians for counseling or psychotherapy. The physician should not call upon a social worker to give initial explanations of the patient's illness to the relatives, or to interview the relatives before he himself has done so.

# INDEX

Acceptance of patient, by physician, 16–18
Accidents, history of, 92
Activity, minimal, in the interview, 172–174
Adjustments to new situations, as stress factor, 60
Adolescence, history of, 99
Adulthood, history of, 100–102
Age relationships of family members, 84
Alcohol, use of, 67
Anger towards physician, 17, 258–259
Anorexia, symptom of, 49
Anxiety of patient,
   about illness, 68
   failure to uncover, 262
   interview methods for, 220–221
      markedly anxious patient, 248–249
   physiological components of, 10
   reduction of, 25–26, 177–178, 203–212
      direct questions, 210–212
      disguised questions, 203–205
      indirection in questioning, 206–210
      rapid questions, 212
      tact in questioning, 205–206
   special fears, 31
   symptoms of, 49–51
Anxiety of physician, 13, 182
Arranging of interviews, 22–24
Aspirations and goals, 112
   frustrated, 119
Association of items, importance of, 122–123
Attachments, development of, 7, 10, 250–251
   excessive, 12
   insufficient, 12–13
Attitudes,
   of patient, 5, 12, 88, 111, 256–258
   See also Personal history
   of physician, 13–21, 248

Attitudes (continued)
   of relatives, 23, 94, 253, 268, 271
Authority of physician, 7–8

Bacteria, as stress factor, 60
Beginning of interview, 24–26
   in later interviews, 33–34
Behavior of physician toward patient, 9
Bowel functions, and sphincter training, 96
   as symptoms, 52
Breathing difficulties, as symptoms, 52

Characteristics,
   of patient. See Personal history
   of physician, 8, 15–21
   of relatives, 152–155
Chart, chronological, 164–165
Chief Complaint, 41–42
Children, interviewing of, 219–220
Chronological chart, 164–165
Cigarettes, use of, 67
Clarification of terms, 139–141, 213
Coffee, use of, 67
Communication,
   of emotion, encouraging of, 124, 181–187, 199–203
   of experiences, limitations in, 116–117
   See also Difficulties in interviewing
Community affiliations of patient, 105
Compensation for disability, 69
Conditioning experiences of patients. See Personal history
Consciousness, loss of 53–54
Constipation, as symptom, 52
Cough, as symptom, 52
Cultural influences on illness, 77, 81–82
Current life situation of patient, 103–108
   how to take history of, 167–170

275

Dates, use of, 161–163
Death of relatives, 60, 84
Delusional patients, 242–245
Dependency of patient upon physician, 7, 10, 12–13, 250–251
Depressed patients, 215–219
Diarrhea, as symptom, 52
Dietary factors. *See* Eating
Difficulties in interviewing, 248–263
  attitude of patient toward physician, 12–13, 255–258
  excessively dependent patient, 250–251
  inaccessible patient, 253–255
  involuntary patient, 251–253
  markedly anxious patient, 248–250
Direct questions, 118, 198
  reducing anxiety, 210–212
Disability from symptoms, 46
  anxiety about, 68
  compensation for, 69
Documentation, adequate, 163–166
Dreams, 123
  *See also* Sleep patterns
Drugs taken by patients, 47, 72–73, 147–148
Duration, of interviews, 28–30
  of physician-patient relationship, 10–11
Dyspnea, as symptom, 52

Ear symptoms, 65
Eating, and diet habits of patient, 58
  enjoyment of, 66, 109
  in infancy, 95
  nutritional deficiency, 67
  stressful, 59
  symptom of anorexia, 49
Economic status and security of patient, 80–81, 107–108
Emotions of patient, 111, 123–126
  correlations with symptoms, 60–62, 128, 221–237
  direct questions about, 118, 198,
  encouraging expression of, 181–187, 199–203
  fear of, 260
  muscular activity expressing, 125–126
  thought content of, 127–132
  to rapid exposure of, 262–263
  verbalized indications of, 124
  visceral activity expressing, 126
  vocal changes indicating, 125
  *See also* Psychological aspects of illness
Empathy of physician, 18–19
  failure to communicate, 261
Employment history, 101–102, 106–107

Ending of interview, 30–33
Endocrine changes, history of, 65
Environmental changes, stressful, 59–60, 76
Evasiveness in patient, 212
Exercise,
  enjoyment of, 109
  stressful, 59
Expression. *See* Communication
Eye changes, history of, 65

Failures in interviewing, 258–263
  discussion of, 258–259
  fears of patients, 259–261
  patient's contributions to, 259–261
  physician's contributions to, 261–263
Family history, 75–86
  age relationships of members, 84
  attitudes towards family, 5–6, 101, 155–156
  biologic family, 79
  economic background, 80–82, 107–108
  how to take, 149–156
  individual members, 78–80
  interviews with relatives. *See* How to interview relatives
  loss of supportive relationships, 60, 84–85
  parents, attitudes of, 94, 96
  psychological characteristics of relatives, 152–155
  racial and cultural origins, 77, 81
  religion, 82, 112
  social family, 79
  social habits and values, 80, 82, 85, 106
  structure of family, 82–85
  topics for, 78–86
  value of, 75–78
Family tree, 82–84, 150
Fantasies,
  of patient, 9, 12
  of relatives, 271–272
Fatigue, history of, 57
Fears of patients, 259–261
Feeding, in infancy, 94–95
  *See also* Eating
Flexibility of physician, 19–21
Fluctuations in symptoms, 222–223
Frequency of interviews, 28–30
Friendliness of physician, 18–19
  failure to communicate, 261
Frustrated goals and aspiration, 119
Functions, review of, 63–67, 145–148

# INDEX

Gains from illness, 69–71, 240–241
Gastrointestinal symptoms, 65
Generalizations of physicians and patients, 6
Goals and aspirations, 112
 frustrated, 119
Group affiliations of patient, 101, 105
Growth changes, stressful, 39
Guiding of interviews, 189–213
 *See also* How to guide interviews
Guilt and shame feelings of patient, 71 217
 hypochondriacal patients, 241

Habits, of family, 85
 of patient, 67, 108
Headaches, 65, 110
Hematopoietic system, symptoms of, 65
Hereditary factors in illness, 75
 pseudo-heredity, 77
History-taking technique, 137–273
 difficulties and failures, 248–263
  *See also* Difficulties in interviewing
 family history, 75–86
  *See also* Family history
 how to guide interviews, 189–213
  *See also* How to guide interviews
 how to help patient talk freely, 172–187, 199–203
  *See also* How to help patient talk freely
 how to interview patient, 22–25
  *See also* How to interview patient
 how to interview relatives, 23, 94, 253, 264–273
  *See also* How to interview relatives
 how to take history, 26–28, 137–170
  *See also* How to take history
 personal history, 88–113
  *See also* Personal history
 present illness, 41–73, 137–145
  attitude of patient towards illness, 68–72
  chief complaint, 41–42
  description of symptoms, 43–49
  patient's concept of illness, 67–68
  recording history of, 144
  reviewing history of, 144–145
  stresses, 58-63
  syndromes, recognition of, 142–143
  terms used by patient, 139–141, 213
  understanding of illness by patient, 143
  previous treatments, 47, 72–73, 91–92, 145–148

History-taking technique (*continued*)
 variations in interviews, 215–247
 *See also* Variations in interviews
Home of patient. *See* Residence
Hostility of patient, 17, 258–259
How to guide interviews, 189–213
 clarification of meanings, 139–141, 213
 difficulties in, 248–263
  *See also* Difficulties in interviewing
 direct methods, 192–193
 facilitating responses, 181–187, 199–203
 full answers to questions, 212–213
 indirect methods, 189–192
 procedure of interviewing. *See* How to interview
 questions asked, 194–199
  *See also* Questions used in interview
 summarizing words of patient, 213
How to help patients talk freely, 172–187, 199–203
 anxiety of patient, reduction of, 25–26, 177–181, 203–212
  *See also* Anxiety of patient, reduction of
 breaking silences, 176–177
 eliciting relevant information, 174–175
 encouraging emotional expression, 181–187
 opening new topics, 174
 minimal activity, importance of, 172–174
 reducing irrelevant material, 175–176
 resistant patients, stimulation of, 235–237
How to interview patient, 22–35
 arranging of interview, 22–24
 beginning of interview, 24–26
 in later interviews, 33–34
 difficult patient. *See* Difficulties in interviewing
 duration of interviews, 28–30
 ending of interviews, 30–33
 frequency of interviews, 28–30
 note-taking, 34–35
 number of interviews, 28–30
 phases of history-taking, 26–28, 137–170
  *See also* How to take history
 relieving anxiety of patient, 25–26, 177–179, 203–212
  *See also* Anxiety of patient, reduction of
How to interview relatives, 23, 94, 253, 264–273
 about examinations and treatment, 269–273
 about history, 264–269

How to interview relatives (continued)
  preparation of patient, 265–267
  reasons for interview, 264–265
How to take history, 137–170
  current life situation, 103–108, 167–170
  family history, 149–156
    See also Family history
  personal history, 88–113, 156–167
    See also Personal history
  present illness, 137–145
    See under History-taking technique
  review of functions, 63–67, 145–149
Hypochondriacal patients, 238–242

Ideals and religion of patient, 82, 112
Identifications, role of, 77, 79–80
Illness,
  attitude of patient towards, 68–72
  gains from 69–71, 240–241
  present. See under History-taking technique
  previous, 72–73, 91, 145–149
  psychological aspects of, 116–132
    See also Psychological aspects of illness
  severe, interviewing patients with, 249
  shame and guilt over, 71
  will to recover from, 71
Imitation of symptoms, 77
Inaccessible patient, 253–255
Indirection, use of, 169, 189–192, 206–210
Infancy, history of, 94–96
Influence of interviewer, 35, 189–190
Insane patients, 6, 42, 250, 252
Insomnia, as symptom, 53
  See also Sleep patterns
Integument changes, history of, 64
Intelligence of patient, 109
Interest of physician in patient, 15–16
  failure to communicate, 261
Interpretations, premature, 202–203
Interruptions, by physician, 172–173
Interviewers, effects of different, 35
Interviewing methods. See How to interview
Involuntary patient, 251–253

Language,
  of patient, 139–141, 213
  of physician, 20–21
Life chart, 164–165
Life situation of patient, current, 103–108, 167–170

Limitations in communication of experiences, 116–117
Loss of supportive relationships, 60, 84–85

Malingering, 70
Mannerisms, 126
Marital relationships, 101
  See also Sexual experience
Medicines, in previous treatment, 47, 72–73, 147–148
Memories, changes in, 113
Menstrual changes, history of, 59, 65
Metabolic changes, history of, 65
Meteorological changes, stressful, 59
Misperceptions of patient, 6
Moods or emotions. See Emotions of patient
Moral judgments by physician, 17
Mouth changes, history of, 65
Muscular activity, emotions affecting, 125–126
Musculoskeletal changes, history of, 65
Mute patients, 253–255

Nausea and vomiting, 54–55
Needs of patient, 7
Nervous system changes, history of, 66
Nose, changes in, history of, 65
Notes, taking of, 34–35
Number of interviews, 28–30
Nutrition, See Eating

Obesity, 58
Objectivity of physician, 19
Occupational history of patient, 101, 106–107
Old age, 102–103
Orientation of patients, 254

Pain, as symptom, 55–57
Paranoid patients, 242–245
Parasites, as stress factor, 60
Parents. See Family history
Patient, relationship with physician, 3–21
  See also Physician-patient relationship
Personal history, 88–108
  adolescence, 99–100
  adulthood, 100–102
  attitudes of patient, 90–91, 111
    towards physician, 5, 12, 255–258
  basic personality, 108–113
  comprehensiveness of, 90
  content of, 92–103
  current life situation, 103–108
  how to take history of, 167–170

# INDEX

Personal history (*continued*)
  dates, use of, 161–163
  direct questions about attitudes, 118, 198, 210–211
  documentation, adequate, 163–166
  economic status and security, 78–81, 107–108
  emotions. *See* Emotions of patient
  family, attitudes toward, 155–156
    *See also* Family history
  goals and aspirations, 112
    frustrated, 119
  habits and use of time, 67, 110–111
  how to take, 156–167
  illness, attitude towards, 68–72
  infancy, 94–96
  intelligence, 109
  life chart, 164–165
  occupational history, 101, 106–107
  old age, 102–103
  past life, attitude towards, 103
  pleasures and satisfactions, 66, 109–110
  positive aspects of history, 89
  prenatal period, 93–94
  preschool period, 97–98
  previous illnesses, 72–73, 91–92, 145–148
    *See also* Psychological aspects of illness
  puberty, 99–100
  recording of, 161
  relations with other persons, 111–112
  relevancy of, 90
  reliability of informant, 166–167, 268
  religion and ideals, 82, 112
  residence, 104–106
  responses to stimuli, 89
  school years, 98–99
  skills, 110
  stress factors, 88, 141–142
    *See also* Stresses
  therapeutic effect of, 89
  training period, 96–97
  value of, 88–92
  variations in, 113
Personality before illness, 108–113
Physician-patient relationship, 3–21, 172–174
  acceptance of patient, 16–18
  attitude of patient, 5, 12–13, 255–258
  attitude of physician, 13–21, 248–249
  authority of physician, 7–8
  behavior of physician towards patient, 9
  characteristics of physician, 8, 15–21
  duration of relationship, 10–11
  excessive attachment to physician, 12
  factors influencing, 5–12

Physician-patient relationship (*continued*)
  flexibility of physician, 19–21
  insufficient attachment to physician, 12–13
  interest of physician, 15–16, 261
  language of physician, 20–21
  needs of patient, 7
  meaning of patient's experience, 18
  and past experiences of patient, 5–6
  self-study, by physician, 13–15
  shared experiences, 11
  warmth and empathy of physician, 18–19
Pleasures and satisfactions, 66, 109–110
Poisons, as stress factor, 60
Pollens, as stress factor, 60
Posture, stressful, 59
Pregnancies, 59, 92–94, 101
Prenatal history, 93–94
Preschool period, history of, 97–98
Procedures and processes of interviewing, 22–37
  *See also* How to interview
Pseudo-hereditary factors in illness, 77–78
Psychological aspects of illness, 116–132
  association of items, importance of, 122–123
  avoidance of topics, 121–122
  clues to significance of topic, 120–126
  confusion and distortions of thinking, 122
  direct questions, 118, 198, 210–212
  dreams, 123
  emotional changes, 123–126
    *See also* Emotions of patient
  favorite topic of patient, 120–121
  free-flowing interview, 119–120
  frustrated goals and aspirations, 119
  limitations in communication of experiences, 116–117
  thoughts and emotions, 127–132
Psychophysiological reactions, 221–238
  correlations of stresses, emotions, and symptoms, 60–63, 128, 222–237
  fluctuations in symptoms, 222–223
  thoughts correlated with reactions, 237–238
Psychotic patients, 6, 42, 250, 252
Puberty, history of, 99

Questionnaires, use in history-taking, 36–37
Questions used in interview, 194–199
  advantages of, 194
  asked by patients, 31

Questions used in interview (*continued*)
  direct, 118, 198, 210–212
  disadvantages of, 35, 195
  disguising of, 203–205
  full answers to, 212–213
  indirection in, 206–210
  limitations of, 194–195
  rapidity of, 212
  suggestions in, 195–199, 202
  tact in, 17, 205–206

Reassurances offered, 178
  harmful, 33
  premature, avoiding of, 179–181, 183
Recovery, incentives for, 71
Recurrent topics, 121, 123
Relationships,
  of family members with each other, 5–6, 85, 101, 155
    *See also* Family history
  of patient with other persons, 111–112
  of physician and patient, 3–21
    *See also* Physician-patient relationship
Relatives interviews with. *See* How to interview relatives
Reliability
  of patient, 166–167
  of relatives, 268
Religion of patient, 82, 112
Reproductive function symptoms, 65
Residence of patient, 104–106
  community and group affiliations, 105
  inhabitants of, 105
  location of, 104
Resistant patients, stimulation of, 235–237
Respiratory symptoms, 65
Review, of functions, 63–67, 145–148
  of history of present illness, 35, 144–145

Satisfactions and pleasures, 66, 109–110
School years, history of, 98–99
Self-diagnosis, dangers of, 68
Self-esteem, loss of, 60
Self-study, by physician, 13–15
Sexual experience,
  attitude toward, 66, 109, 148
  indirect questioning about, 208
  urges in adolescence, 99
Shame and guilt feelings of patient, 71, 217
Shared experiences, of physician and patient, 11
Shy patients, 245–246
Siblings, birth of, 84, 97
  death of, 84–85

Significance of topic, clues to, 120–126
Silences in interviews, 176–177
Skills, special, of patient, 110
Skin changes, history of, 64
Sleep patterns, 53, 59, 66, 109, 123
Smoking, habitual, 67
Social background of patient, 80–82, 85, 106
  stresses in, 60
Sphincter training, 96
Starting the interview, 24–26
  in later interviews, 33–34
Stresses, 58–63, 88
  correlation with symptoms and emotions, 60–63, 128, 222–237
  external, 59–60
  inquiring about, 141–142, 168–170
  internal, 59
  physical, 59
  precipitating, 62
  predisposing, 62
  social, 60
Suggestion, influence of, 77–78, 195–199
Suicidal risks, estimation of, 218–219
Summarizing words of patient, 213
Suspicious patients, 242–245
Symptom(s),
  anorexia as, 49
  anxiety, 49–51
    *See also* Anxiety of patient
  consciousness, loss of, 53–54
  constipation, 52
  correlation with stresses, 60–63, 128, 222–237
  cough, 52
  date of onset, 46
  description of, 43–49
  diarrhea, 52
  disability from, 46–49
  drugs taken for, 47, 72–73
  dyspnea, 52–53
  factors influencing, 46–47
  fluctuations in, 222–223
  insomnia, 53
  location of, 45
  nausea and vomiting, 54–55
  pain, 55–57
  patterns of disorders, 47–48
  precipitating factors, 58–63
  review of functions, 63–67, 145–149
  severity of, 45
  stress factors in, 58–63
    *See also* Stresses
  syndromes, recognition of, 142–143
  weakness, 57

# INDEX

Symptom(s) (*continued*)
  weight changes, 58
Syndromes, recognition of, 142–143

Tact, importance of, 17, 205–206
Technique of history-taking, 137–273
  *See also* History-taking technique
Teeth, changes in, history of, 65
Tense patients, 245–246
Terms used, by patient, 139–141, 213
  by physician, 20–21
Therapeutic effect of history-taking, 89
Thoughts and emotions, 127–132
  correlated with psychophysiological reactions, 237–238
  *See also* Emotions of patient
Throat changes, history of, 65
Tobacco, use of, 67
Tolerance of patient for symptoms, 42, 46, 55
Toxins, as stress factor, 60
Training period, history of, 96–97
Trauma, as stress factor, 60
Trust in physician, lack of, 13

Unconsciousness, 53–54
Understanding of illness by patient, 143–144

Urinary symptoms, 65

Variations in interviews, 215–240
  anxiety states, 220–221
    *See also* Anxiety of patient
  children, 219–220
  depressed patients, 215–219
  hypochondriacal patients, 238–242
  paranoid patients, 242–245
  psychophysiological reactions, 221–238
    *See also* Psychophysiological reactions
  severely ill patients, 246–247
  shy and withdrawn patients, 245–246
Viruses, as stress factor, 60
Visceral changes in emotions, 126
Vital functions, 64–65, 145
Vocal changes in emotions, 125
Vocational history of patient, 101–102, 106–107
Vomiting and nausea, 54–55

Warmth and empathy of physician, 18–19
  failure to communicate, 261
Weakness, as symptom, 57
Weight changes, 58
Will to recover, 71
Withdrawn patients, 245–246

71 72 73 74 75 10 9 8 7 6 5 4 3 2 1

**DATE DUE**

| FEB 18 1986 | | | |
|---|---|---|---|
| FEB 0 6 1986 | | | |
| | | | |
| | | | |
| | | | |
| | | | |
| | | | |
| | | | |
| | | | |
| | | | |
| | | | |
| | | | |
| | | | |
| | | | |
| | | | |
| | | | |
| | | | |

DEMCO 38-297